ADVANCE PRAISE FOR

Democracy Deficit Disorder

"*Democracy Deficit Disorder* is a brilliant book that takes on not only the current war on youth, but also illustrates how young people are writing themselves back into the future at time when democracy is under assault. Combining a language of critique and hope, the book offers a sobering analysis of the ongoing struggle over agency, identity, social values, and justice young people now face. The book makes clear how crucial critical education is to this current crisis and offers an indispensable guide to both understanding it and meeting the call for a democracy in which justice, equity, and compassion matter."

—Henry Giroux, Ph.D., Chair for Scholarship in the Public Interest,
Department of English and Cultural Studies, McMaster University

"This book uniquely suggests positioning young people as solutions to the democracy crisis. When I've asked progressives if they would prefer that the president and Congress be elected by 16-year-olds or by 66-year-olds, I'm surprised again and again at how hostile the liberal-left is toward youths. Easily half would rather see far-Right leadership than more teenagers voting. In 2022, opposition to lowering the voting age to 16-years-olds in a California city was led by a Democrat who argued that we didn't need more 'far left' voters. This book might convince more progressives that youth are not 'a problem,' and instead part of the solution. I'm happy to bestow my endorsement."

—Mike Males, Ph.D., Senior Researcher,
Center on Juvenile and Criminal Justice

"Fletcher is a leading expert in youth leadership and democracy. Adding depth and perspective to both areas, this book is a must-read resource to understand the possibilities for young people to make a difference in engaging in their communities and beyond. It contains substantial contributions for students, practitioners and researchers focused on young people changing the world, improving our communities, and making society a more just, equitable and empowering place for all. I highly recommend it."

—Dana Mitra, Ph.D., Professor of Education,
Department of Education Policy Studies, Penn State University

Democracy Deficit Disorder

<COVNTERPOINTS ▶

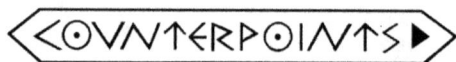

Studies in Criticality

Shirley R. Steinberg
General Editor

Vol. 540

Adam F. C. Fletcher and J. Cynthia McDermott

Democracy Deficit Disorder

Learning Democracy with Young People

PETER LANG

Lausanne • Berlin • Bruxelles • Chennai • New York • Oxford

Library of Congress Cataloging-in-Publication Control Number: 2023017957

Bibliographic information published by the **Deutsche Nationalbibliothek**.
The German National Library lists this publication in the German
National Bibliography; detailed bibliographic data is available
on the Internet at http://dnb.d-nb.de.

ISSN 1058-1634
ISBN 978-1-63667-384-4 (hardback)
ISBN 978-1-63667-385-1 (paperback)
ISBN 978-1-63667-386-8 (ebook pdf)
ISBN 978-1-63667-387-5 (epub)
DOI 10.3726/b20903

© 2023 Peter Lang Group AG, Lausanne
Published by Peter Lang Publishing Inc., New York, USA
info@peterlang.com - www.peterlang.com

Dedicated to Hannah, who is being and becoming every day. I love
you Petey.
—Adam

To my kids who have taught me how to listen: Jason Krieg, Dana
Krieg, Liam Meluso, Mason Dudash, Isabella Krieg, Maggie Krieg, and
Mia Krieg.
—Cynthia

Contents

Introduction

"Our understanding of children as immature may lead us to focus on capabilities they lack rather than what they have."—John Dewey (1916, p. 46)

When Richard Louv's book *Last Child in the Woods: Saving Our Children from Nature Deficit Disorder* was published in 2006, it helped many of us begin to look at the natural world differently particularly for young people. His statement quoting a child who said that he would rather play indoors because that is where the electrical outlets are is a very memorable image. The choices before the youth of the world are narrow because of our adultist perspectives about them.

A title like democracy deficit disorder conjures up similar concerns. But what is meant by this? Synonyms for deficit include absence and deficiency and paucity. The news is resplendent with increasing concerns about the death of democracy not only here but also around the world. There is increasing evidence that there is a democracy deficit and this book has many suggestions about why that is and what can be done about it.

The musician called Sting, born as Gordon Sumner, said in concert recently,

Democracy is under attack. It's under attack in every country in the world. It's in grave danger of being lost unless we defend it. The alternative to democracy is a nightmare, a prison, of the mind. That alternative is tyranny. All tyranny is based on a lie. The greater the tyranny, the bigger the lie. Disagree with the tyrant and you risk imprisonment, torture and death. Yet that is what we must do, all of us. We must protect our right to speak the truth. The war in the Ukraine is an absurdity, based upon a lie. If we swallow that lie, the lie will eat us. The lie is terrified of the truth. We must not lose this battle. (Associated Press, 2022)

A disorder is usually connected in our daily vernacular with medicine and psychology. Here however we prefer to think about it with these synonyms: derangement, disorganization, turbulence, and conflict. As democracy continues to spiral toward its demise, the disordered aspects of it remain out of control and anarchic. Throughout this book, examples of this disordered process are highlighted with suggestions for righting the ship and getting it sailing smoothly are shared.

The main suggestion of this book is how adults can form equitable partnerships with youth around the world to actively support, promote, and engage together in action that fosters healthy democracy. Before we do that though, this book dares to ask what are adults doing that is defeating youth as they enact their complex, interdependent, and just socio-political lives?

To address that question, we discuss the Youth-Industrial Complex, a culture-wide phenomenon that exists to create, facilitate, habituate, perpetuate, and encapsulate the lives of young people. With adults constantly directing the thinking and the management of the young, children and youth today grow to become followers rather than initiators. The democracy deficit disorder is a vehicle that prevents youth from obtaining their rights. It is nothing less than the death knell of the American democratic experiment. At the advent of the American culture that relies on corporate, consumerist, and classist dominance through economic and cultural globalization, young people today have been prevented from enacting what they can and want to do. This book shows that despite that, children and youth around the world are taking powerful, positive, and practical steps to birth, sustain, challenge, and transform the democracy that claims to represent them.

Society has ignored this though, stripping the rights of youth from them and denying them the basic rights of citizenship which they are due. This bias toward adults is the basis of adultism, and throughout this book, the reader will come to understand what this attitude and perspective means for young people. From a child's earliest days, their interest in curiosity, fair play, cooperation, and joy in the unknown is evident. By early school years much of this energy and process has been stripped away leaving young people who no longer ask questions or challenge the status quo. A democracy needs all its citizens to be like those young children with their ability to enact a range of interests and capacities. This book engages readers in an understanding of what is lost as children grow and experience the consistent and dramatic actions that strip them of their citizenship, their agency, their purposes, and their passions. It highlights how others have seen the young differently as this book encourages.

One such example occurred in Poland during the Nazi occupation. A doctor, educator, and writer opened orphanages for Jewish children. His name was Henryk Goldszmit and his pen name was Janusz Korczak. With a unique view of childhood and children, he set out to define the role that children can play in the world. He believed fervently that children were not people waiting to become adults but rather had rights and privileges akin to adults. To him, young people were already citizens and social actors.

Goldszmit wrote about these ideas, but more importantly put them into action with the children. Together, the young people created a government structure, a newspaper, a juris prudence system, and many other ways of self-management. This was indeed a democratic process, ironically taking place within a ghetto. As a doctor and a rebel against the German occupation, he maintained the orphanage for more than 200 children until 1942. That year, he and the children were taken to Treblinka Extermination Camp and all murdered. This hero fought for the freedom and liberty of his orphans and gave his life in protest.

Goldszmit's work is highly regarded, even if largely forgotten. UNESCO declared 1978–1979 the Year of Korczak to coincide with the Year of the Child and the centenary of his birth. Today, a national organization meets yearly to discuss his work and read his writings. The most remarkable outcome of his ideas was the ongoing influence he had on the eventual creation of the United Nations Convention on the Rights of the Child, or UNCRC. Ratified by the United Nations general assembly in 1989, Korczak's ideas remain embedded within the UNCRC as a reminder that children have rights, can use those rights and can be accountable for the actions they take. This is indeed the exact kind of democratic action Dewey wrote about starting in the late 1930s.

This book defines democracy and suggests ways that it can be supported. More importantly, it uplifts youth to examine their potential role in working to end the deficit. There are three main parts in the book: The end of democracy deficit disorder, fighting democracy deficit disorder, and learning to challenge democracy deficit disorder.

Part I, The End of Democracy Deficit Disorder, is a summary of the situations facing children and youth worldwide today. The first chapter makes the case against the democracy deficit disorder, including understanding where it comes from, who it affects most, and why it is such a damning reality today. The next two chapters address the reality of adultism, bias toward adults, is examined in-depth, giving readers more than a passing glance at the framing construct for youth/adult relationships throughout society. Chapters 4, 5, and 6 reinforce the role of democracy as an organizing principle for our society, calling into account the actionable, practical necessity of democracy in every individual's life, particularly the young.

In Part II, Fighting Democracy Deficit Disorder, the book provides a deep dive into what matters most to young people today, and explores the roles adults can play in curing the deficit. Deeply examining the perspectives of youth, this section provides pragmatic, actionable examples and positions the challenge of saving democracy in relationship to other great battles in the lives of children and youth. Ultimately, this section lays the foundation for the final part of the book.

Learning to Challenge Democracy Deficit Disorder is the third section of the book. It details how adults can meaningfully and substantially partner with young people as equitable partners in order to save democracy. Providing a useful typology of action, it also identifies where, when, and how young people are curing the deficit right now, along with showing where it can happen in the future. Finally, it positions this entire discussion in the realm of social change and education transformation, leaving the audience with the challenge of becoming active, wholistic actors rather than passive, forgetful readers.

This book is intended to reach a broad audience of young people and adults who are interested in doing more, but do not know how. It is meant to challenge the intransigence and seeming indifference of adults who maintain the status quo while complaining about the state of the world today. Finally, it seeks to inspire, motivate, and demand action. No matter what our response is to democracy deficit, we must push the entire conversation another step forward immediately, and waiting is no longer an option. This book charges readers to preserve, expand, and transform democracy by learning with young people and from young people for a future we will all share.

Part I

The End of Democracy Deficit Disorder

1 | Young People and Democracy

To say that the world is suffering and in toil is an understatement. So many issues compete for attention and strive to be front and center on the world stage in order to find resolution, build possibilities, and transform the future. In the midst of all of this, though, is a bright hope that is rarely acknowledged. That hope is the positive, purposeful power of children and youth.

Young people everywhere are fighting blatant hatred against them because of their ages. They are challenging apathy toward them because of their race, gender, and sexual identities, and making active, engaged, empowered choices to secure freedom in this generation and beyond. They are doing all of this despite and because of the oppressive forces they face. They are doing all of this because of democracy.

This hope is evident throughout this book through myriad accounts of children and youth fighting to cure the democracy deficit disorder worldwide right now. It shows how young people are working without knowing or particularly caring that they are part of a global movement, planning and challenging, fighting and transforming the endless litany of problems facing them, their families, and their communities. Throughout these chapters, light is shown on media accounts of their actions that are tucked away on the internet, dissected in the academy, and ignored by politicians and pundits who do not value young people as humans, let alone as powerful agents of social change around the world today. Each chapter shows that this routine dismissal and silencing does not make what young people are doing any less impactful though. Instead, it makes their work even more powerful as it digs deeper and has more effect than anything previously acknowledged. This book is not merely philosophical either. Instead, it summarizes pragmatic, current action that moves readers from theory to practice with deliberation.

The work of young people has been ongoing for a long time. For more than ten generations, children and youth have been promoting the values, ideals, operations, and outcomes of democracy in the United States and around the world (Hoose, 2001; Fletcher, 2014a; Barrett, 2015). In reflecting on his own experience as a youth activist in the 1950s and 1960s, the iconic Bob Moses took the distance of youth activists further back, saying, "We SNCC field secretaries in the Civil Rights Movement understood how young we were, but... we were no younger than nineteenth-century insurgent runaway slaves, over three-quarters of whom were *also* between thirteen and twenty-nine years of age... It never occurred to us to think of runaway slaves as [youth activists]" (Moses, 2014, p. 1). There are histories of youth changing the world extending back to the American Revolution and further, too (Hoose, 2001).

There has never been a shared definition of democracy that all young people everywhere have agreed on; instead, every child, youth, and adult comes to understand it for themself in their own unique ways. Informed by all their identities, positions, responsibilities, recreations, and more, these notions of democracy have animated generations of thinkers, leaders, citizens, youth, and everyday people. They have lived, loved, and determined that living in a democracy matters to them personally and is worth fighting for every day in every way possible.

Accepting an image of civically, culturally, and socially engaged young people who are positively changing the world can be challenging for many adults. Conditioned by popular media's consistently negative portraits of children and youth, adults today have been doubly misled about their own children and youth. The forces of capitalism require controlling mechanisms of adultism and its roots in infantilism, patriarchy, protectionism, and other damning forces to be codified through the curriculum and assessment in schools, rules and laws in society, and behaviors and attitudes at home and throughout communities. Challenged by the overwhelming force of these oppressive realities, children and youth themselves often take on the weight of low expectations and dismiss their own capacities and actions to build democracy.

These oppressive realities are doubly true of young people of color, low-income children and youth (McGuire, 2007), neurodiverse young people, and children and youth who do not identify on the binary spectrum (Hope & Hall, 2018). Negative perceptions of children and youth also depend on where they live, what their socio-economic background is, and who they interact with. As Postman (1994) suggested, the idyllic images of childhood harbored by so many people are simply historic artifacts that allude to popular consumer consciousness more than any reality young people in these conditions ever experienced.

Instead, young people have fought literal wars for democracy, and not just on a lark, but as concerted warriors for the ideals of democracy. The breadth of their actions to cure the democracy deficit disorder can be astonishing to the uninitiated. It includes children and youth fighting in wars, organizing for political change, directing popular attention to important issues, becoming systemically involved in democratic institutions including governments and schools, and personally enhancing democracy in their own lives (Lesko & Tsourounis, 1998; Kim et al., 2002; Checkoway & Gutiérrez, 2012; Cammarota et al., 2013).

Hoose (2001) illustrated effectively how children helped fight in the American Revolutionary War and helped ensure the early forms of American democratic government happened. Other scholars have named the roles young people played in putting their lives on the line for democracy by fighting against slavery in the Civil War (Murphy, 2017); for democracy in the world wars (Sharrow, 2000); and for African American civil rights (Hoose, 2010; Sugarman, 2009; Franklin, 2021; Levine, 2000); and for Native American rights (Peters & Strauss, 2009).

As importantly, generations of children and youth have worked to build democracy through political change. During the 1930s, the American Youth Congress challenged popular intransigence toward young peoples' perspectives through political lobbying and popular organizing among youth for social justice (Wikipedia, 2021a). Their "Declaration of the Rights of American Youth" was ratified at a 1935 event in Detroit, Michigan, by "1,205 delegates from 853 organizations representing 1,350,000 American youth" (American Youth Congress, 1935). Starting in 1959, a national organization called Students for a Democratic Society, or SDS, organized young people to fight against American imperialism and more (Wikipedia, 2022a). Their credo called for nonviolent civil disobedience across the United States in order to foster participatory democracy, and the organization is credited with introducing that concept into mainstream parlance today. Their 1962 manifesto was called the "Port Huron Statement" and it was credited with highly influencing the anti-war "hippy" movement of the 1960s (Students for a Democratic Society, 1962; Wikipedia, 2022b). In the

1970s and 1980s, young people fought for the freedom of expression, against abstinence-only brainwashing, and for Title IX in public schools (Barrett, 2015). At the turn of the millennium, the anti-globalization movement was attributed to being organized by youth activists (Welton & Wolf, 2001), while the Arab Spring (Wikipedia, 2022c) and the climate crisis (Klein, 2021; Bachelet, 2022) movements are readily attributed to the leadership and engagement of young people. The student organizers of the Never Again MSD who survived the 2018 Stoneman Douglas High School shooting in Florida continue their anti-gun violence campaign today (Wikipedia, 2022d), and many youth organizers have activated to transform schools and mental health after the COVID-19 pandemic ravished their lives for more than two years. These youth movements have been misidentified (Roberts, 2015) as purely reactive to simple stimuli and as snapshots in moments of time, when they are actually part of the long-standing tradition of young people everywhere to challenge authoritarianism, overthrow autocracy, and build democracy (Hoose, 2001; Barrett, 2015; Welton & Wolf, 2001; Kim et al., 2002; Elrich, 1971; Reulecke, 2001).

As in many succeeding decades, when youth activists are acknowledged by the mainstream media, they are generally uplifted as exemplary and phenomenal, and indeed some of them are. Along with the huge popularity of Malala Yousafzai (born in 1997) and Greta Thunberg (born in 2003) during the 2010s, there are numerous other children and youth throughout the centuries who have had the spotlight, including Sybil Ludington in the 1770s (Barrett, 2015); Sonia Yaco (Wikipedia, 2021b) and Mary Beth Tinker (Barrett, 2015) in the 1960s; and many others. In 2023, young people are even writing their own manuals to promote youth taking action to change the world (Wray, 2021). However, these young people are not the entirety of youth activism. Indeed, the media treat them as avatars representing some adults' expectations for youth, and politicians treat them as tokens for civic engagement.

Instead, when youth build democracy it is not as simple as young people who make the news, lead large-scale movements for social change, or the young going off to fight in wars. Instead, children and youth have been and continue to be the sustainers, educators, challengers, advocates, and leaders of democracy in countless ways. They are massively important to the function, form, and effects of democracy in their own lives as young people, as well as whole communities and the world at large. There are countless ways that children and youth are learning, exercising, growing, and transforming democracy in their own lives, at home, and throughout their communities every day. New technologies used by young people are facilitating new democracy, too, with increased self-expression and newly varied activities leading to new visions of democracy. Coupled with increased access to technology worldwide (Garcia & Philip, 2018), more children and youth are experiencing more democracy than ever before.

These dynamic realities can be exhausting to adults who cannot imagine the implementations, benefits, re-envisioning, and outcomes of what is happening today. Faced with the sometimes-overwhelming challenges of seeing beyond their own points of view, adults sometimes seemingly cannot imagine why, where, when and how this work happens. Beyond imagination, it can be challenging to imagine the depths of young peoples' substantive, sustained, and essential roles and belonging throughout society—not simply on playgrounds, at schools, or at home. Even though it is limited at best, this system approach to young people curing the democracy deficit disorder is happening right now in countries around the world. For almost fifty years, all kinds of organizations and governments at the local, state, national, and international levels have embraced the powers of children and youth to take bold, decisive action (Lesko & Fletcher, 2022; Driskell, 2017; de Kort, 2017; Fletcher, 2007; Hart, 1994).

Reflecting John Dewey's idiom that, "Democracy has to be born anew every generation, and education is its midwife," it is essential for any of these efforts to happen every day in schools, too (Dewey, 2008, p. 139). There is increasing awareness of student voice throughout schools (Fielding, 2004; Mitra, 2014; Fletcher, 2014c). Some educators are systematically engaging young people in deeply democratic activities throughout the entirety of the education system which is essential for curing the disorder this book focuses on (Fletcher, 2005; Fletcher, 2019; Fletcher, 2020).

Not subjected to adults' dilemmas about language, many young people are not distracted when they hear the words "politics," "liberal," "idealistic," or even "democracy." They do not care whether those words are capitalized for emphasis or implication, and they are not interested in whether they are intended to attract or repel certain listeners and readers. Instead, they skip over the verbiage and cut straight to the heart of the issue. Around the world and throughout the generations, young people have sought the purest forms of democracy in their daily lives as well as through grandiose functions of scale such as governments, education systems, and more. In their daily lives, young people of all ages want constant acknowledgment, transparency, accountability, responsibility, engagement, and transformation (Holt, 1974). Whether working online with their peers to build virtual communities in role-playing games, volunteering to raise funds for local homeless shelters, or joining a school district funding committee, children and youth inherently and implicitly strive for those attributes that reflect the most genuine aspects of democratic life—whether or not they know the terms that best suit their desires or meet their needs. Actively building their skills and knowledge in schools, through community programs, online, and in countless other ways, young people today are quickly, deftly, and successfully moving past their own expectations as well as those of preceding generations to continuously reinvent their own roles, actions, and outcomes for democracy, as well as those of other people, systems, and communities around them. This is happening now.

Each generation tends to see the one succeeding it as actively suffering its own existence (Epstein, 2010). Faced with the burdens of modernity, adults of all ages damn children and youth to their lives, proclaiming that they are growing up harder, having a worst time, and living at the end of the world. This leads to the romanticization of the past, where history seems like a fantastic dream and the present is a terrible nightmare. But treatment is true of the eons, with millennia of writers, politicians, and others giving the same treatment to the present (Jenks, 1996).

What is changing from time immemorial until now is the nature of being young itself. Many scholars have examined the roles of children around the world throughout the centuries (Jenks, 1996; Heywood, 2018; Marten, 2018) and others have extensively researched who and what the role of youth has been throughout history (Gillis, 2013; Jobs & Pomfret, 2016; Willard & Austin, 1998) and have arrived at several different conclusions. They have alternately found that children were oppressed and romanticized, subjected and lionized, demonized and typified, treated as inconsequential and essential. Seemingly bound together by the negative sentiment of popular 19th century pediatrician and author Luther Emmett Holt, so many of the viewpoints of these childhood and youth historians rely on the need for young people to conform, be nurtured, adhere to the hierarchy of authority, be prevented from harm, rely on parents as the primary adult, and believe in traditional child development beliefs and practices (Bernier, 2013). Driven by belief in eugenics, Holt once professed, "We must eliminate the unfit by birth not by death. The race is to be most effectively improved by preventing marriage and reproduction by the unfit, among whom we would class the diseased, the degenerate, the defective, and the criminal" (Meckel, 1998, p. 118). This man who was largely credited with the development of modern pediatrics also shaped the negative perceptions many people have of children that has lasted nearly a century after his death. Sometimes these findings were independent of one another, and other times they were woven together throughout the assumptions and findings informing these histories. However, what none of these historical researchers seem to have revealed are the continuous patterns of revelation and transformation that seem successive across the eons. As this book will show, young people of all identities and communities worldwide continuously reveal themselves to be more capable, powerful, active, and progressive than they are ever given credit for.

Similarly, looking at the condition of democracy today it might be tempting to make such a generalization by saying that things have never been worse and need more control than ever before. But to say this would be to say that tyranny of being taxed without representation is not that bad; the terror of being enslaved for your race was not the worst; the manufactured necessity of genocide is passable; and all the endless suffering of humanity throughout the eons be damned—today is the worst day ever. None of that is true though. There are reasons why so many people, young and older, have fought so determinedly and passionately for democracy and all its component parts, including personal and political freedom.

More than a generation ago, Kurth-Schai (1988, p. 120) proposed that youth "possess an unparalleled potential to catalyze positive social change through the development and expression of diverse, exploratory, and optimistic images of future societies." Her point illustrates why adults need to move beyond simply acknowledging young people toward wholly reconceiving what being young means in our world today. Because of sociological and technological advances, society must make broader surveys of current action, modern thinking, and practical actions in relation to history. Reality will become more obvious by revealing the actions happening today to secure democracy and defeat the malaise, indifference, and antipathy demonstrated by so many people. It could fulfill Woods' desire for holistic democracy, which he defined as, "meaning for personal agency, enabling individuals to grow as whole people who aspire to truths, are connected spiritually, socially and ecologically and learn co-creatively; and participation that enhances power sharing and inclusive dialogue to promote mutual understanding and transcendence of disagreement and diversity of interests" (Woods, 2013, p. 343).

Youth-serving individuals and organizations can take the long view much more easily and see the actions of children and youth much more seriously than ever before. This book scans the current realities facing young people and contextualizes them against the pragmatic, actual efforts being taken by them and with them to cure the democracy deficit disorder. Premised on Giroux's (2011) contention that, "Young people need to be educated both as a condition of autonomy and for the sustainability of democratization as an ongoing movement," this book posits itself as an expansive map toward taking practical action. It provides numerous explorations of the individual and collective actions being taken, work that can be replicated and reinvented, and inspirations for future action, as well as acknowledgment for the current generation. As Dewey said, "The very idea of democracy, the meaning of democracy, must be continually explored afresh; it has to be constantly discovered, and rediscovered, remade and reorganized..." (Dewey, 1987, p. 182)

None of this is to say that young people are without fault. Instead, it is to acknowledge the inaccurate popular assumptions that children and youth are apathetic, incapable, and disengaged from democracy. However, accepting the mature proposition that "young" is a fluid state of being insists that adults see the potential of children and youth, rather than as stagnant, fixed beings within understandable though historic frames of reference rather than their realities right now. Rather than centering on condemning them to the perpetual misjudgment of every adult around them, often including parents, educators, counselors, and others, adults in all positions learn to ask children and youth what their realities are right now.

Describing what happens by curing the democracy deficit disorder offers fascinating prospects for the future. In simplistic terms we can refer to the process outlined in a democratic school improvement process created for European schools, which said,

> When students are listened to, they are more engaged with their school and their building. As a result they are better behaved and achievement is raised. As a result teachers are more respectful of students and more fulfilled in their jobs. As a result the ethos of the school is improved. (Klein, 2003, p. 116)

While this is a simplistic and hyper-localized strategy, it reveals the potential of what can happen through the processes described throughout this book. When children and youth are engaged throughout democracy, they are more engaged throughout their families and communities and the organizations that directly affect them. As a result they become better members who contribute actively and achieve success benefiting everyone. Because adults are more respectful of young people and more fulfilled in their membership in families, communities and organizations, the ethos of democracy is improved. That improved ethos is the cure for the democracy deficit disorder.

The challenge presented by all of the actions of children and youth with their adult co-conspirators as presented in this book and far beyond is to create more opportunities for every young person to become actively engaged, deeply committed, and substantially empowered to cure the democracy deficit disorder. As

Kohn (1993) wrote, "[S]tudents should not only be trained to live in a democracy when they grow up; they should have the chance to live in one today." Beyond seeing token examples or positing hypothetical approximations, it is necessary to actualize real possibilities by developing practical responses to real situations. This means imagining the potential, taking action, reflecting on what has been done, re-imagining possibilities, and taking action again in an unending cycle of democratic hope. The perpetual motion that drives that cycle is the power of young people. It always has been and always will be.

2 | Understanding Democracy

All young people today live in ways never experienced before. Instead of having predictable, comfortable, and linear sequences to follow into adulthood, middle class white youth are experiencing non-linear lifestyles that are upending historical socio-economic expectations. Young people of color are fighting for justice, freedom, and peace in sophisticated, sustained ways that are transforming political outcomes worldwide. Low-income youth are challenging traditional trajectories by overcoming negative circumstances with mass determination and action.

Technology is upheaving all parts of the societies where children and youth live, learn, and grow every day. Global communication is instantaneous. Media is manipulation. Culture is more fluid than ever. Didactic learning is dying worldwide because of mass access to knowledge. Commercialism and consumerism are destroying the planet, and hyper capitalism has combined with crass oppression and adult undermining to undo the gains of generations of youth activists, youth leaders, and everyday young people who struggled so hard to challenge intransigence and blatant disregard. Civic engagement has become an ethereal luxury of the wealthy who have enough time and energy to care.

Contrary to what fascists and authoritarians say, the only solution is more democracy, not less. Democratic lifestyles, democratic governance, democracy education, democratic culture, democratic families, democratic communities, and democratic idealism are the only tools to overcome the aristocratic oligarchy that is surging worldwide. The adultist political hegemony has forced autocratic homogenization, alienation, and oppression into the hearts, minds, and hands of children and youth everywhere, and it can only be stopped with democracy. Young people have to be taught this reality in no uncertain terms, as Giroux suggested when he observed, "All too often the worst thing that can happen to the young is to depoliticize them. When that happens, not only are young people told that they do not count—your agency is worthless, your experiences are worthless, and your voice should remain silent—but they are also told that there is no alternative to the current state of affairs" (Johannsen, 2011). They must learn there are alternatives to their current treatment, and that that alternative is democracy; anything otherwise just perpetuates the problem.

Democracy is a practical and theoretical problem that has to constantly be solved anew. Standing at the intersection of daily living and politics, democracy is a signpost that can give us practical actions, shows us cautious boundaries, and help us meet complicated challenges. However, the thing itself requires conscious, deliberate, and constant searching and researching, practice and failure, education and reinvention.

To understand democracy, everyone has to examine the most grandiose conceptions of society, including its myriad purposes and implications. Everyone has to explore the most banal aspects of its applications from the hyper-local to the transcultural, global interpretations that dominate the news. Young people of all ages and adults in all positions also must grapple with the realities facing people everywhere as they try, fail, and try again to secure democracy for themselves and succeeding generations, from America to the other side of the world and back again. All of these have to be examined for their personal, political, and powerful purposes, including how they affect us individually, at the local and national levels and across the globe. Only from this place can adults who support children and youth successfully begin to understand democracy in pragmatic terms.

Democracy is more than a form of government. It is more than an individual attitude, a group process, and a way to educate people. It is all that, as well as the thread that ties together individuals, groups, and society through our thoughts, words, and actions. Democracy is a way of life. Undergirded by the values, beliefs, and attitudes of everyone within a definable community, democracy is made visible in the personal interactions, the organizing structures, and the shared cultures among people (Dewey, 1916; Eriksen, 2018; Golarz & Golarz, 1995).

Even though it is often misunderstood as just the operational process for government, democracy is much more. It is apparent in the ways individuals visualize themselves and society, and it is observable in the interactions between people at home, within communities, across nations, and around the world. It is also obvious throughout the values, operations, and outcomes of places shared among people.

In the lives of young people, democracy is a living, breathing function that can constantly guide their lives, inform their thinking, and drive their actions. While that is not the reality for most young people today, it is the possibility of that reality that drives so many children and youth today to take action to change the world. The democratic potentials in the lives of the young include family life, where democracy can take root, grow, and expand dramatically, in education, where learning, teaching and leadership expand the present capacity of democracy every day, and in community, where the voices of children and the voices of youth can be fully expressed in governance, social capital, volunteerism, and more.

Democracy can be practically expressed within family life, whether in the parent-child dynamic, sibling relationships, or the valuation and devaluation of birth families and chosen families. Expressed through culture and attitudes, democracy at home or the lack thereof is evident in the ways parents communicate with their children, the everyday treatment of kids, and overarching parenting philosophies that are revealed consciously and unconsciously. Unfortunately, these same places are where democracy deficit disorder is most prevalent throughout society.

Explore Democracy Deficit Disorder

It is important to understand the realities facing children and youth today. The theoretical and social underpinnings of youth drive every perspective toward youth today, whether in schools, nonprofit organizations, government organizations, or beyond. White supremacy has its fingers throughout efforts to challenge what Malcolm X referred to as the "miserable condition that exists on this earth" through neoliberalism (Ambar, 2016, p. 24). Neoliberalism informs the belief that young people are a commodity to be produced, manufactured, bought, and sold throughout society. It makes inequality a necessity, creates unfair and unjust outcomes for youth and communities, and relies on the pain and suffering of some to benefit others. According to Giroux, through neoliberalism, "choice is reduced to the practice of endless shopping, fleeing from any sense of civic obligation, and safeguarding a radically individualized existence" (2015, p. xiii). Neoliberalism drives the democracy deficit disorder.

Maybe Howard Zinn explained it best in his autobiography, *You Cannot Be Neutral on a Moving Train*, where he wrote,

> To be hopeful in bad times is not foolishly romantic. It is based on the fact that human history is a history not only of cruelty, but also of compassion, sacrifice, courage, kindness. And if we do act, in however small a way, we do not have to wait for some grand utopian future. The future is an infinite succession of presents, and to live now as we think human beings should live—in defiance of all that is bad around us—is a marvelous victory. (Zinn, 2018, p. 123)

Defeating the values of democratic society, neoliberalism actively teaches young people that their intuition, knowledge, ideas, and actions are wrong. These values, including truth, freedom, fairness and equality, respect for others, the promotion of well-being, and tipping the balance of power and control are not just irrelevant, but are actually seen as negative because they challenge the democracy deficit disorder. As will be shown later on, there are people who will benefit from the end of democracy. Worse still, there are people right now who do not see young people as needing democracy right now. As Giroux writes, "The ideals that inform a substantive democracy are utterly at odds with the current shameful condition of America's youth" (2015a, p. 113). Worldwide reports show that sentiment echoing globally, too (Izsák-Ndiaye, 2021; Foa et al., 2020; Vora, 2022).

Neoliberal views of young people rely on broad political, economic, and social force to drive them. Children and youth around the world have been assaulted by neoliberal forces hellbent on destroying the imaginations of young people and the democratic empowerment they were supposed to inherit. It replaces democracy with money-making through authoritarianism and certainty.

As has been long made obvious by authors such as hooks (2013, 2014), Freire (2004), Giroux (2018), and others, neoliberalism in schools is nearly obvious through large scale political actions designed to increase the wealth of a few while taking away the benefits of education for the masses through standardized testing, fascist curriculums, and depersonalized teaching that results in underpaid labor, dehumanizing jobs, and fractured social fabric. However, neoliberalism is tethered in smaller and subtler, yet no less political, actions that happen daily in education systems and in youth work. These include the ways many classrooms and programs are designed by looking at young people as incomplete, unformed, and in need of adult direction; the treatment of students as disposable populations that should be removed from mainstream society and fed predetermined programs, purchased from corporate publishers and refused roles throughout their communities and families; school and nonprofit funding reveals the exchange of money for production, as children and youth are taught certain skills, led in particular activities and directed through specific pathways in order to produce finite outcomes that are needed by businesses in order to make money; the school-to-prison pipeline enacted through microaggressions of white adults against students of color and low-income students starting in preschool and stemming throughout the school day throughout their primary and secondary school years; the way schools and youth programs communicate with parents, communities and young people themselves. Talking about "youth at risk," "opportunity youth," and "high risk youth" directs young people to act needy, helpless, and incapable; and decisions made by adults for young people without any intention, desire or designs to engage young people in making the decisions that affect them most are neoliberal to their core by removing the public, democratic function from society and replacing it with authoritarian beliefs enforced by dictatorial mandates rather than democratic functioning.

Of course, neoliberalism is most obvious throughout society at large, too. Young people are clearly and deeply affected by the family settings, schools, and other places they spend their time. However, youth programs should be a haven for young people to rest and recuperate from the onslaught of vicious opportunism haunting them.

Instead, many education systems and nonprofit youth-serving organizations view children and youth as opportunities to make money, either on purpose or by accident. Undoing generations that said, "Youth are the future," program after program and organization after organization simply gives up on that idea, let alone the radical notion that "Youth can be the leaders of tomorrow, if we procrastinate." Instead, young people are simply seen as potential funding magnets for K-12 schools and many nonprofits, and potential profit centers by the elected officials who ensure funding, support and evaluation for education and youth work.

James Baldwin (1979) wrote, "It must be remembered—it cannot be overstated—that those centuries of oppression are also a history of a system of thought." It is because of this reality that educators, youth workers, and parents today are routinely forced to go backward in current thinking about youth. Instead of being filled with never-ending possibilities, adults today tend to see young people as fixed to their identities, positions, and roles in societies. Depending on their roles, either as parents, educators, social workers, counselors, or otherwise, adults address young people in singular fashions only: Parents see children, educators see youth, social workers see young people in need, counselors see clients, and so forth. These static positions limit choices, reel in perspectives and discourage hopefulness for and among children and youth, as well as among adults. Young people are more than these fixed identities (and so many others) and limiting adults' acknowledgment of their diversity can limit their possibilities.

This happens because of the neoliberal desire to reduce people to their economic value only. Young people who do not fit into conventional boxes are merely "failed consumers" (Giroux, 2009, p. 27) in the neoliberal model because they are inconvenient to the adults who are trying in any way to profiteer off children and youth. In nonprofit organizations this might mean receiving grants; in government education agencies, administering standardized assessments; in community organizations, relegating youth volunteers to menial tasks. In some way, each action reflects neoliberal adult perceptions predetermined for children and youth.

As a result of neoliberal education within and outside of schools coupled with fascist popular culture propaganda on the internet and elsewhere, young people today sometimes grow up believing:

- The welfare state—which created youth programs originally, ensured young people had food, shelter, and healthcare, and allowed youth to be seen as future citizens—is not worth maintaining;
- There are forces working deeply within communities to ensure youth are looked down on while cynically using language that sounds empowering;
- Democracy means being able to make all the money a person wants to without any regard for the people around you, whether they are in your family or neighborhood, within your culture or society, or on the other side of the world;
- Money invested in youth must be obviously beneficial to the donors who gave it; in the same way, money invested in the public must benefit every taxpayer directly or it was not worth paying;
- Surveillance through closed-circuit television, adult supervision, internet snooping, and countless other ways should be an expected, normal part of life that is not questioned, challenged or otherwise looked down on;
- Widening gaps between wealthy people and everyone else are okay and to be expected because of determination and rights, not because of white supremacy and indoctrination;

- The rights of children and youth rights are only what adults are willing to extend to young people in certain circumstances, and not inalienable or unable to be taken away; and
- The public no longer believes in the future of society, so their investment in children and youth should be squeezed and squeezed away until there is no more.

The results of these perceptions are terrifying, both for the individual well-being of young people today as well as their families, communities, and the world. Democracy is on the ropes, with double- and triple-blows punching at it from crass consumerism and runaway capitalism. All of this leaves young people in the cross-hairs of politicians, executive directors, funders, and evaluators, each of whom is ready and eager to pull the trigger. By doing this, they lay waste to the present as well as the future, sacrificing children and youth to line their own pockets, perpetuate their missions, and dismantle society as we have known it.

Seeing neoliberal education and youth work for what it is means taking off the rose-colored glasses and addressing this scourge for what it is, which is the rapid, completely engulfing, and undeniable effort of a few to make money from the masses of young people in schools and social services. Unfortunately, the few are winning while children and youth are losing as a whole.

Schools and youth-serving nonprofits are much more than a site for work-force development, public health promotion, community service completion or athletic competition. They are places where adults can foster democracy in its most obvious forms, where young people and old can find allies and abilities they did not know they had. These places are where the fiery caldrons of disruption and imagination are borne to fruition, with unquantifiable youth engagement and social change emerging *en masse* throughout society and across futures any adult has yet to imagine.

In his 2021 treatise called *Give Children the Vote: On Democratizing Democracy*, sociologist John Wall proposed that "A new theory is needed of democratic reconstructionism that can understand democracy as responding to people's differences of lived experience" (Wall, 2021, p. 8). This book sets out to establish that theory. To do that, we must understand the context which makes it so essential.

3

Demolishing Democracy

The Damage of Democracy Deficit Disorder

Democracy deficit disorder happens when classrooms, programs, roles, and activities actively raise the barriers to sustainably connecting youth with the world around them. Some of the barriers young people face include: bias, which is prejudice in favor of or against one thing, person, or group compared with another, usually in a way considered to be unfair; sexism, which is prejudice, stereotyping, or discrimination, typically against women, on the basis of sex; transphobia, the dislike of or prejudice against transsexual or transgender people; adultism, which is bias toward adults leading to discrimination against youth; or the addiction to the ideas, actions, appearance, and position of people over the age of majority; classism, the prejudice against or in favor of people belonging to a particular social class; discrimination, the unjust or prejudicial treatment of different categories of people or things, especially on the grounds of race, age, or sex; homophobia, which is the dislike of or prejudice against homosexual people; ableism, discrimination in favor of able-bodied people; favoring, which is to feel or show approval or preference for; and anti-Semitism, which is hostility to or prejudice against Jews.

Most insidiously, democracy deficit disorder positions people who are not seen as adults as secondary, tertiary, or otherwise not relevant to the conception, practice, transformation, or sustainability of democracy in its myriad forms throughout society. This starts with the youngest among us, infants and toddlers, whose earliest conceptions of the world necessarily revolve around immediacy and outcomes. From there it becomes enshrined in the lives of children through low expectations, infantilizing assumptions, and demeaning treatment by adults throughout the lives of young people. Whether it is parents at home, childcare providers before and after school, educators within schools, or youth workers and others during out-of-school time, the democracy deficit is obvious through actions, intentions, and outcomes.

The terms above may not be surprising or unfamiliar. However, the concept of specifically and pointedly raising these barriers to defeat democracy is what should concern us. When children, youth, and adults deliberately address these barriers, everyone can work together to make it easier to engage young people on purpose. When adults intentionally or unintentionally ignore these barriers, they proceed to enforce, reinforce, and perpetuate the oppressions that are destroying the democratic possibilities throughout society.

There are simple questions that demonstrate these barriers at work. Do youth have transportation to programs? Do youth have adults of their race leading activities? Are there other youth from their culture in the room? Do all youth have the ability to be engaged? Does the program assume youth have the knowledge they need to be engaged? Do youth have jobs or other commitments that prevent them from getting to programs or activities? Are these programs and opportunities capable of paying young people to attend and participate? Do children and youth understand the larger function of these programs in society? All of these reasons can keep young people from becoming engaged in democracy. Often, youth have no option but to become engaged outside of schools, youth programs, and other activities.

To lower the barriers to democracy, youth should be presented with opportunities reflecting their interests. They are allowed to become engaged how they want to, instead of having to do what adults want them to. In some schools and youth-serving programs, children and youth are allowed to come and go freely and given bus passes that encourage their freedom. Low-barrier democracy offers off-hours activities as well as typical activity times and creates ways for youth with babies and jobs to attend, too. There are mental and behavioral health services, programs for food and housing, recreational activities, skills and knowledge-building activities and other resources, often all in one location. Life coaching is valued above mentorship, and facilitation is more important than teaching.

The absence of these factors, and even more simplistic elements of democracy such as basic civic education, local civic engagement activities, and opportunities to volunteer form disastrous circumstances for sustaining democracy, let alone growing it. Today, these elements exist in singular places referred to as "civic deserts." According to a leading source of research on youth civics at Tufts University called CIRCLE, "'Civic desert' is a new term that we coined to describe places characterized by a dearth of opportunities for civic and political learning and engagement, and without institutions that typically provide opportunities like youth programming, culture and arts organizations and religious congregations" (CIRCLE, 2017).

When adults learn to stop seeing youth outside of their schools, programs, and priorities as the Other, they begin to lower these barriers and make space for youth engagement to happen. However, the challenge of adults engaging with children and youth is always evident, as witnessed by Mark Twain when he wrote, "We are always too busy for our children. We never give them the time or interest they deserve. We lavish gifts upon them, but the most precious gift—our personal association, which means so much to them—we give grudgingly and throw it away on those who care for it so little" (Paine, 2006, p. 378).

Society can continue to lower the barriers to engaging children and youth in democracy by becoming deliberate and intentional in every activity throughout communities. Learning about and understanding concepts such as Student/Adult Partnerships, children's voices or youth voice, adultism, ephebiphobia, and youth empowerment can help us move toward ending the democracy deficit disorder. Student/Adult Partnerships are intentionally equitable learning relationships based on fostering and sustaining mutual respect (Fletcher, 2005).

Understanding Adultism

Throughout society, children and youth routinely experience alienation, segregation, and silencing. This discrimination has stifled and damaged democracy for generations. Today, that damage is in hyper speed, with the needs of young people cynically and brutally belittled by adults everywhere, all of the time. However, succeeding generations have also taught that this suffering has to end, if not for democracy then just for human decency. As sociologist Zygmunt Bauman wrote, "The main point about civility is...the ability to interact with strangers without holding their strangeness against them and without pressing them to surrender it or to renounce some or all the traits that have made them strangers in the first place" (Bauman, 2000, p. 104).

Young people have been made into strangers throughout society today for many reasons, mainly capitalism. Driving difference into the hearts and minds of parents, teachers, youth workers, government workers, police officers, counselors, and others, adults in all sorts of positions have been made to see children and youth as others, different, unknowable, and alien for many decades. This has proven to be a profitable strategy for politicians who use this alienation, segregation, and demonization as a ploy for votes; businesses who use this fear, separation, and demoralization as a selling point; and others who would manipulate adults everywhere into believing that young people are unfair burdens, easy scapegoats, ready cannon fodder, and ignorant dupes waiting to eat from the hands of the heinous who would readily exploit them at every turn. In the meantime, adults are accumulating power and authority without considering children and youth as serious contributors throughout society (Taft, 2019, p. 80).

Every adult is complicit in this bias, either intentionally or accidentally (Fletcher, 2015). In order to address it, adults must name it and identify it wherever it happens, whenever it happens, for whatever reason. Adult hegemony is a stabilizing factor throughout society, insisting that the attitudes, beliefs, wisdom, and experiences of adults are the dominant factors in nearly all parts of life, including family life, housing, food, economics, recreation, education, mental health, and so much more. This is not to say that adults have ever been conscious of their bias toward other adults, and the resultant discrimination against children and youth. Instead, adults today have been enculturated by a society where the language used, the built environment, policy-making, healthcare, school curriculums, afterschool programs, mental health counseling, libraries, and parenting can all invalidate the worth, depth, ideas, knowledge, actions, and opinions of children and youth.

This bias toward adults and discrimination against young people is called *adultism*, and it is a major cause of democracy deficit disorder. It has a lot of causes, takes many different forms, and creates a lot of different outcomes. Within schools, every single teacher, parent, cafeteria worker, school psychologist, education administrator, afterschool worker, summer schoolteachers, playground monitor, speech and language therapist, math tutor, and school principal discriminates against youth. Throughout society, adultism is an oppressively nefarious reality facing young people at home, throughout society, across government systems, and beyond. As this section explores, discrimination against young people is implicit and inevitable today. Because of its interrelation with democracy deficit disorder, that means both are implicit and inevitable throughout communities. Age-based segregation, age-based discrimination, and age-based exclusion are all demonstrations of adultism, and so much more.

This is not a screed against adultism. Instead, it is intended to be a careful study of the phenomenon of adultism, a failure of modern society which prohibits young people from participating democratically throughout their own lives as well as their communities and the entire world. Different from other writing about adultism (Stoneman & Bell, 1988; Checkoway, 1996; Cummings, 2001), the goal of this section is not to stigmatize, demonize or bastardize adultism; instead, the goal is to acknowledge it exists, root it out where it fails and acknowledge the necessities of it when appropriate.

Adultism in Society

Bias toward adults happens anytime the opinions, ideas, knowledge, beliefs, abilities, attitudes, or cultures of adults are held above those of people who are not considered adults. It is obvious in the language, actions, policies, and many other elements of society which adults use to emphasize their bias toward themselves. Because of this, the very concept of schools, many out-of-school-time programs, and most structured summertime activities are adultism at work. Adultism happens throughout society, and should be addressed as a systemic, cultural, and attitudinal challenge facing education, child development and youth development. Anyone who works professionally in schools or throughout communities with young people as an adult is inherently adultist. This idea is reinforced by Cushman and Cervone who wrote, "Secretly, adults—outside schools as well as in—generally believe that they know best" (2002, p. 99).

The causes of adultism are often oversimplified or overlooked and have not been thoroughly explored. In the literature that currently exists, little or no psychological schema are presented to explain the presence of adultcentrism throughout society, and there is no work that rationalizes the extent to which adultism is present (Fletcher, 2015). However, reinterpreting DiAngelo's (2018) exploration of white fragility as a basis for understanding the source of adultism, it becomes apparent that adult fragility might be the conductive force behind adultism. Adult fragility is a state in which even a minimum amount of age-based stress can become intolerable and trigger a range of emotional and behavioral reactions intended to restore a sense of age-based comfort. Understood as the motivating force for adultism, adult fragility is on the backside of every adultist behavior, attitude, structure, and outcome in society today. Afflicting both young people and adults, adult fragility can leave children, youth, and adults "feeling drained, exhausted, unsafe, and, to a lesser extent, attacked and confused in the same contexts" (Roos, 2021). Occurring in every situation throughout society—including home, school, the community, government, and elsewhere—the adult fragility that leads to adultism can pummel organizations, institutions, communities, and individuals everywhere.

Ultimately, adultism is the reason schools exist. It is the reason youth programs, childcare, and many other formal activities for young people exist, too. All of these activities constantly and consistently demonstrate adultism by discriminating against children and youth. This discrimination happens through: national, state, and local laws; educational, health, nutritional, and funding policies; curriculum, pedagogy, and leadership practices; and cultural norms and social customs.

Adultism is reflected in many things in passive and active ways, from cafeteria table heights to laws mandating compulsory education to the school levies that fail. Seeking to conform young people to adult visions, social leaders, psychologists, and others invented the concept of childhood to ensure that kids were comprehendible and controllable (Jenks, 1996; Marten, 2018). Because of that, the status of young people has become passive, static, and predictable.

Well-meaning educational adultism is intended to keep young people or others safe, force learning, and show what taxes pay for public schools. If a building is burning down, as an adult it is the responsibility of every adult to grab everyone and make sure they are out of the building, regardless of age. However, adults in schools and beyond constantly act like the building is constantly burning down, and that is what must change.

Adultism is actualized by interrelated phenomena which are similar but not identical to adultism. These include adultcentrism, which is the exaggerated overemphasis of adults for the benefit of adults specifically intended to undermine people not seen as adults; ephebiphobia, which is the fear of youth; infantilism, which happens whenever a person is made unable or assumed to be incapable of something because of their age, making them feel, act, think, believe or otherwise less capable than they actually are; adultification, which is making out a young person to be more mature than they actually are; and adultocracy, which is a governing system that assumes power should be concentrated in the hands of adults at the expense of children and youth having authority (Freechild Institute for Youth Engagement, 2016).

People who want to change the state of adultism affecting democracy throughout society must take action immediately, consistently and continuously. bell hooks wrote, "True resistance begins with people confronting pain...and wanting to do something to change it" (hooks, 2014, p. 215). Challenging the ineptitude of adults and common intransigence toward the changing abilities and roles of young people throughout communities requires pushing back against age-based assumptions that have nothing to do with the capacity of learners today. Education is adultism—but it does not have to stay that way. Democracy deficit disorder does not have to exist either.

Adultism in History

Back when children and youth packed factories, farm fields, mines, and service jobs around the western world in the late 19th century, many adults could not find jobs. This caused adults to rally against child labor and for public schools, led by Mother Jones who implored, "The employment of children is doing more to fill prisons, insane asylums, almshouses, reformatories, slums, and gin shops than all the efforts of reformers are doing to improve society" (Gorn, 2015, p. 139). A lot of adults said they wanted to end children ending up on the streets without an "occupation"—especially after newspapers reported that was the case. Schools suddenly became popular as places where young people could have productive experiences throughout the day. In the early 20th century they were made compulsory in many Western nations. Moving children from compulsory labor occupations into compulsory learning occupations without their input, ideas, or contributions in any way paved the way to the state of education today. That is why adultism is the reason schools exist today.

Bias toward adults is so heinous because it discounts the validity, personhood, and importance of young people themselves. Creating exclusive control and domination, adultism forces children and youth to feel unjustly inferior, encourages adults to believe they are unduly powerful, and creates a cascading imbalance of authority that can impact young people negatively for the rest of their lives. Adultism drives adult behavior throughout society, as well as a lot of young peoples' behavior. The approaches adults use to work with young people—whether teaching styles or counseling methods or parenting strategies—frequently represent adults' values and skills rather than the perspectives and capabilities of the children and youth affected. Adults determine what is valuable for young people to learn and how young people need to show their outcomes. They enforce inequities between young people and adults in everyday behavior, too. When adults yell at youth, they are controlling unruly heathens. When children or youth yell at adults, they are creating unsafe environments.

Ultimately, children and youth are subjected to adults' assessments of their performance in any given space without any formal input into grading, awards, reports, or graduations. Searching for adult approval in order to receive the most praise or achieve the best grades, children and youth routinely seek to appease adults with sufficient work without actually engaging in the content being taught. They find solidarity with the adults who control their lives while betraying the trust of their peers as they tattle and compare each other.

In addition to those such as Montessori, who was almost uniquely oriented against adultism in schools, educators have rallied against adultism in schools without naming it as such for hundreds of years. It was 1762 when Rousseau wrote, "Nature wants children to be children before they are men... Childhood has ways of seeing, thinking, and feeling, peculiar to itself, nothing can be more foolish than to substitute our ways for them" (Rousseau, 2013, p. 64). This situates him squarely on the side of anti-adultist educators. The same can be said of many, but not all, progressive and radical educators. In the 1970s, Paulo Freire justly sought authentic learning for students, too. His attitude could be summarized by his singular belief that, "the educator for liberation has to die as the unilateral educator of the educatees" (Freire, 1974, p. 8). This positions the student as the holder, creator, and determiner of learning, and that is anti-adultist.

While some theories address youth roles indirectly, and others head-on push against the overbearing domination of adults, in schools, all are valuable as allies in this struggle. The work of hooks (2013, 2014, 2018) also speaks to her anti-adultist tendencies. While many of her writings reflect this, perhaps it was in *All About Love* that emphasized her position most effectively. Among other things in that work specifically, she wrote, "When we love children, we acknowledge by our every action that they are not property, that they have rights—that we respect and uphold their rights" (2018, p. 30).

There are some educators, researchers, and others in history whose work positions them near the location of being anti-adultist, but not squarely on the mark. Writing by international expert Harry Sheir (Corney et al., 2021) and others in the same vein aims to engender children and youth as equals to adults. While that is an important concept, it will not actually defeat adultism. Instead, it unnecessarily squares with a type of anti-democratic absolutism that is explored later. Facing adultism fosters *equity* between young people and adults, not equality. Practically speaking, the idea of "equality and horizontalism" (Taft, 2019, p. 86) is wrought with extremism, which while appropriate in a few settings around the world, is the exception not the rule. While young people are whole people right now, and while they are complete human beings, it is vital to understand that there are necessary times and places for bias toward adults. Ironically, one of those spaces is in fostering equitable relationships between young people and adults.

Youth equity allows everyone involved, including young people and adults, to be recognized for their impact in the activity, program, organization, or movement (Freechild Institute for Youth Engagement, 2016). No matter what their age, all people have ownership of all outcomes, including particular issues, specific goals, and overarching outcomes. Youth equity requires conscious commitment by all participants to overcoming the barriers involved. Allowing adults and young people to have healthy, whole relationships with each other, youth equity moves everyone forward together through action. These relationships can ultimately lead to creating structures that support differences between and among young people and adults by establishing safe, supportive environments with equity at the center of all activities. In turn, this may lead to recreating the climate and culture of communities, and lead to the greatest efficacy of everyone's involvement.

The Practice of Adultism in Schools

According to UNESCO, corporal punishment is legal in schools around the world (Hart et al., 2005). Corporal punishment is any physical, psychological, emotional, or sociological punishment administered to students (Wikipedia, 2022l). As one of the most brutal and overt exhibitions of adultism in schools today, corporal punishment is the belief that physical abuse has a place in educating youth. In schools where students received corporal punishment, students generally have no format to appeal such punishment. They frequently do not have the ability to raise concerns over the legitimacy of the claims made against them, and they may not have the ability to raise concerns over the severity of the punishment being administered for their presumed violations. Corporal punishment may be one of the most obvious physical impacts of adultism, but it is not the only one.

There are educationalists in history who deliberately sought to enforce adultism by wholly dismissing the personhood of children, including Italian educator Maria Montessori. Her theory actively demonstrates how, in a subtle yet obvious way, the very physical plant of the school is adultist. A hundred years ago Montessori's research and practice encouraged educators to pay attention to the physical apparatuses young people were expected to learn with. Their desks got lower, the chalkboards became handheld, and drinking fountains were built at their height. While these are seemingly beneficial changes for children, this adultism ends at the classroom door and does not acknowledge the interests, benefits, or roles of students outside of the classroom yet within the confines of the education system. The types of accommodation Montessori called for end where young people are expected to stop interacting with adults. In the education system today, the physical environment is most hostile where students themselves are not allowed, encouraged, or accepted. Administrative offices look more like corporate C-suites than like the schools they serve; school board meeting rooms are built for adults; school counselor offices are built for so-called adult conversations; cafeteria food preparation areas are built for adults. Even in high schools, students are generally expected to be "of average adult height" to operate learning instruments such as microscopes, computers, and other devices. Students easily comprise most of the population within an average school building, and there is an inordinate amount of physical accommodation for the minority of that population (Jens, 2015).

Adultism is apparent when large numbers of young people of any age are not allowed to congregate, cooperate, and coordinate. Schools today are rooted in age segregation that disallows young people from socially and educationally interacting with each other. With few formal opportunities to socialize, young people may learn to distrust their peers and seek the approval of adults only. Some adults in schools lose the ability to distinguish between conspiracy and community, and they make continuous efforts to keep students from interacting with each other in schools.

Finally, and perhaps ultimately, adultism undermines the very purpose of educating students in schools. Student engagement has been shown to directly affect academic achievement (Reckmeyer, 2019). When students experience adultism, their engagement is severely affected in negative ways, no matter the environment (Fletcher, 2015). Classroom management, learning activities, and student discipline are all affected by adultism, in all grade levels. In response to all of the bias toward adults throughout their education, some young people completely acquiesce to adult expectations. Others completely abandon or apparently rebel against these expectations by routinely performing poorly in school through behavior or academic achievement and through dropping out. Dropping out of school is the ultimate impact of adultism in schools.

The Engagement Gap

There is an inherent gap in young peoples' engagement that is both implicit and explicit throughout society. In every activity for children and youth throughout society in every community around the world, there are young people who are involved while others are not. This may reflect conscious or unconscious discrimination; it may be completely chosen by young people or not; and may or may not be an inherent outcome of compulsory participation of any form. Regardless of why or how it happens, it happens.

This space between the involved child or youth and the uninvolved young person is often caused by adult bias. Whether it is motivated by age, race, gender, income or otherwise, the gap is real for those who are stuck in it. There is adult bias for engagement styles, with many adults demanding that either children or youth engage the way adults want them to, or not be engaged at all. In other circumstances, adult bias focuses on young peoples' behavior, with adults relying on children or youth complying with any seemingly arbitrary boundaries and expectations laid out by adults. Despite insistence to the contrary, many adults—including parents, teachers, youth workers, and others—are also biased against gifted students, underperforming students, and neurodiverse students. They are frustrated by young peoples' apparent inability to be engaged, whether they are underperforming or differently abled children or youth. At the same time, they are intimidated by highly gifted young people.

The gap that is created by adult bias is as obvious as what happens every day in every activity involving young people, where some children and youth speak up while others look away, and other young people are acknowledged for their contributions while others are punished for not being involved. It extends further toward the heart of democracy when anyone looks at which young people get heard and when they get ignored. This can be addressed as a convenient or inconvenient democracy (Fletcher, 2014a).

Convenient democracy entails children or youth saying or doing things that adults are comfortable with. Democracy is convenient when adults can predict who is going to engage in it, what the young people will express, how it will be shared, where and when it is going to happen, and why students want to share it. When children or youth engage in things that most directly impact them, such as cafeteria food, home conditions, or bathroom usage, they are generally offering convenient democracy. Convenient democracy usually engages children or youth who are already seen by the adults as positive role models in the communities—a youth leadership club, for instance, or members of a youth council.

Inconvenient democracy happens when children or youth bring up ideas and take actions that adults do not expect or are uncomfortable hearing. It is inconvenient because adults cannot predict it, do not expect it, and frequently do not want to hear it. These topics can be those that impact parenting or governance at home or throughout the community, or even be topics that some adults themselves want to discuss but fear bringing up due to their bosses or other outside forces. Inconvenient democracy often comes from young people who are not seen as leaders by adults, or who feel alienated by the community, and it might come at times and places that adults are not expecting.

These realities make the engagement gap wider and more pronounced. Without direct intervention, this gap will spread and devour more young people. This is innately supportive of the insidious goal of democracy deficit disorder, which is to devour the inherent hopefulness, consciousness, and peacefulness of young people by soaking them into the capitalist hegemony that drives violence, injustice, and widespread cynicism throughout society. As bell hooks writes, "Cynicism is the great mask of the disappointed and betrayed heart" (2018, pp. xviii–xiv).

Adultism enables and makes schools and many youth programs today perpetuate the democracy deficit. The only way to begin the massive cultural and structural transformations that are required is through a deliberate plan of action focused on engaging young people as partners throughout the education system, communities, and beyond.

Understanding Adultism and Democracy

There is an implicit and unstated connection between adultism and the democracy deficit disorder. Whether democracy is seen as a personal vehicle, social mechanism, or as a political effect, it relies on the belief that all people should be free to choose. Adultism actively denies that belief simply because a person is not seen as an adult.

Liberal democracy has eight fundamental rights, including "the freedom to form and join organizations; the freedom of expression; the right to vote; the right to run for public office; the right of political leaders to compete for support and votes; the freedom of alternative sources of information; the right to free and fair elections; and the right to control government policy through votes and other expressions of preference" (Wikipedia, 2022e). On first glance, it is obvious that only one of these marginally applies to anyone not viewed as an adult worldwide, and that is the freedom of expression. Each of the other tenets listed is the sole domain of adults in nearly every country around the world. For instance, in the United States (Wikipedia, 2022f) and Canada (Wikipedia, 2022g), it is a lark for young people under 18 to be elected to political office; while it happens, it is extremely rare. In the United States many states actually prohibit anyone under 18 from running for office (Wikipedia, 2022f). Worldwide, while some places are struggling to implement the democratic rights of children and youth, generally the same stringent denial of their abilities, attitudes, knowledge, and actions holds true in the other fundamental rights, too.

Adult fixations on adult ways-of-being and adult attitudes largely drive a lot of adults' responses to young peoples' efforts to cure the challenges facing democracy today. For instance, even proponents of children's participation in democracy are driven by adultism. Biesta (2015, p. 37) reflects this bias by suggesting, "To exist as democratic subjects in a grown-up way is not about acquiring a set of skills and characteristics, or to be in a process of developing democratic maturity [...], To exist as grown-up democratic citizens is an ongoing challenge, not only for children, but also for adults." This notion of "grown-upness" is clearly discriminatory against young people, suggesting that they are not valuable in their current state of being, but only because they are going to become adults in the future. Fetishizing the future by dismissing the present, this attitude is reflected in the popular idiom, "Youth are the future." This viewpoint simultaneously allows adults to dismiss and demonize the current opinions, actions, ideas, wisdom, and creations of children and youth (Nishiyama, 2017). As Kohn (1993) wrote, "Children, after all, are not just adults-in-the-making. They are people whose current needs and rights and experiences must be taken seriously."

Echoing some of that sentiment, the United Nations Convention on the Rights of the Child asserts that young people have many rights simply because they are young. These include the right to be listened to, to freely express their views on all matters that affect them, and to freedom of expression, thought, association, and access to information (United Nations General Assembly Resolution 44/25, n.d.). The overwhelming adult hegemony throughout society strictly prevents this, not only conceptually but as an operating norm around the world. Instead of being granted the rights they are entitled to, young people are systematically excluded from all parts of society because of adultism, routinely denied their rights, and exclusively treated as objects and subjects rather than full members or partners.

There are a lot of opinions about how to do this most effectively, mostly focused on systems change. There are demands for systemic measures that ensure age-appropriate opportunities are provided for children and youth to be involved throughout their communities, governments, and beyond (Lansdown, 2005). Others insist that young peoples' participation should be ensured to always promote the best interests of young people and to substantiate their personal development (Gollop et al., 2000). It is common to want to focus on young peoples' "equal rights to participation" without discrimination because of their identities (Landsown, 2005), and that all young people have the right to be protected from manipulation, violence, abuse and exploitation.

However, what none of those suggestions does is address the reality of attitudinal adultism (Fletcher, 2015; Pease, n.d.). This is the internalized bias toward adults which is seemingly innate to humankind. What makes attitudinal adultism much more insidious than the structural discrimination described earlier is the pervasive and wide-reaching effects it has throughout everyone's life. Anywhere adults and children and youth interact directly or indirectly, attitudinal adultism is present. Adultism at home, in stores, daycares, schools, restaurants, playgrounds, city halls, and far beyond is supported by a psycho-emotional scaffolding that does nothing more than reinforce and extend the undue oppression of children and youth, anyone not viewed as adults.

One of the most subtle ways internalized adultism happens is through gaslighting, which happens when children, youth, and adults convince themselves and other people that young people are not rational, resulting in the belief that children and youth are subhuman, inadequate, incapable, or otherwise undeserving of democracy. Gaslighting is routine in research on young people, educational methodologies, parenting techniques, government policy-making, and many other areas. It is also present among young people who are taught to suspect, doubt, refute, and defeat other young people throughout their lives, including at home, in school, at work, and elsewhere.

Another way adultism happens is by being a "tattle tale" or a bully. More subtle ways include what Alfie Kohn (1993) calls "parroting," when young people repeat what adults say in their own language simply to gain that adults' acceptance; "testing," when children and youth try to find the limits of adults' encouragement to be part of democracy; and denial, where young people flat out resist assuming responsibilities shared with them.

Social cliques that form in community settings throughout young peoples' lives, including schools and community centers, are expressions of attitudinal adultism. Sociologists have long referred to cliques as "youth subcultures" (Brake, 2013), but they are actually forms of internalized adultism because they are prescribed to happen by adults through mass marketing and commercialism. As the American Psychological Association (2004) pronounces, "Identity-oriented branding also encourages disapproval of anything different, be it a different generation, different cultural group or different school clique." Young people start to believe these negative stereotypes of themselves, suddenly joining through language, clothes, music, attitudes, and behaviors that were prescribed for them by whatever adult-driven mass media brought them there originally.

Internalized adultism is doubly harmful because of its social and economic impacts throughout society. Whether the community is made of middle class African American people, working class whites, low-income Latinx, or rural or urban Native Americans, cliques have had their place among young people (Closson, 2009, p. 411). In some areas they are gang-related; in others, popularity-driven; in still others, they were motivated by clubs or athletics or other factors. The internalized adultism driving these cliques are obvious from the manufactured identities assumed by participating youth, most of which are prescribed by popular consumerist culture produced by adults, manufactured in overseas factories, distributed by transnational corporations, and sold by national outlets around the world. In sociology these are sometimes called "ingroups" and "outgroups." Ingroup bias drives young people to oppress one another, both by alienating some at the expense of others, and reinforcing membership through clothing, music, and attitude. The attitudes of ingroups inform how people behave throughout life. Checkoway (1996) asserted that adultism causes youth to "question their own legitimacy, doubt their ability to make a difference..." and perpetuate a "culture of silence" among young people. Additionally, consumer behaviors, social norms, and cultural acceptance are all evidence of individuals' attitudes when people are young. Even if attitudes change drastically as people mature, they are still responding to their exposures when they are young. Ingroups also inform both why young people perpetuate adultism toward other children and youth, and why young people become adults who perpetuate adultism toward children and youth.

Structural adultism is the way institutions, organizations, governments, and other formal entities in society perpetuate bias toward adults (Fletcher, 2014). This happens in businesses, banks, courts, police, schools, nonprofit organizations, churches, mosques, synagogues, and all levels of governments at the local, state, federal, and international levels. Structural adultism happens in many ways, including laws, formal and informal policies, rules and regulations; curriculum and assessments; professional development, credentialing, degree attainment, and training; the physical plant including school settings, architecture and design; and any identifiable structural bias toward adults. Examples of laws and regulations include compulsory education, access to contraceptives, legalized corporal punishment, age-based curfew laws, and anti-youth loitering policies. When the legal system—including schools, police, courts, probation, and re-entry programs—criminalize and demonize children and youth, it is structural adultism. Voting ages and the age of candidacy are examples, as is access to healthcare and age-based mandatory national service. Pundits and academics agree on this, with former Cambridge professor David Runciman saying, "...if there's one group that is really disadvantaged at the moment, it is the group that democracy used to be for and is now against, and that's the young," and political operator James Carville declaring, "This is not class warfare, this is generational warfare. This administration and old wealthy people have declared war on young people. That is the real war that is going on here. And that is the war we've got to talk about" (Cook, 2003). Others including Giroux (1999, 2009, 2011, 2015) and Males (1996, 1999) have continuously and successfully illustrated this point as well, but without focusing on adultism.

Adultism drives children, youth, and adults to do many things. In order to stop it, adults have to learn to identify and fight their own behavior, and to challenge the adultist behavior of their peers. At the same time adult allies need to facilitate learning experiences for young people to identify adultism, challenge it among their peers, and effectively challenge it among the adults in their lives. Only then can true social progress toward curing the democracy deficit disorder occur.

Young People of Color and Adultism

> The idea of citizen participation is a little like eating spinach: no one is against it in principle because it is good for you. Participation of the governed in their government is, in theory, the cornerstone of democracy—a revered idea that is vigorously applauded by virtually everyone. The applause is reduced to polite handclaps, however, when this principle is advocated by the have-not blacks, Mexican-Americans, Puerto Ricans, Indians, Eskimos, and whites. And when the have-nots define participation as redistribution of power, the American consensus on the fundamental principle explodes into many shades of outright racial, ethnic, ideological, and political opposition. (Arnstein, 1969, p. 216)

All of this understanding of adultism is appropriate and according to the experience of every young person around the world. However, there are systems of oppression which amplify the experiences of adultism throughout the lives of some young people that are not present in the lives of other young people. Youth who are taking action for democracy are afflicted by adultism in many different ways. When considering these oppressions and the inequities they cause, we have to consider how children and youth identify, be it race, class, gender, sexual orientation, or other identity categories. For instance, young women often face the intersection of sexism and adultism; neurodiverse children face discrimination against their differences from so-called mainstream young people that intersect with adultism. Acknowledging those intersectionalities are vital to understanding the effects of adultism. However, the experiences of young people of color and adultism are something else.

Stoneman and Bell (1988, p. 33) clearly enunciate this intersection when they wrote about people of color, "As young people they have been denied any power over their institutions or their families or their communities; as Black and working class or poor people they notice that their parents are similarly denied any power, so they look forward to powerlessness as adults." In countries dominated by white supremacy worldwide, this reality is domineering throughout the lives of young people of color. Raised in prolifically white-dominated institutions throughout their communities "including but not limited to education, criminal justice, the military, the media, and religion" (Christian, 1992, p. 177), the internalized chaos of adultism may be predominant in the psyches and physical existences of children and youth who are not identified as "white." This can happen even where there are no white people present, as Christian (p. 181) explains,

> Whiteness is the structuring force that historically shaped the multiple social levels and has found ways to continue in 'deep structures' through new models and systems of malleable signification that maintains whiteness on top even in spaces in which there are no white bodies.

This reality of whiteness is only compounded by adultism where it intersects with other oppressed identities of young people of color as well. If a Black youth is queer, homeless, neurodiverse, and lives in a historically redlined neighborhood, the frameworks of white supremacy can become overwhelming for them personally. Granted the innate discriminations within the white supremacist culture, these young people are often prohibited from any substantive democratic discourse within and throughout their own lives, let alone in the larger world around them. These require a sophisticated interrogation of the civic systems that disempower youth of color, of the cultural patterns which negate and deny their democratic competencies, and the attitudinal indifferences of white people to the realities these young people face constantly.

As James Baldwin wrote, "The brutal truth is that the bulk of white people in America never had any interest in educating black people, except as this could serve white purposes. It's not the black child's language that is in question, it is not his language that is despised: It's his experience. A child cannot be taught by anyone who despises him, and a child cannot afford to be fooled. A child cannot be taught by anyone whose demand, essentially, is that the child repudiate his experience, and all that gives him sustenance, and enter a limbo in which he will no longer be black, and in which he knows that he can never become white. Black people have lost too many black children that way" (Baldwin, 1979).

This denial of the humanity, and the importance and the power of young people of color is at the core of public educations' failures today. Educators and school leaders have knowingly positioned children and youth of color in pre-dominantly white-centric learning environments, eliminated the distinctiveness of the voices of students of color, sustained the school-to-prison pipeline, and taught white supremacist norms, history, and outcomes for generations (Boateng et al., 2021). By doing this, education systems have continuously attempted to eliminate the depth, validity, and power of non-hegemonic learning, and have wholly repudiated the democratic potential of education, let alone its ability to resolve social injustices (Paglayan, 2021). The worst of these repudiations may be the damning intersection of race, ethnicity, and adultism.

There are places, situations, and activities where adultism is being confronted specifically in the lives of young people of color. One study looked at the experiences of African American students in a school with an adultist African American principal (McClellan, 2020). Positioning these Black girls as experts and co-constructors of knowledge on what it means to be a Black girl in a public school, the study makes a compelling case for addressing adultism in the lives of youth of color. Similarly, Black librarian Tamara Stewart finds adultism to be a specifically damning reality in public libraries serving youth of color. She suggests, "The disrespect of young adults is a prevalent social attitude that insidiously infiltrates our libraries and can undermine our best efforts to provide equal access and quality service to all" (Stewart, 2012, p. 78). These findings are accentuated by the ongoing work of organizations and individuals addressing the growing field of youth-led social change driven by young people of color across the United States and around the world. In the United States, the Funders Collaborative on Youth Organizing, or FCYO, is "a dynamic collective of social justice funders and youth organizing practitioners dedicated to advancing youth organizing as a strategy for youth development and social change" that focuses primarily on supporting "...some of the nation's most marginalized youth, including poor youth, youth of color, and out-of-school youth" (Funders Collaborative on Youth Organizing, n.d.). Their work and the work they support frequently and directly addresses the intersection of adultism and other oppressive forces throughout the lives of young people of color and the communities where they live. These children and youth are not mere victims of adult oppression who are sitting by the wayside awaiting well-meaning white people to stop the discrimination and bias afflicting them every day in every possible way. Instead, they are empowered and seeking more power to rectify the white supremacy they face daily (Black Youth Project, 2012; Hipolito-Delgado et al., 2022).

Similarly, the fixation on adults' bias toward other adults has been shown to particularly afflict young African American girls through a phenomenon called "adultification." A 2017 report from the Georgetown Law Center on Poverty and Inequality stated,

> Adultification is a form of dehumanization, robbing black children of the very essence of what makes childhood distinct from all other developmental periods: innocence. Adultification contributes to a false narrative that black youths' transgressions are intentional and malicious, instead of the result of immature decision making—a key characteristic of childhood. (Annie E. Casey Foundation, 2017)

It also, "showed that even in the age bracket of 5–9 years old, adults perceive Black girls as needing less nurturing, protection, and comforting than white girls of the same age, and that they are more independent" (Georgetown Law Center on Poverty and Inequality, n.d.). The reality of adultification had prior been exhibited in studies on low-income children and youth in general (Burton, 2007). However, the Georgetown study specifically identified that young Black girls were targeted disproportionately to their white peers, thereby showing again the intersection between adultism and white supremacy is particularly heinous.

Adultification reiterates the point that young people of color are not monolithic (Ray, 2020), and because of that all action to engage young people in democracy must critique, invent, and reinvent children's participation and youth engagement anew in every setting and at every time possible.

Flanagan's research shows that in addition to the underlying effects of adultism on young people of color and other marginalized children and youth can deeply inform the construction of their political identities while they are young (Flanagan, 2013, p. 21). Adults in power can shape their senses of negative and positive influence, affecting their perception of governance, police, teachers, and more. As Flanagan states, "[C]hildren who are members of groups that are marginalized from mainstream power learn that the terms of the social contract might not apply equally to all groups." They also found that studies show, "…the interests and needs of more privileged groups in society receive far more attention in policy formation than those of the disadvantaged" (p. 21). This reinforces any sense of discrimination young people may have in general; for children and youth of color the intersection of white supremacy and their age may have compounding effects unlike others in society.

Additionally, Flanagan also finds, "there is a class and racial divide in the civic opportunities available to young people: cumulative disadvantage built up over the kindergarten through twelfth grade (K-12) years depresses civic incorporation and action later in life; events such as school dropout or arrests have an especially negative effect" (p. 32). From this viewpoint it becomes obvious that young people of color start out unequal to white youth, further implicating the roles of adultism and the democracy deficit throughout their lives. The generational effects of white supremacy and the transgenerational commitment to adultism are wholly unparalleled.

At the intersection of adultism and white supremacy, ephebiphobia and adultification lies a very specific type of hysteria afflicting young people of color. Sociologist Mike Males (Males, 1996, 1999) has repeatedly found how this media myth-making machine endlessly diverts America's complacent, established middle class voters by propagating demographic myths about age and race and "sensational scapegoating" to avoid facing its own violence. This scapegoating portrayed a generation of young African American men as "superpredators" while ignoring the threat of suburban white males shooting up schools and movie theaters. According to Giroux (Giroux, 2009, 2015) and others, results included the entrenchment of the school-to-prison pipeline, the eruption of private supermax prisons and the militarization of police departments across the United States. Showing the perplexing realities of this intersection of racism and adultism, Males has shown that even when young people of color are performing favorably in and toward society, media and politicians continuously demote their contributions and wellbeing (Males, 2023).

These are just some of the nameable oppressions trying to condemn young people of color. As this book shows, the forces upholding this oppression and trying to compel Black, Brown, and other young people of color to be defeated in each succeeding generation are nefarious and subversive. However, there is hope. Perhaps the most forthright prescription for responding to adultism in the lives of young people of color comes from Bettina Love when she writes about the difference between abolitionism and reform. Advocating for the former, she wrote,

> Abolitionists strive for that reality by fighting for a divestment of law enforcement to redistribute funds to education, housing, jobs, and healthcare; elimination of high-stakes testing; replacement of watered-down and Eurocentric materials from educational publishers like Pearson, McGraw-Hill, and Houghton Mifflin Harcourt with community-created standards and curriculum; the end of police presence in schools; employment of Black teachers en masse; hiring of therapists and counselors who believe Black lives matter in schools; destruction of inner-city schools that resemble prisons; and elimination of suspension in favor of restorative justice. (Love et al., 2020)

In order to face adultism fully, adults who say they support young people of color need to be abolitionists who fight white supremacy in all forms, everywhere it occurs. Love gives practical actions to take to do that. Expanding her analysis with an understanding of adultism can increase the abilities of Abolitionists' efficacy, as they strive further to foster youth-driven civic engagement, challenge age-biased laws, transform courts and systems of care which disproportionately affect young people of color, and ultimately defeat adult apathy toward young people.

Similar to white supremacy, the harrowing effects of ephebiphobia cannot be easily dismantled with simple actions. It is only through sophisticated, multi-faceted analyses of existing structures that practical and effective transformation can be conceptualized. Toward that end, the next section identifies one avenue that maliciously enforces, reinforces, and transmits adultism across generations.

Identifying the Youth-Industrial Complex

There are malevolent forces driving the democracy deficit that are undermining youth and democracy right now. This phenomenon is the Youth-Industrial Complex, which determines the nature, cause, and effect of relationships between activities of any kind for children and youth on one hand, and on the other hand, businesses, governments, and nonprofits, as well as the functions between public and private sectors. Acknowledging the history and future of the phenomenon, it is essential for this knowledge to become core learning among people within and affected by the complex (Fletcher, 2014a). This includes parents, educators, youth workers, mental health providers, and youth themselves.

As others have identified, there is a nonprofit industrial complex that affects billions of people worldwide, benefiting and detracting from efforts to make change all while avoiding appearing innocuous and indifferent (Samimi, 2010). However, this posturing is ineffectual for any critical examination of the impact of these organizations. A close look at their own impact evaluations as well as the commentary of politicians, activists, and others shows how many local and international nonprofits can have broadly negative outcomes in the short-term and long-term (Helmig et al., 2014). Because of their age and role in society though, young people might be the most heinously affected. Their experience is so finitely affected that it needs to be addressed as the Youth-Industrial Complex.

The Youth-Industrial Complex is a phenomenon that summarizes the overlapping interests of nonprofits, businesses, and government agencies which use public and private resources to create youth-serving activities to address economic, social, and political problems. It is reflected in the relationship between the three components of governments, nonprofits, and businesses. These activities reinforce each sector's mutually beneficial interactions with young people.

Each individual component gains from addressing specific problems in society with specific activities for youth, while the other two aspects gain from ensuring young people have those specific problems in the first place. This looks like government agencies getting increased budgets for issues affecting youth; nonprofits receive funding and create jobs that address those issues; businesses earn profits by ensuring those issues exist in the first place; government entities regulate those businesses ensuring taxation that supports government agencies. Government agencies get increased budgets, and so forth. The issues are vast, and include the school-to-prison pipeline, cannabis usage, athletics, suicidal ideation, school vending machines, and much more. The government agencies address all of those issues in several different fields, including juvenile justice, economic development, mental health, community recreation, elementary education, and other areas. The nonprofit organizations are as expansive as the fields involved, focusing on community improvement, unmet human needs including food insecurity, housing, afterschool programs, and educational services. Businesses that profit from all of this include consumer goods and services including security services, technology, clothing, entertainment, and other industries such as weapons manufacturers, construction, physical fitness, and more.

There is an inherent tension between these relationships. While presenting themselves as "saving children" or "helping youth," many nonprofit organizations, government programs, and even schools benefit from perpetuating the problems afflicting young people today. They benefit through funding, social capital, and other profits. This section explores how they perpetuate the problems in many ways. In what could be applied globally today, in 1932 George Counts said,

> America is the scene of an irreconcilable conflict between two opposing forces. On the one side is the democratic tradition inherited from the past; on the other is a system of economic arrangements which increasingly partakes of the nature of industrial feudalism. Both of these forces cannot survive: one or the other must give way. Unless the democratic tradition is able to organize and conduct a successful attack on the economic system, its complete destruction is inevitable. (Counts, 1978, p. 41)

The tension throughout the Youth-Industrial Complex is tearing at the very fabric of democracy today by incentivizing the democracy deficit disorder, giving tools for the habituation of anti-democracy, and maintaining the economic situation that entirely disincentivizes the strengthening of democracy throughout society. Every single young person is affected by this complex in countless visible and invisible ways, extending from their home lives to sports, schooling to hanging out, from technology to clothing, and music to communication. So many aspects of young peoples' lives are touched upon by the entwined, non-linear forces of the Youth-Industrial Complex that it can be hard to identify exactly what it is.

Identity segregation, rather than intersectionality, is key to the Youth-Industrial Complex. Youth are frequently identified by governments, nonprofits, and businesses by way of their age, sexuality, class, ethnicity, race, and gender, in addition to geographic location, family status, academic achievement, and more. In business, each identity is addressed as a potential "market segment" with products, advertising, and pricing that are targeted specifically at them. In governments, identities may appear less segmented, but still have programs, activities, policies, and policing targeted at them. The very existence of many youth-serving nonprofits is based on youth identities. This specification reinforces the appearance and realities of youth diversity; ironically, it both supports and challenges the very institutions addressing youth to become more effective.

As already identified, the Youth-Industrial Complex consists of three components which form a unique "iron triangle" (Adams, 1981) with each component a solid factor made of several layers. The components of the iron triangle in the Youth-Industrial Complex are:

- *Businesses*, including large corporations and sole entrepreneurs; direct sales and consultants; marketers and social media; curriculum designers, program developers, and assessors; lobbyists and gaming; clothing and counseling; and any other profit-oriented transaction.
- *Nonprofits*, including all sorts of formal and informal activities that build, foster, and otherwise change communities at the local, regional, state, national, and international levels, including social services such as community education, food subsidies, healthcare, job training and supported housing, and adoption.
- *Governments*, which are systems that operate to organize local, state, national, and international jurisdictions. The three primary parts of government include the legislature, executive, and judiciary on all levels, and their activities are central to designing, implementing, and regulating policy and regulations which govern economies, policing, education, public utilities, businesses, healthcare, transportation, sanitation, and much more.

The Youth-Industrial Complex can be identified in several subsequent relationships, too, including the education industrial complex, the sports industrial complex, the youth/police industrial complex, the juvenile justice industrial complex, the video game industrial complex, the music/movie/television/entertainment industrial complex, the voting industry complex, and the child welfare industrial complex.

There can be many other activities of each of the components of the Youth-Industrial Complex. Ignoring the subsequent relationships, refusing to see the interconnectedness of each of them, and denying the negative impacts they can have can be confusing to the people who work within these places; to the people affected most by them, seeing each one individually or as disconnected from the others can be disorienting and ultimately disabling. Unfortunately, this segregation of interests and isolation of approaches is commonplace today, with its proponents arguing that it is necessary. However, that is inaccurate at best; at worst, it reveals the insidious nature of neoliberalism and the disparities inherent throughout the Youth-Industrial Complex by obfuscating their true natures. Henry A. Giroux writes how,

...the popular demonization of the young now justifies responses to youth that were unthinkable 20 years ago, including criminalization and imprisonment, the prescription of psychotropic drugs, psychiatric confinement, and zero tolerance policies that model schools after prisons. School has become a model for a punishing society in which children who violate a rule as minor as a dress code infraction or act out slightly in class can be handcuffed, booked and put in a jail cell. (2008, p. 18)

While Giroux addresses the aspects of the Youth-Industrial Complex that are plainly oppressive, the overarching aspects of this reality are obtuse throughout the lives of children and youth. In addition to its dominance over their democratic potential, the Youth-Industrial Complex functions as the tool of total control and adult dominance over young people, embodying Goffman's concept of the total institution (Davies, 1989). This means it wholly disallows their innate human rights, let alone their specific rights as children and youth. As Deleuze explained about institutions, this relationship "cannot be identified with any one institution or apparatus precisely because it is a type of power, a technology, that traverses every kind of apparatus or institution, linking them, prolonging them, and making them converge and function in a new way" (Deleuze, 1986).

This complex relationship and the intricate and interwoven interactions therein are apparent in almost every youth activity in North America. Connecting these sectors within the iron triangle are three bridges:

1. Youth activities include every type of activity that serves young people in society, from consumerism to volunteerism; youth development to education; culture building to social media; and so-forth. These can be formal and informal; charitable and profiteering; individual and corporate.
2. Public resources are the money, time, property, facilities, equipment, and supplies of any level of government.
3. Private resources are nearly identical, but come from profit-focused nongovernmental places, including sole proprietor businesses, corporations, individual donors, philanthropic foundations, and so on.

Just because nonprofits, businesses, and governments are operating in a relationship does not mean they are sitting in a smoky backroom making deals, either. Instead, they are operating in seen and unseen ways that subsequently affect young people in a variety of ways that are both good and bad.

The relationships between nonprofits, government and businesses include subtle and overt interactions between: laws, rules, policies, and regulations; products, programs, curricula, projects, plans, and activities; evaluations, assessments, analytics, and oversight; training, professional development, certifications, and degrees; books, articles, reports, websites, and blogs; associations, affiliations, partnerships, coalitions, networks, districts, and regions; funds, sales, grants, allocations, set-asides, donations, and foundation programs, as well as; schools, faith communities, stores, factories, parks, jails, and much more. All of this is just part of the depth and breadth of the Youth-Industrial Complex.

Looking closer, it is plain to see that the Youth-Industrial Complex is obvious among nonprofits, including community-based organizations and national nonprofits, as well as local coalitions and international networks; governments, including K-12 schools, higher education, and agencies and programs on the federal, state, county, and local levels; and businesses including privately owned companies and transnational conglomerates, foundations, and individual donors. There are other entities, too.

The relationships between these entities are driven by three elements, which are private resources, public resources, and youth-serving activities. These elements are clear in the money given, the money spent, and the money obtained between governments, nonprofits, and businesses. They become obvious when observing the leverage between the lobbying and bureaucracies that control sophisticated measures and contracts, which in turn go to private businesses that shift and transition youth culture and the social climate where it belongs. In the meantime, the same elements are apparent within the entire network of support for parents, opportunities for privileged young people and the oppression of other children and youth. All of these rely on the ecosystem of nonprofits, governments, and businesses in order to exist.

The Youth-Industrial Complex exists to create, facilitate, habituate, perpetuate, and encapsulate the lives of young people throughout society. Whether it is beneficial or detrimental is not the point of this analysis; the point is that it simply exists in myriad forms, driving the lives and outcomes of children, youth, and adults throughout the world today.

The Youth-Industrial Complex is a vehicle of the democracy deficit disorder, effectively and continuously delivering indifference, ineffectuality, and near despair to generations of young people. The death knell of the American democratic experiment was sounded with the advent of American corporate/consumerist culture and its dominance through economic and cultural globalization (Giroux, 2009, p. 32). The Youth-Industrial Complex exists to undermine, destabilize, and otherwise dismantle democracy for the sake of economic efficacy for the extremely wealthy.

The Youth-Industrial Complex did not simply pop into existence one day. Instead, it has slowly come to exist over a century of political and economic machinations that made individual families, governments, schools, churches, and other locations that form the social fabric serve private financial interests. Within this entanglement emerged the fields of public health, education, youth development, public safety, parenting and family development, healthcare, and sustainability. Taking advantage of their interdependent natures, private financial interests first used these fields to commodify the notion of "youth." Then obligating these fields to their funding masters, private financial interests were able to carve out profit margins from the social fabric. This is evident in each field. For instance, before there were youth behavioral rehabilitation camps and other sites of explicit profiteering within the "troubled youth" industry, there were family farms and family-owned businesses where non-conforming students could apprentice, learn trades and work for a living rather than being penalized for their differences.

At the same time, the establishment of manufactured and commercialized culture established the position of "youth" within society, which did not exist in prior centuries. Socializing, policing, education, environmentalism, empowerment, workforce development, culture building, civic governance, neighborhooding, and volunteerism began interacting among themselves, and eventually became wholly entwined with commercial youth culture, which today includes music, clothes, hair styles and language, as well as social media, technological devices, connectivity, and so much more.

All of these functions were originally embedded as democratic in their nature and intended to build the efficacy of democratic citizenship in democratic societies. As that happened, it became essential to heal the wounds young people faced. This included stopping forced child labor, ending youth homelessness, defeating educational ignorance, and demanding social justice for all young people, regardless of their identities and because of their belonging in the world.

In turn, this increased adult intentions and deliberations about the status of youth, including who they are, what they do, where they are at, and why they exist. The Youth-Industrial Complex became essential for determining what the answers to these questions are, how they are enacted, and whether they are successful.

However, what emerged was a crisis of purpose wherein so many activities became anti-democratic by forcing youth, either through legal compulsion, cultural tradition, family pressure or economic machinations, to become involved in them. In turn, succeeding generations of young people have become disengaged and disillusioned in much of society. While this was once seen as happening only to college-age students, it became the providence of high school students, and now has reached into elementary years. Jaded, life-weary children and youth are saturated by adult-devised, adult-implemented, and adult-mandated activities throughout their young lives. This leaves young people at risk of becoming wholly divested in the democratic process while forming deeply disturbing attachments to the habits of consumerism (Giroux, 2009, p. 67), including accepting what is handed to them, accepting authority unquestioningly, and believing the mainstream social, cultural, and economic narratives that dominate society.

Understanding the Youth-Industrial Complex can be as intricate as attempting to wholly comprehend the present reality of the situation facing young people, if not more so. Political and economic forces have realized the profit potential of every component of the iron triangle. There are few areas in the lives of children and youth around the world left to exploit for profit by either government, businesses, or nonprofit organizations. Without naming it as such, Giroux (2008, 2009) and others have deftly diagnosed and analyzed the indisputable role of neoliberalism within and throughout the Youth-Industrial Complex. The continuing rise of neoliberal youth services in all functions of society seems inevitable and nearly unstoppable, presenting itself as the engine for all innovation. Youth services have been reduced from their essential roles in building democratic society to become mere profit centers responsible for ensuring successful consumers within nonprofit organizations, government agencies, and philanthropic foundations that lack vision and misunderstand their dictums, inadvertently cloaking neoliberal marketplace investors' interests and intentions.

This positioning has established a battle between the forces of crass capitalism and socially minded community-builders. This is not a false dichotomy. Instead, it is inherent and apparent in the positioning of youth throughout society. While crass consumerism insists that youth simply arrive, partake of predetermined activities, products, and services, and then complete their terms as temporarily young, democratically minded people are repositioning young people as active co-creators throughout society who live in interdependent cultures supporting and sustaining their personal and collective possibilities, potential, and powers as members of the greater communities which all people belong to.

The future of the Youth-Industrial Complex is mired in this battle, positioning all nonprofits, all levels of governments, and all businesses as the beneficiaries of the dichotomous relationship they have with young people everywhere, all the time. This is not a conspiratorial relationship either. Instead, it is largely coincidental and circumstantial. However, coincidences and circumstances are nearly always present and affect every single person in society today.

Youth workers, teachers, businesspeople, doctors, organization administrators, elected officials, government workers, mental health counselors, police, and store staff all have to determine for themselves where, when, why, and how they interact, benefit, and critique the complex. However, it is youth themselves who offer the greatest possibility for challenging and defeating the invariably nefarious outcomes of the Youth-Industrial Complex. Rachel Jackson was a youth organizer fighting against the school-to-prison pipeline in California when she said,

> Our youth are not failing the system; the system is failing our youth. Ironically, the very youth who are being treated the worst are the young people who are going to lead us out of this nightmare. (Fletcher & Vavrus, 2006, p. 6)

These prophetic words demonstrate the greatest hope society has in this battle for the souls, hearts, minds, and hands that can build, recreate, transform, and critique democracy today and in the future. Youth are the only hope. Let us see that and work from that place, now and forever more.

4

Solving the Deficit

"The question which you and I have to settle is this: Can we envision and do we want a democracy where the rights of all citizens are equal? It is not necessary to meet this clear statement with a trite remark that all people are not and probably never will be equal and similar in their abilities, their gifts and their accomplishments. The problem which is now proposed is a problem of legal rights to recognized political, civil and social equality for every citizen."—W. E. B. Du Bois (1947, p. 1)

The democracy deficit disorder must be cured. As the subjects of adult domination throughout millennia, children and youth have been forced to passively accept the outcomes of democracies made without them that excluded them. Curing the democracy deficit disorder requires reimagining the roles of young people throughout society so that democracy is done *with* children and youth instead of done *for* them; empowering young people so democracy is done *by* them instead of done *to* them. Aside from slight sporadic attempts throughout the ages, there has never been a serious reconceptualization of society that included children and youth in democracy. Engaging the youngest members of society with full and active democratic agency is the only way to face the challenges overwhelming society today.

Ultimately, this necessitates what has been coined by Ruthanne Kurth-Schai (1988) as reconceptualizing the roles of youth in society. However, society needs more than a reconceptualization; communities, nations, and the world need pragmatic action (Nishiyama, 2017). This reality is examined throughout the rest of this book, and while it sounds like a massive, society-wide intervention, it is essential to understand that curing the democracy deficit disorder is intensely personal as well. Curing the democracy deficit disorder requires meaningful wisdom, practical action, systems changes, and personal accountability.

Personalizing Democracy with Meaningful Wisdom

In the aftermath of the January 6, 2021, insurrection at the U.S. Congress, Rep. Jamie Raskin gave testimony in the House during the second U.S. Senate impeachment of President Donald Trump as to what he saw that day. Describing the harrowing reality of his daughter visiting and saying after the attack that she never wanted to come back to the Capitol again, Rep. Raskin introduced the idea that "democracy is personal" ("U.S. Senate Impeachment Trial," 2021). He used this phrase to describe the intensely personal effects of the coup attempt on his daughter. There is value to expanding on this idea to acknowledge that every single person in every single country around the world should internalize and personalize democracy this way—not for its colonizing effects, but for its expansive possibilities. This embodies the popular tenet of democracy that, "People affected by decisions should have a share in making those decisions" (Golarz & Golarz, 1995, p. 16). Expanded further, it means that people affected by government should choose the governors; people learning in schools should select the teachers; people experiencing poverty should choose what types of relief they experience. This is not a charity, but justice. Democracy on the personal level is justice.

Defeating the democracy deficit disorder is not just about stopping violently radical insurrections from ever happening in the U.S. Capitol again; it is much more than that. It is not just about volunteering or running for political office, either, especially for young people who are often disallowed from doing either. Instead, making democracy personal means that all people come to understand democracy within themselves, their families, communities, states and nations, and around the world. Every institution throughout society has to be understood for its role in that democracy too, including formal and informal, government and private institutions, and beyond. This is the deepest implementation of direct democracy imaginable because it thrusts upon every individual the rights and responsibilities of membership within a democracy at the hyper-personal level as well as the global scale.

Imagine each individual throughout society living without oppression. Envision every person in their complete, entire, and whole lives without anyone acting as an unnecessary intermediary or interrupter of their life experience. This oppression happens in the mind and heart; in the physical and corporeal self; in families and homes; in communities; at recreation and jobs; in formal and informal education; and across entire lifespans. Imagine personal and public decisions being made by every individual with full consciousness and understanding of their public implications and effects. Imagine that the practicality of daily democracy is no longer questioned for its relevance or potential. Instead, the benefits to the individual and the smallest groups of people are equitably recognized and redistributed to benefit all people throughout society. This is not just an exercise in voting, either; instead, it is the wholesale reimagining of the roles of *every* individual in every corner of society today.

Recognizing the modern aspects of democracy can be essential for this understanding, no matter where people are seeking to defeat this disorder. These traits include but are broader than the popular consensus of governmental democracy, which include "electoral politics, rule of law, open markets, flexible labor, fiscal restraint, political and economic stability, and transparent and corruption-free public administration" (Ryder, 2013, p. 253). Others are more prescriptive, declaring that democracy is a system for choosing and replacing the government through free and fair elections; active participation of the people, as citizens, in politics and civic life; protection of the human rights of all citizens; and a rule of law in which the laws and procedures apply equally to all citizens (Stanford University, 2004). The former UN Commission on Human Rights defined democracy in 2000, saying it includes "Respect for human rights and fundamental freedoms; freedom of association; freedom of expression and opinion; access to power and its exercise in accordance with the rule of law; the holding of periodic free and fair elections by universal suffrage and by secret ballot as the expression of the will of the people; a pluralistic system of political parties and organizations; the separation of powers; the independence of the judiciary; transparency and accountability in public administration; and free, independent and pluralistic media" (United Nations, n.d.).

All of these traditional traits are important and offer a basis for understanding what is in disarray in today's democracy. However, they do not speak to the personal effect of democracy within the lives of every person, everywhere, all of the time. This "personal democracy" is an increasingly obvious yet deeply internalized perception of how individuals operate within themselves and see themselves operating throughout the world around them. With increasing verbiage present throughout their lives, children and youth are the latest generation to inherit this innately esoteric notion of personal democracy. While this is deeply private, technology also makes personal democracy a public phenomenon by amplifying children's voice and youth voice in meta-spaces on the Internet. Other activities discussed later in this book provide a similar service in the real-time lives of young people and the communities they live in. In this way, the traits of democracy include "liberty, equality, autonomy, reciprocity, fallibility, experimentalism, transparency, and practical reason" (Ober, 2013, p. 1). As young people seek to embrace, advocate, and embody these characteristics, they are neither seeking more rights or privileges; instead, they are seeking the Kingian notion of interdependence (King, 1968, p. 191) reflected when he said, "we must develop a world perspective…as nations and individuals, we are interdependent… It really boils down to this: that all life is interrelated" (Dellinger, 2017).

However, as one researcher found, "Students who not only learn about democracy but also experience aspects of it may be more likely to articulate more complex definitions of democracy" (Avery et al., 2012, p. 31). More people can more thoroughly understand the breadth of these democratic traits by experiencing democracy in its broadest sense. In order to do that, the public must stay public.

Keeping the Public Public through Practical Action

There is a fire burning in the commons today. It was started in broad daylight by unnamed perpetrators who look like everyone else and act in familiar ways but have different motivations. They are making money from ignorance, peddling lies and hatred, and promoting violent revolution and active discrimination. The fires they light are fueled with books they hate and laws they overturn; they keep burning with the motivations of evil, spite, contempt, and hurt. Ultimately, these actors would end any sense of collectivity, any joint concern for mutual success, and every idea that works against their agenda of separation, segregation, and suffering for profit. These forces are best summarized as neoliberal, and they rely on anti-democratic sentiment in order to propagate and perpetuate the fires that burn.

The work of curing the democracy deficit disorder is not wholly individualistic. Instead, it also necessitates a collective strategy to improve the shared spaces everyone co-occupies throughout society. This is true of everything from the smallest and most intimate family or home-setting to the largest global, international, and cross-cultural institution. In their important book, *Re-envisioning Education and Democracy* (Kurth-Schai & Green, 2016, p. 121), Kurth-Schai and Green asked the essential question, "Given commitments to deeper democracy in schools and society, how can we develop feasible collective visions?" The sweeping breadth of this question is the heart of the challenge that is asserted in this section. Instead of doing it alone, how can society do the work of curing this disorder together? This book asserts that any adult who wants to support children and youth must begin with empowering them to do the work individually and collectively. However, that action must not be wholly theoretical; it must be active, practical, and actually empowered.

Differences among young people necessitate a plurality of approaches to every action detailed in this book. However, there are some basic, pragmatic steps all adults who are committed to democracy can and must take in order to begin to realize the positive, powerful potential of all young people to engage in democracy, everywhere, all of the time.

Defining the purpose of any activity for children and youth *with* children and youth must happen before engaging in any attempt to challenge the democracy deficit disorder. This includes parenting, schooling, afterschool programs, summer camps, sports, extracurricular activities, and all other manner of serving young people. Young people and adults should engage in practical, purposeful conversations about the focus of activities for them and the adults who serve them. Being forthright and honest about the purpose of activities—whether to provide basic learning for successful democratic citizenship, to support the economic workforce, or some other reason should be named by everyone involved. As Gillen writes, "We start each year in the standardized school with no consensus at all among our students about what we are there for. No common purpose; no sense of a shared task freely undertaken; no agreement on how our work should be structured beyond the idiotic routines of drills, course requirements, tests, and grades" (2014, p. 28). This same absent rambling through the days can be said of most activities for children and youth today outside of schools, as well as within. Educational goals and "success" have become defined by student performance on standardized tests, along with student attendance and graduation rates. While these might be part of the purpose of education and young peoples' programs, a growing number of adult allies to children and youth today want to broaden the goals of education, social services, and more to include students' social, emotional, and intellectual development, as well as helping young people gain the skills needed to build a better and more democratic world.

The first step is for each person to recognize their roles in curing the democracy deficit disorder. To do this, young people and adults should see themselves as democratic agents who are empowered within their own life and throughout the society around them. Then they should see themselves as both the targets and perpetrators of adultism.

Then, each person should acknowledge and validate the whole humanity of children and youth. This means actively and critically countering any personal belief and professional obligation that lessens, dehumanizes, or otherwise shuts down young people in any way. Every domain in the life of a young person adds up to 100%, including the emotional, social, cultural, intellectual, recreational, moral, and other parts. This does not overburden them with unrealistic expectations but sees their humanity by treating them as whole people right now, whatever their age, capabilities, or actions. It allows children and youth to be seen as democratic agents who can and should fully contribute, criticize, reimagine, advocate, and empower other people.

The next step in this process is to validate what young people are doing right now in order to challenge the democracy deficit disorder. Throughout the world there are countless moment-by-moment, day-by-day, and year-by-year actions being taken by children and youth that positively impact democracy. Adult allies of young people are morally charged to acknowledge, uplift, and advocate for these young people and their actions, no matter what the magnitude of the action or outcomes is.

Each person should then educate themselves about how to empower children and youth in democracy. By doing this every child, youth, and adult can confront the inaccurate, sensationalistic, and otherwise unrealistic portraits of young people painted by popular media. Confronting this can stop the daily terrorism facing children and youth in society, including being simultaneously infantilized, criminalized, minimized, incapacitated, segregated, isolated, and denied their existence, their whole humanity, and their capacity to change the world. Self-education is the key here, as each *democrat* is empowered to protest, advocate, and advance democracy without permission or acknowledgment from others.

Taking a step by recognizing places within and throughout daily life to engage young people happens next. Seeing daily life as a canvas for both young people and democracy, it is vital to situate the attitudes, actions, and potential of children and youth throughout individual homes, neighborhoods, businesses, institutions, governments, and beyond. This entails making young people into normalized, expected, and accepted agents of change throughout the world, illustrating the greatest possible outcomes for social change affecting democracy and adultism at the same time.

The next step can be the most obvious or subversive in anyone's life because it is educating children and youth about democracy and adultism. Whether it is through literature such as children's books, poetry, or song lyrics, using the internet for research and creation, or making art that proves the point, everyone can educate others about the power and potential of stopping age-based discrimination and building democracy. All kinds of media and any kind of methods can be used to educate and elevate conversations throughout our lives.

After that step, the next one is to transform the world through practical, meaningful, and productive action in any given situation. This step focuses on the pragmatic and practical journey from theory to practice and from talking to transformation. At whatever scale and to whatever effect, taking action can look like changing our own lives or changing the world. It can happen on the micro-personal level even by challenging our own discriminations against young people at home, on a grander scale by addressing adultism and anti-democracy affecting children, and on the grandest scale throughout international efforts designed to confront adultism at the United Nations, World Bank, or other global institution.

Reflecting on what has conspired and the difference it made and planning to apply what each individual can do with what they have learned is the final step. This means allowing critical engagement with the actions that have been taken, the assumptions informing them, and much more, as well as the essential re-envisioning of whatever has been completed into something more just and equitable between young people and adults.

This practical, personal action can provide an essential avenue for pragmatic engagement with the democracy deficit disorder.

5

Democracy Matters in Many Ways

Arguing for freedom and against authoritarianism may seem passé, but with the January 6 insurrection in the U.S. Capitol, the climate crisis, white supremacy, the war in Ukraine, and so many other issues smashing at the bedrock of democracy worldwide right now, in these times it is more relevant than ever. What is more irreverent is arguing for democracy for young people. Working to educate parents, teachers, youth workers, nonprofit executives, government officials, and people in dozens of other types of adult roles throughout society about this idea has shown the abilities of these people to apply a holistic approach of democracy to young people to be lacking at best; at worst, the broad ineptitude and indifference of some of these people can be astounding. This is not to say that they do not try, or are wholly intransigent; however, it does mean that there is a lot of work to do if democracy deficit disorder is to be overcome.

Ultimately, liberal democracy insists that the moment-by-moment expression of freedom is essential. Surely, through deliberation and process, that democracy takes on larger connotations for the operations of society and the machinations of governments. However, its ultimate effect is on the individual young person, and without individual freedoms the function of democracy in a society is purely a display with no real substance. This is doubly so for young people who generally apparently live such autocratic, authoritarian realities that experiencing democracy in their daily lives is often the only opportunity they have to feel the joy of freedom. This reality is true throughout their lives, from their family lives to their education, from out-of-school time to religious expressions, and in those exacting motions of daily living, including their speech, technology usage, clothing, and friendships. This makes it vital to ensure that children and youth are actively engaged in every aspect of planning, organizing, implementing, and sustaining every effort throughout their lives in order to transform society into a true democracy (Chomsky, 2013).

There are even some proponents of children and youth involvement who insist that their involvement is contingent on the implementation of direct democracy rather than the tradition of representative democracy that so many of the world's democracies rely on. In an interview about youth and democracy from 2018, David Runciman said, "There are lots of ways we could do it: more deliberation, citizens juries, using new technology to give people more of a say. Many different forms of participation that we've barely even tried because representative democracy was designed to prevent it" (Carr & Runciman, 2018). In saying this though, he revealed the bias he has toward existent practices rather than the dynamically responsive activities young people are engaging in today. Despite adultist viewpoints like this, democracy can give society a framework for understanding the depth and breadth of what young people are doing today to cure the disorder.

Democracy matters in many ways because of the diversity and evolving capacities of children and youth today. The vast array of possibilities, potentials, and purposes of young people necessitate holism throughout all the functions in a young person's life. From a similar perspective, in 1958 Eleanor Roosevelt wrote,

> Where, after all, do universal human rights begin? In small places, close to home—so close and so small that they cannot be seen on any maps of the world. Yet they are the world of the individual person; the neighborhood he lives in; the school or college he attends; the factory, farm, or office where he works. Such are the places where every man, woman, and child seeks equal justice, equal opportunity, equal dignity without discrimination. Unless these rights have meaning there, they have little meaning anywhere. (American University School of International Service, 2017)

Envisioning what that can look like is challenging, but not impossible. In order to do that though, it is vital to acknowledge that most things happening on the grand scale today to teach democracy are not effective in engaging every young person in every community in democracy.

Failures of Democracy

Democracy is no perfect potion. The simple truth is that democracy allows the current situation—one rife with totalitarianism, neoliberalism, and fascism—to exist. The inherent tension of democracy is that it is flawed and imperfect, yet because of that there is room for it to grow to become something greater than it is today. What lies between here and there is the question, and that is what makes it essential to recognize the roles children and youth can, should, and are occupying throughout society.

When it comes to young people, there are plenty of failures of democracy. They include the failure to meet the basic needs of young people, the status of young people in the electoral system, the moral discrepancies in civic life, and the wholesale effects of adultism. As Delgado and Staples (2008, p. 96) wrote, "Democratic principles have been developed exclusively by adults for adults, and youth either have been ignored totally or told that their time would come if they are patient."

However, by the nature of their age, experiences, and what their roles are in society, young people have particularly dynamic and responsive lenses to see the world through. Because of their inexperience, they contain a multitude of possibilities for a new world that has never existed before. Most importantly though, it is their energetic wisdom that can teach adults new ways of seeing and doing that have never existed before. While there are certainly limits to this, it can be said that most children and youth innately have new viewpoints and hope that adults do not.

Systemic roadblocks to democracy in the United States that are cited in the media include historical and obvious elements such as voter suppression, inconsistent voting rights for the incarcerated, gerrymandering, campaign financing, and the electoral college system. They are even said to be intentional within the American democracy (Emmerson, 2020). Others insist that "real" democracies are nearly nonexistent, with "American kleptocracy and plutocracy" dominating the American experiment with democracy and causing "endless wars, colonialism, capitalism, plunder of the poor, restriction on free speech and censorship, imprisonment of political opponents..." and so forth. Used as a rationale for so many undemocratic activities, the term is said to have no real meaning in western society. Internationally, observers cite these and other issues. Recent research from Harvard suggests there are five major challenges to democracy today. They are overcoming polarization; immigration and sustaining multiethnic democracies; globalization, economic inequality, and democratic discontent; causes and consequences of populism; and debates over institutional solutions (Ziblatt, n.d.). A 2016 article from Switzerland says that around the globe, the biggest failures of democracy include, "outdated electoral systems; low election quality in established democracies; unregulated campaign funding; completely failed elections; autocratic characteristics in presidencies; declining political and civil rights; rising populism; increased personal sovereignty; lack of identity; and undemocratic role models for young people" (Longchamp, 2016). It is the last issue in this list that is most egregious.

There are several ways democracy has failed children and youth. The most poignant way to find out what those failures are is to ask young people themselves; in lieu of that, following are some specific ways.

The first failure is that the basic needs of children and youth are not met worldwide right now. That means that no nation on the planet is 100% successful in ensuring that every young person is safe and has access to food, water, shelter, and clothing. Those needs are amplified by the failures to ensure the effectiveness of the Convention on the Rights of the Child. Even if the tool was complete, it is still not signed by the United States, which effectively allows every other nation to treat children's rights as supplemental, rather than primary, to their national wellbeing. These are cornerstones of understanding how young people are being undermined right now worldwide.

The perpetual silencing of children and youth throughout society in formal and informal ways is another failure of democracy. This form of adultism is absolute, nearly suffocating children's voice and youth voice in countless ways and in nearly every situation, including at home where the power and authority of adults is treated as absolute; in government where there are few roles for children and youth beyond that of "passive recipient" and when there are roles, they are tokenistic at best; in education where the experiences of young people are treated as irrelevant and the judgment of adults is complete; and in countless other settings. This silencing is always violent: Nonphysical silencing is manipulative, tokenistic, and belittling; physical violence is often unquestioned and held tantamount to "good parenting" when it is employed. As Freire (2004) wrote, "Any situation in which some individuals prevent others from engaging in the process of inquiry is one of violence. The means used are not important; to alienate human beings from their own decision-making is to change them into objects."

Another failure of democracy comes in the status of children and youth in the election process. Within that process, they are neither the voters nor the elected. As Wall (2022, p. 3) wrote, "Democracy is an ideal. It aims to hold those in power accountable to all, instead of just a few." As people whose capacity to make the choices required within a representative democracy are constantly called to question, young people are taught they are less than fully human and irrelevant to the societies within which they live. The absence of any kind of a vote for young people is an absolute failure in our society. Similarly, children and youth are not elected to be represented by children and youth within any legislative bodies at any level around the world. Because of that routine exclusion, the issues young people value are routinely and wholly dismissed by those who are supposed to represent them. If young peoples' voices are taken seriously, they are often treated as a single-issue phenomenon with actions taken to appease and pacify rather than acknowledge, amplify, and empower broad civic ability.

Throughout the structure of civic life today, children and youth are treated as an afterthought to more "serious" adult issues, with the opinions of young people almost wholly dismissed by elected officials, government workers, community leaders, and others. This is despite the fact that according to the U.S. federal government, 55% of young people ages 12–19 volunteer every year. By comparison, 29% of adults do the same (AmeriCorps, Office of Research and Evaluation, 2021, p. 3). This means that in the United States young people are contributing their energy to the wellbeing of their communities at nearly double the rate of adults without the benefits of being seen as serious contributors to their communities. Even the benefits espoused by neoliberal advocates are not treated seriously enough to warrant the wholesale support of the U.S. federal government for youth programs, as one federal website said, "Afterschool programs also provide a significant return-on-investment, with every $1 invested saving at least $3 through increasing youth's earning potential, improving their performance at school, and reducing crime and juvenile delinquency." The same website attested to the reality that there is one single federal program supporting afterschool programs for children and youth (Youth.gov, n.d.). All that is to say that despite the best actions of young people, their interests are not being served by the federal government in the United States today. Surely there are many federal programs dealing with the gamut of issues affecting children and youth today; however, what of these responds to what young people want for themselves throughout communities across the country every day, rather than what adults have determined are what they need? No study is available to share children's voices or youth voice about federal spending. Arriving at the absence of young peoples' voices is not a coincidence, because it is a failure of democracy worldwide. Seen as anomalous or special, aside from a few exceptional circumstances around the globe there is a nearly complete blackout on engaging young people as policymakers worldwide. Surely there are small numbers of children's parliaments and youth councils, student school board members, and other forms of representation. However, the value of these programs is negligible at best, as their influence and authority is regularly trampled under the heel of adultism.

Overarching, domineering, infantilizing, and complete, the power of adultism is unparalleled for its completeness throughout society today. In nearly every situation affecting children and youth, adultism rears its compulsive authoritarianism to render irrelevant young people today. This distinct phenomenon occurs in so many places and is enforced by so many people that it is nearly impossible to envision a world without it. However, therein lies its distinct possibilities: unlike other oppressive -isms, adultism can be employed for the good of society too. Adults can use the bias toward adults as a tool for uplifting the status of children and youth, and as is commonplace, adults can influence, educate, and empower other adults to do better. However, it is a failure of democracy to have enshrined, enculturated, and codified adultism in every function of society today, even ones that should be serving young people most effectively.

Failures of Current Democracy Education

It can be argued that democracy education has largely failed (Torres & Assié, 1998; McGuire, 2007). Democratic education has been apparent throughout public schools around the world for generations (Straume, 2016), with much of the approach today attributed to John Dewey. As one of the direct extensions of his efforts to make public education more relevant to every student, his work is credited for contributing to the development of the field of career and technical education (Gordon & Schultz, 2020, p. 42), as well as the integration of collaborative learning, critical thinking, and problem solving throughout K-12 education and beyond (Sanborn & Thyne, 2014). However, Giroux (2018) argues that there is a fetishization of techniques and methodologies as a consequence of these strategies. The absence of critical engagement with education as a topic, process and outcome has led to the rise of authoritarianism and the anti-democratic movement sweeping the globe right now (Aquarone, 2021).

There is no single form of democracy education that all people everywhere adhere to; indeed, the phrase "democracy education" means many things to many people (Kahne & Westheimer, 2003, p. 35). Rather than oversimplifying it as a simplistic set of activities or methods, this plurality seems to demand overarching frameworks to invent and reinvent democracy education in every setting for each generation. To this point, many approaches reflect Hendrick's three methods for teaching democracy: "encouraging children to make decisions, building children's autonomy, and fostering children's trust in the individual, authority, and the group" (Hendrick, 1992). While this offers a convenient summary, it easily dismisses the breadth of actions used throughout history to educate children and youth about democracy. Worse still, it might perpetuate the attitudes informing a lot of theory and practice today (Zheng, 2022), which reflect the invasive presence of adultism within democracy education. The ultimate goal of democracy education must be to teach more than teach children and youth about humanity. Flanagan found that "people who believe human beings are generally trustworthy and fair tend to vote, join organizations, lead groups, and actively support the rights of others to hold and express their own religious beliefs, cultural traditions, and lifestyles" (Flanagan, 2013, p. 163).

It is not enough to simply be anti-authoritarian though, which is a core assumption in the tradition of democratic education (Dewey, 1987, p. 460). Said to be synonymous with white supremacy, eurocentrism, and other forms of ethnological terrorism (Torres, 1998), democratic education has been depoliticized to the point of irrelevance in the overall social discourse dominating daily interactions (Expósito, 2014, p. 231; Johannsen, 2011). Its authoritarian roots are laid bare (Sanborn & Thyne, 2014, p. 774), reflected in the adultism inherent throughout its functions (Fletcher, 2015). It is as if the very act of educating children and youth about democracy was intended to keep young people from being essential agents of democracy in their own lives and throughout their communities (Torres, 1998). Consequently, the young people who manage to graduate from programs and institutions with any commitment to democracy are rare; those who fulfill their democratic responsibilities are rarer still; and those who advocate, perpetuate, and actively engage with democracy are rarer still. The rarest are people who critically engage with democracy, challenging it to become a more perfect engine for daily living, as well as governance and social structures.

Traditional, longstanding approaches to teaching young people about democracy are barely relevant to the conversation in this book. Claiming to teach youth about the origins of democracy, democratic ideals and practice, the ideals of justice and freedom, the difficulties of democracy and so on, these programs are often mere recitations of the U.S. Constitution, the Eurocentric timeline of democratic development culminating in American democracy, and an emphasis on the male-dominated U.S. presidency. Moreso, the practices therein are increasingly said to reinforce white supremacy, patriarchal beliefs, sexism, heterosexism, classism, and much more.

Rather than teaching democracy, many current activities may simply placate the innate interests of children and youth and satiate their desire for formally and informally engaging as active agents of change in their communities. These activities are often conducted out of context as some kind of pacification, inserted almost recklessly into the lives of young people and given undue expectations of having anything to do with the substantive development of democratic skills. They are often couched in the cloak of problem-based learning, with adults feeding young people problems to be worried about in the way that Freire explored as "myths fed to the people by the oppressors" that ultimately secure power for the oppressors by falsely frightening the people (Freire, 2004, p. 172).

This type of democratic education actually serves to impose adultism throughout the lives of children and youth by providing stability based on adult ability, adult knowledge, and adult authority. Because of this, civic education is taught as decontextualized technical skills that have nothing to do with the day-to-day realities facing young people; in turn, this actually prohibits the development of substantive knowledge about democracy. This can actually be detrimental to young people in communities where democracy is undervalued by reinforcing the negative perception of choice as an unnecessary burden. In these situations, young people practicing activities devoid of the context of a larger democratic project are taught to believe it is better to passively receive democracy rather than actively be the drivers of democracy.

Some of the activities that are used in the name of democratic education today lack any substance and are merely stand-ins for what should be long-range, planned out, sophisticated opportunities for children and youth to study, criticize, and transform democracy today. For instance, simple mock voting in schools or doing adult-led service-learning projects is not enough to educate for democracy. Instead of showing their impact on the world around them or weaving them into the lifeblood of their surrounding communities, these activities isolate children and youth from adults, reinforce a sense of ignorance, inability, and worse, infantilize them. Similarly ineffectual activities can include parents taking children to the voting place; talking about political candidates at home; and writing letters to elected officials as a family. At school or in after school settings such as childcare or youth programs, other typical activities include talking about protest as patriotic; encouraging children to speak up when they do not agree and to ask questions about what they want to; talking about times when countries do not live up to democratic ideals; talking about voter suppression; and reading books about democracy and citizenship as a group. There can also be voting on rules, punishments, and decorations, or giving false choices that present young people with options without giving them real authority to choose (Kohn, 1993, p. 19). International authorities concur on the importance of providing young people with substantive opportunities to act on democracy in real ways, too, with the United Nations Committee on the Rights of the Child declaring,

> Any decision that does not take into account the child's views or does not give their views due weight according to their age and maturity, does not respect the possibility for the child or children to influence the determination of their best interests. (Eriksen, 2018)

The age-based segregation implicit in all the aforementioned activities is at the core of their failure (Jenks, 1996, p. 57). By separating the young from the older people throughout society for the majority of waking hours, education institutions, out-of-school time organizations, government agencies, and others inherently tell children and youth their presence is not welcome in the adult world (Holt, 1974). Further, it perpetuates negative stereotypes about young people by implying they are not worthy, deserving or otherwise in need of being involved in democracy's activities in all their forms. Instead, age segregation tells young people they need to be shuttled off, cordoned away, and locked up for their own safety and everyone else's, too.

Understanding what needs to happen in order to respect children this way is not a mystery. As Counts (1978), Freire (1985), hooks (2013), and others taught, young people must learn to read the word through the world by becoming critically engaged with issues that matter right now, not as an exercise but as a way of living. While this was radical forty years ago, today there are decades of research that has shown that contextualization is essential for young people to build connections between their learning and their lives (Rathbun, 2015). Working with children and youth as partners to identify where, when, why, what, and how they learn not only lends credence to the educational processes they are engaged in, but also to the democratic experiment they are simultaneously and perpetually inheriting and inventing. Understanding this empowers learners, substantiates educators and nullifies naysayers, the adultists who believe there is no real place for children and youth within democracy beyond being Marshall's classic notion of young people as "citizens in the making" (Marshall, 1992, p. 15).

Adultism in Democracy Education

Addressing something as "democracy education" does not automatically mean it is safe and free, or particularly encouraging of young peoples' involvement. That reality alone makes democracy education adultist, as it reflects an adults' perception of what young people want or should want, rather than asking fully informed, fully invested young people what they want for themselves.

In some forms of democracy education, adults create specially isolated spaces for kids to "learn in freedom." This is adultist on many levels. One reason for this is that learning environments that isolate young people from so-called real-world interactions by creating singular experiences where young people have the capability to supposedly "do whatever they want" in the name of learning that are actually expressing the will of adults. As explored previously, society instills a number of inalienable rights on everyone because of their age. Intending to rectify a perception of diminished rights for young people, there are educators both within schools and outside schools who seek to create rebalance by instilling similar rights in the young people they interact with—to an extent determined by those adults. But children and youth need to do more than *learn* about democracy and rights; they need to enact and live democracy.

In a number of gestures, adults in schools and community organizations who adhere to democracy education grant young people the right to voluntary class attendance, voting through class meetings, and in some cases, "all aspects of the school" are led jointly by participants in these meetings. This is why Scottish progressive education innovator A.S. Neill dismissed early efforts to replicate his famed Summerhill School in the United States, because he thought the Americans were granting license, not freedom (Bailey, 2014). He was wrong though; they were granting the right to self-governance, which is not freedom; it actually reflects the "tyranny of freedom" (Deresiewicz, 2012). The right to self-governance is a premise of American liberal democracy.

Neill fetishized freedom for children (Neill, 1990), and his belief has become the premise for a lot of democracy education in Western countries today. This was perhaps best understood in his concept of the "free child," in statements like "Free children are not easily influenced; the absence of fear accounts for this phenomenon. Indeed, the absence of fear is the finest thing that can happen to a child" (Neill, 2010, p. 138). Achieving this absence of fear is unattainable for many young people today though. Instead of focusing on that, democratic educators often focus on self-governance instead.

However, the right to self-governance, when applied to children and youth, is wholly adultist, as are all forms of governance. Adultism is bias toward adults, and so far as history shows, no form of governance has ever been proposed and enacted upon by children or youth. It is not merely discrimination toward youth; instead, adultism is bias toward adults, and it is not always wrong (Fletcher, 2015).

In the case of democracy education, adultism informs its very existence. As Neill showed in his refutation mentioned above, revealing the very premise of his understanding of freedom was adultist since it was he himself who determined its necessity rather than the young people he worked with. This same reality is true in other democracy education settings, too, whether they are afterschool programs, at-school classrooms, or other spaces where democracy is taught.

So many well-meaning but poorly informed program workers, educators, community organizers, and activists form their opinions of the world and then impose them on young people. They then call those opinions "democracy education" rather than allowing young people themselves to form their own conceptions independent of adult manipulation. In an ironic twist, these adults propagate and promote these limited conceptions without the input of the very people who are intent on learning about democracy. Without a thorough examination, one could easily conclude that almost all schools, youth-serving nonprofits, community groups, and social movements do this exact same thing.

The final important distinction to make about adultism in democracy education is regarding the difference between capacity and capability. Capacity is the ability a single person has to understand information, use it in doing something, and foresee the outcomes of that thing. Because of the ways that each person evolves, the boundaries of an individual's personal capacity are largely unknown throughout their life and can only be seen on a person-by-person basis. In an important difference, capability is a specific level of skill, knowledge, or ability relative to a task. It is a continuum that is best measured by degrees to allow for appropriate and just differentiation between people. In these ways, capacity refers to what could be, while capability refers to what is.

As the natural world around us routinely reflects, young people are not born with the capability to operate in the world around them. However, every child and youth has infinite capacity to live according to their own terms. The dilemma is that well-meaning adults throughout the field seem to mix up these two words, capability and capacity. They assume young people are capable of leading themselves whenever, wherever, and however they want to, without working to intentionally increase the capacity of young people to do this. This wholesale handover is a deep expression of adultism, whereupon adults assume that young people have the same capability as adults just because adults have the capacity to do it. This is an unjust assumption at best. At worst, it is a cynical ploy to abdicate responsibility and set up young people for failure (Cockburn, 2007, p. 452).

Perhaps Neill's ultimate belief about children was best though. In his seminal work called *Summerhill: A Radical Approach to Child-Rearing* he wrote, "A child is innately wise and realistic. If left to himself without adult suggestion of any kind, he will develop as far as he is capable of developing" (1990, p. 4). The hope implicit in that belief should continuously inform any further development of the project to educate children and youth for democracy, and to cure the democracy deficit disorder.

Beyond Adultism

In his novel *Turn Coat*, Jim Butcher (Butcher, 2009) writes, "No one is an unjust villain in his own mind. Even—perhaps even especially—those who are the worst of us. Some of the cruelest tyrants in history were motivated by noble ideals or made choices that they would call 'hard but necessary steps' for the good of their nation. We're all the hero of our own story."

Every adult who educates for democracy positions themselves as the "hero of their own story," as with much of society's work with young people in general. The fields of youth development, K-12 education, social services, counseling and therapy, and public health among many others are all littered with heroes like this, adults who are unjust villains trying to save the world. It is adultism that imposes, enforces, and substantiates this tyranny.

Democracy education, in all its myriad forms, can only be anti-adultist by making young people fully equitable partners. This means that in addition to the self-governance over educational operations, all children and youth of any age in any space must have full ownership over fundraising, the mission, and higher levels of organizational operation through an equal or greater number of full voting positions on boards of directors for the schools and nonprofits that are practicing democracy education. In many states across the United States, those roles are fully against the law for young people to occupy. In other places where young people can legally hold those positions, in organizations ascribing to the values of democracy education, young people are often thrown into these positions by well-meaning adults without the knowledge and skills to fully contribute. They have the capability; they lack the capacity (Lansdown, 2005). This justifies adults' rationale proclaiming young people have nothing of substance to contribute in these positions.

Every adult practices adultism. By confronting the situations and naming what they are, democratic educators can successfully challenge themselves from an informed place of critical awareness instead of a naïve place of self-satisfaction with status quo.

Holistic Youth Development

The primary failure of democracy education is adultism. Adultism is a failure of hope in young people that cynically posits that their present is worthless. The primary failure of adultism is that it *dehumanizes* young people, forcing them to accept the banking approach to democracy.

Freire's concept of banking education is a method of schooling where teachers "deposit" information in youth, who simply store it and retrieve it on demand (Freire, 2004). Adultism embodies that by actively denying that children and youth are whole human beings who can engage their whole selves in the active pursuit of democracy.

This antithesis of this cynicism was named by radical educator John Taylor Gatto who proclaimed,

> Whatever an education is, it should make you a unique individual, not a conformist; it should furnish you with an original spirit with which to tackle the big challenges; it should allow you to find values which will be your roadmap through life; it should make you spiritually rich, a person who loves whatever you are doing, wherever you are, whomever you are with; it should teach you what is important, how to live and how to die. (Gatto, 1992, p. 75)

If all young people experienced education about democracy the way that Gatto so thoroughly hoped for education in general, they would genuinely grow into well-rounded, fully capable citizens of the world who would not only rule themselves justly, but feel bound and determined to be fair, empathetic, and nonviolent toward all other humans, other creatures of the earth, and the planet itself. Gatto's vision reflects an innate awareness of holism, which is "the idea that various systems should be viewed as wholes, not merely as a collection of parts" (Wikipedia, 2022i). There needs to be a concept reflecting this perspective which makes the disparate activities currently done in the name of education and positive youth development more effective and more relevant to all young people, in addition to becoming more precise and applicable throughout their lives. This concept is called holistic youth development.

Holistic youth development is a framework for considering the myriad ways children and youth grow, learn, and evolve while they are young (Fletcher, 2014b). As introduced in the beginning of this section, there is an inherently complex and oftentimes contradictory relationship between every young person and the world in which they are born that is imposed by adultism. Idealized for being young, youth are also infantilized for being under-experienced. Scorned for being childish, children are praised for being playful. Lionized as "the future," youth are also scandalized for not respecting the past. Children who are precocious are labeled gifted but held in suspicion by adults who do not trust their intelligence (Zheng, 2022). Rather than conveniently stagnating because of adult contentment, young people can embody a seeming tornado of perpetual motion which swirls through the "evolving capacities of the child" (Lansdown, 2005) toward adulthood. Along with that is what appears to many adults as randomness, chaos, incoherence, and indifference, or as Audre Lorde once wrote, "I find I am constantly being encouraged to pluck out some one aspect of myself and present this as the meaningful whole, eclipsing or denying the other parts of self" (Lourde, 1984, p. 120).

As opposed to the segregating aspects of traditional theory and practice in the fields of youth development (Schulman, 2006) and child development (Stephenson et al., 2004, p. 14), holistic youth development includes all parts in the life of young people, including the attitudes, activities, cultures, structures, and outcomes that impact, animate, and continuously transform their realities. It recognizes the fluidity of their existence, and instead of treating children and youth as a specific age number interested in a single topic during one time of the day, week, month, or year, holistic youth development sees the entire young person all of the time, from birth to adulthood. This notion of holism challenges the traditional perspectives of child development and youth development that happens on a continuous, convenient, and consistent linear progression. Instead, it is all over for different young people, driven by the ecology surrounding children and youth. That ecology includes the adults, other young people, the environment, social and economic realities, culture, and many more parts.

This holistic perspective must be taken toward educating children and youth about democracy. Several different approaches can ensure that young people and adults are working toward holistic youth development. They include thinking sustainably; having a clear purpose; engaging the non-traditionally engaged; fostering real connections; striving for equity instead of equality; growing capacity;

making a clear path; acting for systemic change; connecting the dots; and keeping your eyes open. Following are details on each of these steps.

First, think sustainably. This should happen from the outset of any activity. There should be specific ways to ensure young people continue to be continuously equitable partners in learning about democracy throughout youth development. Young people should have roles in facilitation, evaluation, research, decision-making, and advocacy throughout the culture of every class, program, organization, or community. If young people must be involved in a onetime activity, they should be informed about opportunities for youth development outside of that activity.

Second, have a clear purpose. Working with children and youth to establish a clear purpose for themselves in a democracy-building program is the beginning. Then, other young people, organization leaders, parents, community members, and local schools know what is being done and why it is happening. Clarity of purpose is often missing from democracy education, as school is done to the young, family is done to them, and stores are done to them. Democracy building activities should be done *with* children and youth, and they should know why.

Third, engage the historically disengaged. Creating space and helping children and youth who have not been particularly engaged before to become involved in democracy education is essential. Both the historically involved and the non-typically involved young can contribute to all of the various aspects of democracy. Training is available for people to learn about youth voice, Meaningful Student Involvement, youth infusion, Student/Adult Partnerships, and other concepts that are central to curing the democracy deficit disorder.

Fourth, form real connections. When young people see themselves in democracy, real connections are happening, and when real connections happen, children and youth become engaged. Repeating this cycle is what affirms its authenticity and brings young people along. While they may have obvious expertise or interests in a specific topic, it can be vital for afterschool youth workers, teachers, parents, and other adults to help young people discover what they already know and to appropriately acknowledge the wisdom of young people.

Fifth, strive for equity, not equality. Developing equitable roles between young people and adults means that adults do not pretend all things between children, youth, and adults are 50/50 split equally. In adult-centered society that is simply never true. Equity allows young people and adults to enter into responsible relationships that acknowledge what each other knows and does not know, and to work from that place instead of assuming everyone has equal ability and capacity. Every person's differences are real and equity acknowledges those differences without pretending otherwise.

Sixth, grow capacity. Growing the existing capacity of children, youth, and adults to become involved in democracy is very important. When young people and adults learn core knowledge about democracy they defeat its deficit. This is also true when they learn essential skills related to democracy, such as their learning styles, how to defeat assumptions, conflict resolution, change management, and more. It is important to have practical opportunities for people to put these new capacities into action as well.

Seventh, make a clear plan. Having a specific pathway for young people and adults to see how their contributions can affect democracy is vital. This can happen when they see how their democracy can affect their lives, organizations, and communities. Creating opportunities for young people specifically to contribute to an existing program, opening a brand-new course of action and learning, working with the same adults in new ways, or partnering with new adults are just a few ways they can experience democracy in new ways. Creating an afterschool program plan with young people is not the culmination of work, but the starting point of an organization's efforts to create more effective programs. A clear plan can include goals, next steps, roles, and responsibilities, an activity outline, and a participant evaluation. Setting priorities, using timelines with target implementation dates, and developing clear benchmarks for measuring success in each area can also enhance a democracy program plan's effectiveness.

Eighth, be systemic. Encouraging active Student/Adult Partnerships beyond any immediate setting is important so that young people can connect meaningfully throughout larger communities. Specific systemic engagement can include researching their democracy in their community, school, nonprofit program, or anything through participatory action research. They can facilitate, teach, and mentor peers, younger people, and adults of all stripes. They can evaluate themselves, their organizations and communities, workplaces and businesses, and other places. They can participate in organizational, family, community, or other decision-making. They can advocate for what they care about. Ultimately, children and youth can be engaged throughout the systems that prevail in every part of their lives for the purpose of curing the democracy deficit disorder.

Ninth, connect the dots. Establishing family-community-organization-school connections when possible, there should be substantial collaborations that reinforce young people's learning and support in-school learning. The partnerships established in these processes can deepen efforts through the future, and mutually support young people in and out of school time.

Tenth, eyes have to be wide open. Opening the doors of critical examination with young people can provide an essential avenue to grow democracy. Learning how to use critical lenses focused on justice in order to examine their assumptions, those of the people around them, the ones driving the systems they are affected by, and more is very important. Children and youth should also explore the effects they have in any given setting. Identifying strengths and weaknesses allow programs, families, schools, and organizations to improve the overall effectiveness of democracy, especially through divergent efforts. Make space by giving young people permission and skills they need to be partners in mutual accountability with adults. In democracy building activities with the young, it can be essential to set clear benchmarks and hold agreed upon celebrations when they are met and consequences that young people can see for when those benchmarks for improvement are not met.

These ten steps following in sequence can establish a firm foundation for holistic youth development because they embody the whole young person. In turn, they can serve as a crucial starting point for understanding the necessary actions that must be taken to cure the democracy deficit disorder.

Sabotaging Democracy

When adults assume and exert power and control over young people, they often dismantle, demean or otherwise harm young people by habituating, enflaming or otherwise causing more of the democracy deficit disorder. Following are several ways adults accidentally or deliberately sabotage democracy.

For all recorded history society has been adult-driven, rarely making space for children and youth in leadership. In the last 20 years though, more adults are considering and implementing roles for young people throughout democracy. Unfortunately, it seems many adults at all levels of authority are keeping just a few young people in the room to remember why democracy exists, instead of actually engaging many children and youth as equitable partners in substantive practices. Their motivations for doing this are not going to be examined here. However, as Gillen says, "Young people know intuitively that they must figure out how to become adults, but that their schools are designed to infantilize them, to simplify and standardize their verbal expression, to restrict and control their bodies, to crush independent, nonconforming thought. Nevertheless, nearly everyone they trust tells them school is the only way out of poverty and dependency" (2014, p. 50).

Whether it is coincidental or intentional, schools can nullify the passion, perspective, and power of young people and particularly stifle their roles throughout democracy in many ways. Luckily, there are many ways young people and adults can work together to make society a better place. However, adults must understand the value of young people as partners throughout social institutions. Following is an exploration of the ways adults sabotage democracy.

To sabotage something is to destroy, damage, or obstruct it, especially for some kind of advantage. Adults and young people can sabotage democracy. This happens when democracy is used as a tool to manipulate, twist, and turn to achieve a goal. Democracy is more than a tool to use in a specific situation. Instead, it is a way of living which can and should be used every day in every way possible, by everyone for every purpose imaginable. In the lives of young people, it should be taught, empowered, and encouraged at every turn. In order to stop sabotaging democracy it is essential to understand the ways it happens. Following are several ways democracy is sabotaged.

The first way adults sabotage democracy with young people is by forcing involvement. When adults in any setting use force to make something happen with young people, it undermines their best intentions by taking away any democratic intention behind their actions. Young people do not depend on adult approval to engage in democracy; instead, they can inadvertently and explicitly compel it within their own lives dozens of ways throughout the day. Similarly, adults cannot force something to be meaningful for children and youth, because they are the ultimate judges. Authoritarianism, totalitarianism, and coercion directly defeat the feeling, effects, and outcomes of democracy, and by forcing involvement adults take away the ability of children and youth to experience what matters most in democracy, anywhere at any time. Introduce democracy to young people and adults, educate them about the frameworks and options, and then allow them to make up their own minds about whether they want to be involved.

The second way adults sabotage democracy with young people is by silencing the voices of children and youth. One of the most insidious ways adults undermine democracy can be very overt and very subversive, sometimes at the same times. When teachers and youth workers ask young people to deposit their cell phones in a box before classes or programs begin, they are silencing young people. Demanding they dress and talk a certain way before a community board or organizational committee is silencing young people. Leaving the experiences of young people out of classroom lesson plans or ignoring the histories of the ethnic cultures children and youth come from are examples of silencing young people, too. Silencing young people defeats democracy every time. Intentionally making spaces for engaging a wide range of young people in activities and creating broad opportunities to learn, teach, and lead in diverse ways is democracy in action.

The third way adults sabotage democracy is through whitewashing young people. In the United States today, there are more than 56 million K-12 young people. There is no single way any one individual, organization, hashtag, or movement can represent all of those young people. In this changing nation, it is more important than ever to honor pluralism. Pluralism is when smaller groups within a larger society maintain their unique cultural identities, and larger groups honor their identities. A characteristic of democracy is personal commitment, which includes honoring all voices for their diversity of experience and knowledge. There is no reason to pretend all voices are represented by one voice, particularly if the single voice does not and cannot effectively represent their peers. Allowing room for diversity and difference is positive and enhances the meaningfulness of student involvement.

Showboating children and youth is the fourth way adults sabotage democracy. Democracy is not the same as basketball or business, and there is no room for showing off, preening or otherwise making someone a star at the expense of everyone else in a team. This is a diverse movement filled with multiple perspectives and broad actions focused on many, many issues. Showboating happens when someone exaggerates their own skills, talents, or abilities. In democracy, individual young people may be tempted to self-promote and make it sound as if they are the only children and youth in the world, or their organization or program is the only democratic activity of value. Instead of focusing on themselves, democracy engages all voices and teaches young people and adults to honor the contributions and abilities of all young people everywhere all the time in order to avoid showboating.

The fifth way adults sabotage democracy is by placing young people on pedestals. Adults can be easy to amaze. Seduced by mainstream media and politicians who routinely dismiss the positive power of youth, adults often feel like they have discovered gold when young people stand up for themselves and work together to create change. In some instances, they lean on these children and youth constantly and raise them to the point of infallibility. This is pedestaling young people. It includes romanticizing, which is making someone always right and unquestionable. Focusing on our shared humanity, democracy has room for disagreement and mistakes, and model consensus and collaboration. It is a continuous learning process engaging all participants including adults and young people as equitable partners without artificially or superficially elevating one voice above all others.

Making young people into heroes is the sixth way adults sabotage democracy. In a room with too few representatives, a particularly loud voice standing above all others can sound brave and unique, especially when they represent an under-acknowledged majority. This is especially true in democracy. Just because a young person puts on a suit and discusses social change in a way which makes adults listen to them does not make them heroic or a superhero. It makes them dressed right and well-versed. In the same way, there are organizations and programs in democracies which are made heroic too. These organizations insinuate that they represent young people particularly well or are "right" whenever they talk. Among the 56 million young people in the United States though, adults do not lionize programs or organizations making them uncomfortable or ideas which are too far from their acceptance. The ones uplifted are generally satisfactory to adults who make decisions about funding, data usage at home, and community leadership. Organizational heroism is also a danger to democracy. Democracy makes room for young people who do not please or appeal to them so easily and emphasizes teaching young people about the society affecting them so much.

The seventh way adults sabotage democracy is by lowballing young people. Many organizations and individuals today are calling for young people to be informants to adult decision-making in society. They want democracy, and they do not want to be underestimated. Lowballing happens when adults deny, mis-understand, or underestimate what, why, when, where and how young people are curing the democracy deficit disorder. Children and youth want more than a seat at the table, because there is a lot more at stake for them than simply being able to talk or be represented somewhere. Young people make up significant percent-ages of nearly every population in the world and they should be fully integrated into the operations of every single community, if only for their energy and to educate them about democracy. Every layer of government bureaucracy should infuse young people as well, positioning them in powerful roles affecting not only young people, but all people; not as recipients, but as active partners who design, implement, critically assess, and make substantive decisions about the democratic system as a whole. Additionally, while organizations may have a sophisticated, deep analysis of the complicated status of democracy throughout society today, many people and programs in those organizations often simply do not get it. Reduced to reacting, they rally young people around the apparent problems in society without recognizing the deeper issues. Reaching much further than simply acting like the flavor-of-the-day, democracy positions young people as constant, deliberate, and fully engaged partners throughout all of democracy, all of the time.

Using youth and adults as sockpuppets is the eighth way adults sabotage democracy with young people. A literal sockpuppet is made of a hand inside of a sock with a face drawn on it. Figuratively speaking, sockpuppetry happens when one person manipulates another person to say what they want the other person to say. The other person allows this because they do not understand what they are part of, because they want approval or acceptance, or for myriad other reasons. The puppeteer does this to portray the illusion of acceptance beyond themselves. A lot of adults use children and youth as sockpuppets when they give them verbiage and handpick the issues expected to be addressed. Intentional or not, this usage of children and youth is designed to deceive the people who are listening to make them think what is being said is genuine democracy, sockpuppetry is often coupled with manipulation. If young people do what adults say, they will be rewarded; if they do not follow expectations, they will be punished in some form. They often do not know they are being used to prop up an adult's perspective. Sometimes adults use young people to provide an alternate or opposite perspective to their own. This is called strawman sockpuppetry. Having no real authority to enact anything in organizations without adult approval, adults may deliberately position young people to say outlandish or contrary things, only to show their perspective as more valid, valuable, and important.

Each of these eight ways sabotages young people in democracy. They actually negate democracy entirely, as democracy, when authentic, deliberately positions both traditionally and non-traditionally engaged people in safe and supportive environments, ensuring young people speak for themselves and are treated as equitable partners with adults throughout society. When adults sabotage young people, they end democracy.

Adults can learn to stop doing this though. The key to preventing negative actions from undermining democracy is to follow the pathways described throughout this book. However, it is equally important to move beyond these pathways by inventing and re-inventing democracy in every situation with every young person all the time. Maintaining critical vigilance for purposeful or accidental sabotage is vital, as is taking deliberate steps to address the ways described above. Preventing sabotage may require what poet Audre Lorde refers to as, "transformation of silence into language and action [as] an act of self-revelation" (Lorde, 1984). Paying attention to the dangers within democracy by engaging organizations through democratic action honors the legacy of past and present efforts. With more young people and more adults working together to transform society, the very least adults can do is honor their contributions.

Democracy moves by powerfully enshrining, codifying, and infusing transformation. More importantly, meaningfully involving young people in curing the democracy deficit disorder gives space for children, youth, and adults to share in the deliberate and ongoing critical examination of enshrinement and codification. Not only does this discourage organizations from stagnating and becoming irrelevant, it makes consistent critical thinking the norm and effectively elevates the roles of both young people and adults throughout society.

Denying Democracy

While sabotaging young people is diabolical, denying democracy is even worse. Unfortunately, this has been the reality for children and youth through time immemorial. There are many ways adults deny democracy, including hyperbole and invisibility.

Using hyperbole to deny democracy to young people is a popular trope that uses a vision of an upside down kingdom in order to scare, startle, and otherwise frighten adults into maintaining adultism. This trope says that given any power and authority, all children and youth will automatically be akin to inmates running the asylum, or monkeys flinging feces in every direction given the opportunity. While scholarship on the historical culture of children and the evolution of youth throughout the millennia is nascent (Jenks, 1996), there is enough available to begin to understand this frequent hyperbole has been intact for a long time. Beginning with ancient times, the youngest people have been seen and treated as idyllic in good circumstances, but a potential firestorm given the right circumstances (Carroll, 2021). While emerging into normalcy during the Middle Ages, there were still portrayals of childhood and youth as wild times barely controllable by adults. Children were seen and treated as feral creatures needing the interventions of adults in order to be raised "acceptably" (Crawford, 2009). Fast forward to more recent times and we have the crass exploitation of *Wild In The Streets*, a 1968 movie featuring the story of a youth-inclusive society. Given the ability to vote, young people vote in youth leadership and quickly ruin the country, driving the economy into shambles and destroying civil society. Called "cautionary," both the media and academics generally accepted its ridiculous premise for a generation (Doherty, 1984; Wikipedia, 2022n). Denying democracy through hyperbole continued into the 1990s with the emergence of youth "superpredators" and the painting of Gen X "slackers" by scholars, poli-ticians, and popular media (Males, 1996; Giroux, 1999), and continues today with the fixation on standardized education, the denial of young peoples' gender identities and more, and is maintained with the weaponry of the Youth-Industrial Complex identified earlier.

The effects of this hyperbole on children and youth in democracy are wide-ranging and deeply affecting. For generations, young people have been taught to doubt their own self-efficacy and resilience by this kind of messaging. Unable to rely on themselves, many children and youth have been forced into maintaining abusive relationships with adults, whether their birth parents, teachers, religious leaders, or others. In the face of irresponsive political systems that do not govern for their benefits and does routinely discriminate against them, young people in need of a social safety net often find themselves without a social shoulder to cry on, whether that is systems responsive to their needs or laws abiding to their own self-determination. This happens because young people are not taken as serious political, social, cultural, or economic actors in society—even in places and times when they clearly occupy those roles (Jenks, 1996; Taft, 2019). Instead, they are made subjects to the wills, whims, and worth of adults and merely treated as humans-in-the-making, instead of being seen as full human beings right now.

The effect of this dehumanization is invisibility (Books, 2015). There are many children and youth around the world right now who are rendered invisible by the democracy deficit disorder. These include homeless children and youth, refugee children, children of incarcerated parents, children and youth in war-affected countries, young people in minority populations, urban children and youth, non-white young people, and many other identities and belongings. These young people have been more than silenced by adults; they have been made invisible.

Becoming invisible even happens beyond the disparities and inequities pres-ent with various identities around the world. It happens specifically because of age in many parts of the world. One study shows how in Hong Kong, youth have been made invisible by social isolation from adults in many ways (Wong, 2012, p. 430), while another reviews how the COVID-19 pandemic enforced youths' invisibility around the world (Beaumont et al., 2021, p. 123). However, the met-aphor of invisibility might apply to any political process that erases someone sim-ply because of their age—especially when that process constantly proclaims its democratic orientation. Voting, elected offices, and special interests are just part of that. Unfortunately, for people under 18 in the majority of Western nations the extensions of invisibility seep into daily living where children and youth are treated as the property of their parents or guardians with little or no civil rights due to them. This is despite the UNCRC and myriad local and national laws intended to engender young people with those rights. In addition to political rights, children and youth suffer from a media landscape that routinely paints them according to whatever profits best via criminalization, infantilization, homogenization, and other oppressions meant to reinforce the bias toward adults throughout society (Books, 2015).

This crisis of invisibility is reinforced in countless ways to endless effects. Perhaps the most egregious of all is the democracy deficit disorder.

How Action Cures This Disorder

In his 1835 classic *Democracy in America*, Alexis de Tocqueville wrote, "Once a people begins to interfere with the voting qualification, one can be sure that sooner or later it will abolish it altogether" (Tocqueville, 2006, p. 60). This same notion should be extended from voting to all of democracy. Once society starts eliminating anything keeping people from being active in democracy, everything should be eliminated that keeps people from being active in democracy. As applied to the ages of young people, that means that eliminating anything that prevents the engagement of children and youth in democracy will lead to eliminating everything that prevents young people from engaging in democracy.

Seemingly expanding on Tocqueville's presumption in the way described above, United Nations Secretary-General Kofi Annan once said, "No one is born a good citizen; no nation is born a democracy. Rather, both are processes that continue to evolve over a lifetime. Young people must be included from birth. A society that cuts off from its youth severs its lifeline" (United Nations, 1998). Everyone has the human right to engage in democracy regardless of age. There is no single activity within the democratic process that should be dependent on a person's age (Lister, 2007, p. 695). Age-based voting, eligibility for political office, lobbying, and other restrictions are arbitrary barriers that wholly disenfranchise a large minority of people in order to promote the power of a majority. Age limits are meant to keep children and youth in check, behaving according to adult expectations for reasons only adults are supposed to know (Holt, 1974, p. 168).

For almost the entirety of the existence of most Western nations though, there have been ways to disqualify minority populations—and sometimes majority populations—from being engaged in democratic activities. Scholar Harry Boyte finds that many traditional democratic mechanisms are tools used by the powerful to maintain power over others, including voting, consumption, and political representation in general (Boyte, 2018, p. 103). Slowly, these tools are failing and eroding. Around the world, the constraints of birthright, race, gender, or previous condition of servitude, or taxes no longer serve as legal barriers to democratic action, even if cultural bias and political intentions limit them still. Real barriers continue to affect people because of those realities, but legally they are not supposed to keep citizens from voting—except for age.

Everyone who wants to engage in democracy should be allowed to do so. There is no such thing as "knowing enough" about politics, democracy, elections, or the process. Simply speaking, democracy is each person engaging in the act of choosing what best represents their personal interests in the public sphere. In a more complex fashion, it is the acknowledgment that children, youth, and adults share responsibility for the society they share. Boyte found that this public democracy includes engaging people as co-creators throughout society, "developing civic agency [and] negotiating a common life" as the tasks and integrating self-interest "with making work more public" are the mechanisms for fostering this reality (p. 103).

Is there an appropriate role for the consideration of mental, intellectual, or emotional competency in democracies? According to Wall (2022, p. 199), "Children are full human beings and fully democratic persons. To be human is to be part of the political sphere... Democracies at present do not imagine children as equal political beings. But...democracies can be imagined differently. They can be imagined as spaces of responsiveness to the people." The young people who politicians and the courts have declared mentally incompetent currently experience this. However, in an age when courts are continuously hammering young offenders with adult sentencing, age is not a worthy barrier to competency. In these same times, corporations are feasting off young peoples' buying powers, politicians are fear mongering against young peoples' collective image, and businesspeople use the fear of youth to scare adults into buying things. This shows how age is an arbitrary measure that is used as a convenient kludge over and over. When taken in light of technology and social change though, everyone can see that the role of age discrimination in society is rapidly diminishing.

Luckily, children and youth today are not waiting for an invitation to exercise their traditional and expected democratic responsibilities, including paying taxes, volunteering, and voting. People under 18 in the United States pay 2% of all employment taxes on their jobs (Hodge, 2010), despite higher youth unemployment rates than ever. Youth volunteering to benefit the public good continues to happen in record numbers, with research showing, "Even as they've been battered economically by the pandemic, with their educational and professional lives upended, young people are deeply engaged in trying to help their communities during the COVID-19 crisis" (CIRCLE, n.d.). In the United States, young people who can vote are voting in record numbers, with successive election cycles showing increasing numbers for the last decade (CIRCLE, 2021). Internationally this is even more true, with rates of youth voting generally continuing to rise worldwide (Symonds, 2020).

Action cures the democracy deficit disorder because it directly, systematically, and specifically works to infuse young people into portions of the world once wholly preoccupied by adults.

The Timing of Democracy

Time affects the roles of young people in democracy in a number of ways (Jenks, 1996, p. 109). Young people invariably lose their childhood as they grow older. Children implicitly become more capable of consciously experiencing democracy (or the lack thereof) as they age. Adults often forget, disconnect, or deny young people as they grow older. Despite that complexity, it is essential to think about the variety of ways time affects children and youth in democracies, from hour-to-hour, day-to-day, year to year, generation to generation, and beyond (Jenks, 1996, p. 109). There are important developmental, social, educational, familial, and cultural considerations that affect their democracy experiences, understandings, implementations, criticisms, and actions. As Epstein observed, "When you spend your day doing things you believe are important, your life has meaning. Conversely, when you spend your day doing things that make no sense to you, you feel empty, frustrated and angry" (2010, p. 76).

Rather than just expecting them to adapt to adult perceptions of time, adults need to acknowledge that young people have their own understandings of time. Children and youth can have important times during their days when they are responsible for showing up, attending, participating, leading, watching, or belonging in certain places (Jenks, 1996, p. 107). They also have their own priorities including self-care, mental health, play and recreation, and more.

Developmental research about children and youth shows that people literally see time differently at different ages. That means that while infants have no conception of time, young children are beginning to try and comprehend the structure of time. By the time they are seven or eight, many children are reading clocks—however, they have little conception of what "future" or "past" means, particularly over the long range. While they are able to comprehend the future, by their early teens most people are focused on the present. That is particularly important for action to cure the democracy deficit disorder because young people have a particular need to see immediate outcomes. By their late teens, young people are becoming more future-focused, and need opportunities to learn responsible future planning skills. Young adults are often solely focused on the future and need opportunities to stay connected with the experiences they had as young people while moving positively forward.

When in life should children and youth start actively engaging in democracy? When should they become agents to solve the democracy deficit disorder? Simply said, this should happen every day starting at birth, and it can happen during infancy. Parents who deliberately respond to their infants' needs in holistic ways lay the foundation for lifelong community engagement. Respecting young babies can mean encouraging their "personhood"—that is, being as attentive, courteous, and deliberate about them as people often are with older people. Close physical time between parents and children can create strong personal attachments that can lead to strong community bonds. A father who nurtures his baby, rather than avoiding or "handing off" responsibilities to the mother supports strong engagement in democracy by developing a strong sense of duty in infancy. Community belonging is important at this phase as well, as exposure to people outside of the household can foster lifelong bonds to the broader ecology around the child. When small children are surrounded by caring adults, they learn that their responsibility is to care.

This can mean that when an infant "goo-goos," adults should listen to them. Learning that when they speak, their voice has impact; in turn, they can learn to engage their voices throughout the communities they belong to as infants and into childhood. Listening to a child's voice is the first step in engaging them. It can also be important for parents or caregivers to give young infants undivided, uninterrupted attention for at least short periods of the day. This can show young children that their presence and activity is important enough for adults to be with them and their concerns only.

Engaging young people in curing the democracy deficit disorder can happen during childhood. Investing in children can mean building their skills and giving the time, resources, and space needed to share democratic responsibility with them. It also means developing the skills and investments adults need to succeed as well. Competent communication with toddlers and children means talking with them, not at them. That is a skill that adults often have to learn, starting with unlearning their previous behaviors. Acknowledging children's voices can be important for self-worth and can help form healthy expectations of family and community. Learning to engage children in democracy can require adults to change their behavior while striving to see children as whole people valuable because of who they are right now, instead of simply seeing them as future adults. Childhood is an essential phase of life where young people form their sense of identity, purpose, and belonging within their larger community. Part of this democratic expectation turns a popular idiom on its head: Instead of, "It takes a village to raise a child," think about what it means to say, "It takes a child to raise a village." That is what curing the democracy deficit disorder requires. When children go through hard times, they usually figure out how to "deal with it." This ability, called resilience, is a powerful skill. However, children need to learn how to use it positively. Design democracy building to teach young people how to rely on their community as a collective benefit that can help them. That will build up the positive power of young people to change not just their own lives, but the communities around them.

Democracy building happens during teen years. Being meaningfully involved in their community should extend throughout a teenager's world: Home, school, community centers, town hall, parks, libraries are all environments where teens belong and could actively strive to cure the democratic deficit disorder. The responsibility for that engagement, or the lack thereof, does not fall on the shoulders of young people themselves. Rather, it is the adults throughout their lives who deny their own obligation to struggle, strive, and drive toward actual, practical, and obvious democracy throughout communities. As teens become engulfed by this expectation throughout their waking (and sleeping) hours, they will develop, sustain, and expand their comprehensive connections to their communities.

There are many challenges, barriers, and pitfalls to consider with the timing of engaging young people in curing the democracy deficit disorder. The first challenge could be called the bandage syndrome. In this, adults may be tempted to see engaging young people as a bandage that provides a temporary fix for serious problems. While it is true that organizations and communities have short-term problems, it is also true that these problems are almost always a part of larger issues. Successful communities engage young people as part of a long-range effort for sustained democracy, no matter their size or scope. The length of action committed to engaging young people can serve as a litmus test for the amount of sincerity there is toward children and youth throughout a community, as well as being an indicator of sustainability.

The second challenge of time is election season tokenism. Election season politics are challenging for the many segments of American society that are tokenized for their votes. As politicians increasingly recognize the necessity of the "youth vote" they become quickly interested in "youth issues." A common approach to this is setting up youth forums or rallies where photo opportunities are all over. There will often be youth speakers, passionately sharing their positions, as well. The dilemma of these approaches is that young people increasingly identify these efforts as election season ploys, and if that politician does not follow through on campaign promises, youth may actually become more disenfranchised than before. To avoid this tokenism, some politicians are working to engage youth throughout the year, instead of just election season.

Time offers many challenges, and the third one identified here is the query of quantity or quality. Many organizations are using "quality management" theories to develop "client-driven" approaches to reform, which encourage them to look to young people to identify problems and solutions. The temporary nature of these emergency responses often stops when everything appears to be functioning, and children and youth are often left by the wayside while the organization's staff roll along without them. Young people need consistent, meaningful action, and democracy requires sustainability. One successful approach to fostering democracy building is to develop regular, meaningful activities with young people that go beyond quick fixes and provide constant feedback and action.

The fourth time-related challenge in curing the democracy deficit disorder can be called seasons of free labor. In communities around the world, engaging children and youth in democracy is used as coded language to disguise trash pick-up or graffiti removal programs. Generally, the assumption is that by being involved in community service activities young people will become invested in democracy. However, the unfortunate reality of this assumption is that young people can generally see through the false advertising. In many of these cases, adults are inadvertently searching for free labor, and automatically turn to children and youth to provide it.

Considering the time of day, the time of week, the season of the year, the year of life, and the time of life that young people and adults are living are all essential to building democracy. While the differences may feel overwhelming, they can be successfully navigated.

Democracy Education as Social Justice

If we accept the contention that democracy is supposed to represent the will of the majority, i.e., majority rules, then we have to understand that public education is the most effective way to engage the majority successfully in self-governance. Education is said to achieve a lot of goals, and sustaining democracy is at the top of the list. Public schools have been seen as the best route to democracy since the founding of the United States, with Benjamin Franklin himself swearing to the inevitable success of schools when he wrote, "I begin to be almost sorry I was born so soon, since I cannot have the happiness of knowing what will be known 100 years hence" (Franklin, 1783).

The "public" aspect of education is vital in Franklin's formula, as is the democratic part. Democracy education happens when the virtues, activities, mindsets, and goals of democracy are taught through practical, purposeful, and poignant action both inside classrooms and out. Combining this with the distinct purpose of achieving justice for all is the highest calling schools can have today. Democracy education is a clear means to achieving social justice in society (Freire, 2004; hooks, 2013, 2014). Democracy educators strive to overcome oppression throughout the lives of young people by emphasizing the challenge, uplift, power, and abilities of learners in many ways, including critical engagement in literacy, action learning for change, and cultural reflections on justice (hooks, 2003; Giroux, 2018; Freire, 2015). Learning opportunities can make life better, bring joy, and create new knowledge, giving democracy educators the ability to support learners in changing their own lives, their communities, and the world. Young people engaged in democracy education learn to critically engage throughout life by seeing the disparities in power present in politics, culture, economics, and much more.

Focused on social justice, democracy education centers the public's role in the distribution of wealth, as well as the roles of race, class, gender, ability, language, and other identities throughout society. These concerns each and all innately intersect with a discourse on age (Freire, 1985, 2004, 2015; hooks, 1994; Giroux, 1981, 2015), and particularly the effects of age in democracy education. Focused on examining power structures throughout society, critical pedagogy offers a particularly apt structure for enacting democracy education (Freire, 2004). This practice offers applications in school settings and out of schools led by young people working along, in partnership with adults, or through adults facilitating activities. Understanding the power structures which engulf and eclipse their own daily realities can empower and enliven young people. But children and youth are capable, desiring, and ultimately needing to do more than *learn* about social justice; they need to enact and live democracy which fulfills the demands of social justice.

The practical application of democracy *as* social justice looks like actively addressing the age-based discrimination inherent within many educational practices in schools and beyond. It means learning about discrimination, segregation, white supremacy, and other tools of oppression—as well as taking action to improve the situation faced by young people, led by learners for the sake of social justice and democracy. At the core of social justice education is the practice of children and youth taking a stand, declaring what is fair, nonviolent, and good, and struggling to create a more just and equitable society. This entwinement is embodied by learning spaces that meld "multicultural education and critical pedagogy, Freireian dialogic education, and Kolb's active, experiential learning" (Nagda et al., 2003, p. 1) into engaged democratic learning.

It has been argued that this melding of democracy education and social justice happens in three primary ways: Participatory democratic structures where all individuals—regardless of age or role—have a substantive say over decisions affecting community life; a culture of democratic values, such as equality and shared responsibility, compassion, and inclusivity; and space for self-directed learning—considerable scope for learners to choose what they learn, when, and how (Aquarone, 2021). Fletcher argues this happens through a constructive approach to youth learning about education in general, about student voice, and about transformative education, including studying the operational functions of learning and teaching as well as taking actions including service learning, participatory action research, restorative justice, and more (2019, p. 60). Perhaps the most important implication of all of this is that democracy education *as* social justice entails critical, conscientious action-oriented learning.

Perhaps the most radical outcome of this learning is that young people may not fit into the society into which they are born. As Freire expounded on in his 1970 *Pedagogy of the Oppressed*, "And since people 'receive' the world as passive entities, education should make them more passive still, and adapt them to the world. The educated individual is the adapted person, because he or she is better 'fit' for the world" (2004, p. 76). Observing the passive "banking" form of education, Freire was describing the popular conception of schooling in the world to that point—and still today. A short time after Freire's book, Jiddu Krishnamurti said, "It's no measure of health to be well adjusted to a profoundly sick society" (Krishnamurti, 1976, p. 131). This is to the advantage of young people who are arriving in a world that is poisoned by the climate crisis, never-ending wars, and a host of social and moral problems that were not acknowledged for their validity just a generation earlier. The world needs new solutions, and children and youth who are engaged in democracy education as social justice show us that another world is possible.

6

Democracy Means Action

"What has been cut apart cannot be glued back together. Abandon all hope of totality, future as well as past, you who enter the world of fluid modernity."—Zygmunt Bauman, *Liquid Modernity*

There is no single way to cure democracy deficit disorder. Democracy is inherently pluralistic and fluid; in order to cure the democracy deficit disorder there needs to be pluralistic and fluid thinking as well.

Democracy relies on people taking action, especially collective ownership and deliberate roles in the societies where they live. From the earliest age children have the interest in their neighbors and communities to warrant actively engaging them in democracy; research, and international practice codified in the Convention on the Rights of the Child (United Nations, 1990), demonstrates that their evolving capacities necessitate opportunities for their active involvement (Lansdown, 2005; Gollop et al., 2000, p. 32). Curing the democracy deficit disorder requires embracing these realities by connecting young people with meaningful opportunities to share their knowledge, ideas, actions, and more throughout society.

There is no one age group that is absolutely responsible for curing the democracy deficit disorder; however, one age group is responsible for perpetuating it. Adults, including anyone over 18 and everyone who interacts with children and youth anywhere throughout society, are wholly culpable for the absence of democracy, the waning democracy, apathy toward democracy, and the obliteration of democracy. However, the same people can become adult allies to young people who assume responsibility for curing the democracy deficit disorder and engage young people to do the same. Speaking of educators, radical theorist George Counts said something true of every adult: "[We] cannot evade the responsibility of participating actively in the task of reconstituting the democratic tradition and of thus working positively toward a new society" (Counts, 1978, p. 13). Simply put, ethically oriented and morally compelled adults of all political backgrounds must strive to engage young people of all ages in democracy building throughout all parts of society in any way possible.

For a long time, children's participation was seen as the obligation of child-serving organizations only. The last decade has seen the expansion of this concept as children's participation is increasingly seen as essential in and by schools (Fletcher, 2017); local, regional, and international governments (Taft, 2019; Driskell, 2017; Hart, 1994); community development organizations; and in other sectors. Initially viewing children's participation as effective marketing, businesses also have realized the necessity of actively engaging young people. Today, they continue to enrich their activities through technology (Garcia & Philip, 2018). As recent developments in the Middle East have shown us, many activists are also realizing the potential of young peoples' participation, as indeed, many activists in that region are children and youth.

Youth involvement throughout communities is democratic participation and serves to nurture all of the skills and knowledge young people need in order to be successful members of democratic society (Zeldin et al., 2000; Payne, n.d.). By increasing the frequency of children's participation, organizations and individuals can deepen the impact children have throughout society. This will help alleviate many of the worst conditions facing the world today and help democracy transition to the new forms it will be required to have in the near future as technology and necessity continue to drive growth. There are several essential elements in this democratic participation.

Essential Elements

There is no singular cure, silver bullet or inevitable way to cure democracy deficit disorder. Instead, people everywhere have to re-imagine, reinterpret, and re-engage in democracy according to their own resources, abilities, and outcomes every time they want to engage young people. Saul Alinsky, widely regarded as the originator of modern community organizing tactics (Alinsky, 2010), taught that in all practical action to challenge oppression people must consider the different elements that make activities effectively democratic or not, including individual attitudes, organizational structures, and shared cultures which affect all of us. These are reinforced by Kohn's findings specific to democracy in schools (Kohn, 1993). Challenging the democracy deficit disorder requires addressing each of these essential elements.

The first element, individual attitudes, reveals that adult allies must believe that engaging youth in a variety of roles is important, possible, and necessary. Individual attitudes are the ways people feel, their beliefs, and the mindsets they hold toward themselves and the world around them. With attitudes that build democracy, youth and adults acknowledge their mutual investment, dedication, and benefit from democracy. Their acknowledgment is made visible in relationships, practices, policies, and organizational culture. Adults do not talk about youth in the third person, use demeaning or adultist language, or otherwise act as if youth are not present, when in fact they are. Adult attitudes show that youth are validated and authorized through adults' regular usage of youths' abilities to improve programs, organizations, classes, schools, and society. Youth attitudes can reinforce all of this by revealing internalized adultism (Fletcher, 2015). All of this can show how addressing individual attitudes can begin to cure democracy deficit disorder.

The second element, organizational structure, is vital in democracy. Group structures are the formal and informal responsibilities, systems, authority, and relations that allow a program, organization, or community to perform its functions. This can happen when the voices, strengths, talents, actions, and achievements of youth are continuously focused on programs or classes, and throughout schools, organizations, and communities. It happens when young people are thoroughly integrated throughout all components of all activities intended to challenge the democracy deficit. Within the structure of places committed to building democracy, important activities focused on youth are done with children and youth as partners, whether they are focused on learning, teaching, or leadership. Structures should be designed to provide opportunities for young people to learn about the issues, agendas, politics, and processes they are going to participate in, and activities should be created that reflect those structures. As Freire (1970) posited, learners need a "deepened consciousness of their situation," to be able to "apprehend that situation as an historical reality susceptible of transformation." Making youth part of plans, activities, and evaluations allows young people to contribute throughout the process, and encourages them to be incorporated into ongoing, sustainable activities. Youth are encouraged and supported to invite other young people or adult allies to support them, and in systematic as well as informal ways, the voices of youth of all ages are engaged. This demonstrates a visible commitment to democracy.

The third element of democracy is shared culture. Shared culture includes the values, beliefs, and patterns of relationships, behavior, and performance that characterize a group. Anyplace and anytime an activity, program, class, or otherwise is intended to challenge democracy deficit, youth should feel comfortable asking for clarification of language and terminology. This includes the acronyms, definitions, concepts, or asking critical questions about assumptions, activities, and other components. Intentionally challenging democracy deficit disorder means youth are never lectured about their behavior, attitudes, input, or other perceptions adults may have of them. Instead, adults and youth are treated as equitable partners, each with valuable contributions to make to the program, organization, or community. Issues addressed with young people are not limited to so-called youth issues; instead, youth are seen and treated as members of the entire community. "Their" issues are the community's issues, and the community's issues are theirs. As Manchester et al. declare, "Young people lead from their values and are not afraid to innovate and transform systems" (2021, p. 76). That is an approach every community benefits from.

Essential Actions

It is essential for everyone—children and youth especially—to see democracy as a personal responsibility and organizational process. However, as Gillen writes, "We have to do away with the idea that young people will be wild without adult control and coercion, but that means that we also have to find ways to teach and develop an alternative relationship. Older adults and teachers cannot simply let go and see what happens" (Gillen, 2014, p. 145). The bias toward adults is an endemic and enduring threat to the future of democracy around the world. Facing adultism and undoing the injustice it perpetuates requires a conscientious and deliberate pathway.

We can nurture new perspectives and actions to cure the democracy deficit disorder through *problematization*. Michel Foucault wrote, "It seemed to me there was one element that was capable of describing the history of thought—this was what one could call the problems or, more exactly, *problematizations*" (Foucault, 1997, p. 117). When we examine the history of democracy, we can see that the process of identifying a challenge, analyzing it, and emerging with new ideas has been essential for people who were afflicted in negative ways by democratic action. This might be the very nature of the democracy deficit disorder: People are negatively afflicted by the very thing that could liberate them from their struggles. This is certainly how many children and youth treat it, with democracy being both demonized and lionized in equal measure according to their challenges. *Problematization* allows young people to come to clear conclusions about where struggles come from, why they matter, how they arrive, what to do about them, how to critically examine responses to struggles, and when to transform action to respond to new challenges. Democracy holds the multitudes of perspectives of young people around the world specifically because it fosters *problematization.*

Working together to *problematize* democracy today, at least one organization found, "an urgency to create transgenerational spaces of critical production that try to overcome experiences where adults teach, children and youth learn, and elders are isolated" (Campus in Camps & Grupo Contrafilé, 2014, p. 7). These spaces work to reposition young people and adults from the hierarchical dynamics that dominate current democratic purposes by moving them away from being passive recipients of programming done to them toward becoming active co-creators of knowledge, opportunity, and action. One of the dilemmas of democracy is its historical structuralization of hierarchical relationships that have relied on patriarchy, racism, classism, and more for their institutionalization, operations, and outcomes. The realities of these historic democracies are that they have fostered a propensity for opportunism whereupon the strong prey upon the weak. Ironically though, it is the very structures that have been oppressive that can be used in order to liberate anyone—particularly children and youth—from the hierarchy. Democracy fails because it can be a tool of the oppressor; it succeeds because it can liberate, too.

Young people are no panacea though. More because of their socio-economic status and political upbringing than their age or maturity, there are many children and youth who exhibit an absence of critical consciousness. Because the democracy we live in marks them as insignificant until they are adults, many young people have internalized helplessness, been conditioned to apathy or hold a self-protective disdain for the world they live in.

In its two-decade-long examination of the actions of young people around the world, the Freechild Institute has identified six essential actions to take in order to cure democracy deficit disorder (Freechild Institute for Youth Engagement, n.d.B).

The first essential action is to be actively and intentionally inclusive and equitable. Youth are showing us that diversity is essential for democracy. Considering gender, race, sexual orientation, socio-economic status, education, behavior, and other identities is essential to fostering democratic reality and fighting the disregard for democracy today. The days of engaging the same people to do the same things that have always been done are over. This is proven by the dynamic, responsive, and equitable actions taken by youth worldwide.

Practicing transparency and mutual accountability is the second essential action. Seeing people, listening to everyone's voice, and encouraging positive, powerful action are parts of democracy building. However, they do not make it meaningful. Democracy deficit disorder requires people of all ages to exercise their critical thinking skills by seeing through the decisions affecting them. Mutual accountability means that powerless people around the world hold the powerful accountable. That is true whether identifying political power, economic power, cultural power or otherwise.

The third essential action to cure democracy deficit disorder is to learn together. Learning together is a key to democracy. Young people are teaching us right now that when the traditionally hierarchical structure of formal education is overthrown, learning together can foster transformative interdependence that includes sustainable connections and shared purpose. When informal and formal learning opportunities happen among people from diverse backgrounds, perspectives, and daily realities, together they can share wisdom, knowledge, and ideas across differences. They can also place their learning into action and reflect on what they've learned through action.

Creating planned processes that are responsive to changes is the fourth essential action. Understanding the processes, activities, organizations, and communities they are part of is essential to everyone throughout society. Through their work to transform these systems, young people are showing us that planning processes can build this knowledge by creating new ways to operate, activate, and explore the vision, mission, and goals of democracy. Meaningfulness can happen when everyone has equitable roles through sustained, evolving, and engaging processes.

The fifth essential action is generating sustainable action, impact, and outcomes. When examining the work of children and youth worldwide, it becomes obvious certain elements make democracy thrive and sustain. The following elements form the "6 Ps" of sustainable democracy: People, Policies, Programs, Practices, Possibilities, and Progress (Fletcher, 2014a). People are those who are consciously engaged in critical action to build democracy. Policies are the formal and informal rules governing democracy. Programs are the formal interactions democracy relies on for operations and outcomes. Practices are the informal interactions which determine the efficacy of democratic homes, communities, cultures, structures, and societies. Possibilities are the anticipated and proven outcomes of democracy. Finally, progress is the continuous evolution of democracy that is intentional, situational, and transformative.

Youth around the world have shown that the sixth essential action to challenge democracy deficit disorder is continuous critical examination. Taking the form of non-technical reflection and assessment, this examination can provide learning, growth, critical engagement, and perspectives that people did not have when they became involved. Meaningfulness in examination like this can be assured by following the other essential actions outlined here but has to be followed up by practical action reflecting the findings.

Seeing Democratic Action

When examining action that challenges the democracy deficit disorder, a typology of democratic action emerges. It is vital to understand these as a logical sequence of potential action, and not as a prescription. As Freire wrote, "Manipulation, sloganizing, 'depositing,' regimentation, and prescription cannot be components of revolutionary praxis, precisely because they are components of the praxis of domination" (2004, p. 126). Instead, democratic action requires thoughtful determination, group deliberation, conscientious planning, practical action, and substantive reflection. At no point, though, is there room for violent reactivism. Instead, young people and adults are internally compelled to consider words like Eldridge Cleaver's as metaphorical instead of literal:

> The only way that the world is ever going to be free is when the youth of this country *moves* with every principle of human respect and with every soft spot we have in our hearts for human life, in a fashion that lets every pig power structure know what when people are racistly and fascistly attacked, the youth will put a foot in their butts and make their blood chill. (Erlich & Erlich, 1971, p. 254)

Right now, children and youth are providing that metaphorical foot in many ways. There are several different ways to engage in democracy that are apparent throughout society, whether within homes, across communities or at national and international levels of governance.

Young people simply benefit from democracy without having to actively contribute or see themselves as contributors. Adults are seen as the primary actors while children and youth have no active input. Children and youth are given opportunities to share and engage in democratic activities, either as advocates for their own best interests or representatives of others they identify with. Adults, whether they are parents, teachers, youth workers, elected officials or others, sometimes seek youth participation.

Through substantive, meaningful empowerment, children and youth are actively engaged in defeating the democracy deficit disorder. This empowerment includes educational opportunities and active positions that intentionally increase the capacity and impact of young people. More than just participating though, young people are infused throughout all parts the democratic action within a class, school, program, organization, and community. Motivating themselves and others, people who drive democracy serve in equitable roles in a majority of authoritative positions, manage the day-to-day democratic activities throughout society, and critically engage with the activities, outcomes, and perceptions of democracy. Social justice is at the heart of driving democracy.

Leading democracy is a powerful way young people are changing democracy. Children and youth are in all major leadership roles, including executive leadership, consulting, lobbying, and more, and have majority membership on boards of directors, with appropriate support from adult allies. They are also critically examining democracy. Developing their lenses for social justice, young people learn to share critical insights that deconstruct, explore, and transform assumptions, ideas, and practices throughout their own lives, their families, communities, organizations, and beyond.

Young people are liberating democracy. Stuck in the confines of adultism and other oppressions, children and youth liberate themselves, groups, and their communities from inequities in a variety of ways through a number of strategies. Engaging in democratic processes, they develop consensus, foster support, gain support, and emerge successful. This liberation might not be explicitly obvious to everyone who looks. They are working to transform democracy, too. In this role young people determine, drive, and delineate what needs to change, where and how it needs to be changed, who should be engaged, and what the outcomes of the transformation should be.

These different types can help youth and adults better understand how to challenge democracy deficit. Often relegated to simply benefiting from democracy, adults should reposition young people as equitable partners in building, transforming, sustaining, and evolving democracy everywhere, all of the time.

Varieties of Youth Engagement

The institutions, culture, and public policy that drive society need to be transformed so that adults and young people share roles more equitably within government, communities, workplaces, and families. With that assumption firmly intact, the development of new cultural and structural avenues to foster the active participation of children and youth takes a firm direction. Such avenues might include the following.

The first avenue are horizontal, non-authoritarian attitudes between young people and adults. This takes the form of stopping the discrimination against children and youth inherent in adultism. Dismantling oppressive cultures and structures that discriminate against young people is no small charge, with the systematic disenfranchisement facing children and youth thoroughly entrenched in all corners (Fletcher, 2015c, p. 23).

The second avenue are fully democratic opportunities for young people throughout society. The institutions society relies on to support and sustain democracy must be made completely accommodating toward children and youth. This extends beyond government, and includes schools, hospitals, non-profits, policing, and so on.

The third avenue are restructuring all educational opportunities, everywhere at any time. The introduction, infusion, deepening, reflection, and critical examination of democracy is a taught thing that must be reinforced throughout the schooling, working, out-of-school, and other activities all people are engaged in.

These are three massive ideas that have to be thoroughly examined. Defeating the democracy deficit disorder can be simultaneously motivated by and motivating for the advancement of technology throughout society. Wikipedia, videocams, Facebook, cell phones, and other sorts of developments are encouraging the development of democracy that is more than participatory; instead, it is owned. An owned democracy—and not one that is owned by corporate overlords, either, although it is a slippery slope between popular ownership and corporate ownership—has the balance of control and benefit, consciousness and coincidence. This idea is expanded on in the next section.

7

The Owned Democracy

The owned democracy reflects the determination of its owners, and the people who own it are everyone who lives in it, occupies it, inherits it, creates it, and recreates it in every succeeding generation. This democracy is confident, persistent, and passionate. In its functions, forms, and outcomes, the owned democracy is confident in their democracy and knows its roles, beliefs, investments, and outcomes. This owned democracy is persistent, necessitating consistent engagement in maintaining, sustaining, transforming, and reimagining the activities, ideas, outcomes, and opinions about itself. The owned democracy is passionate, actively requiring time, energy, and resources and readily securing them because of shared determination for democracy. The passion within the owned democracy is palpable to anyone who observes it.

With this amount of investment though, the owned democracy requires a certain kind of membership which is committed to the democracy wherever it exists, either socially, culturally, economically, educationally, throughout governance, or beyond. Reports on the experiences of young people and their adult allies throughout the fields of schooling, social services, public health, and more grant some insight into what it takes to sustain this concept of the owned democracy (Hoose, 2001; Welton & Wolf, 2001; Kim et al., 2002; Delgado & Zhou, 2008; Cammarota & Fine, 2010; Cammarota et al., 2013; Checkoway &

Gutiérrez, 2012; Erlich, 1971; Fletcher & Vavrus, 2006; Barrett, 2015; Fletcher, 2017; Terriquez et al., 2020; Franklin, 2021). While there are many findings from across the spectrum of young people working to support democracy, several specific findings emerge repeatedly across these studies of children's citizenship, young people's involvement, youth-led community organizing, youth engagement, and more (Lister, 2007; Manchester et al., 2021; Payne, n.d.).

Of the findings from the field, several elements emerge. Following are key traits of members in an owned democracy. They include the skills, abilities, knowledge, and dispositions required between people who talk about changing the world and people who actually change the world. These items are personal "capacities" because they provide definition to life. They determine what everyone can do, who they can be, and where they are at any given point in life. The following traits are observable, useful, and powerful when working to cure the democracy deficit disorder.

Personal Competencies to Cure the Democracy Deficit Disorder

Overcoming the malaise, apathy, and antipathy shown toward democracy and youth in society requires a large number of adults consciously becoming allies to young people. However, in whatever role they have in the lives of young people, it can be frustrating to be an adult ally because it is so different from traditional ways of interacting with children and youth (Checkoway, 1996). It can also be challenging to be a young person with these competencies, if only because consumerist society readily imposes the opposite competencies through consumerist pedagogy within and beyond schools. According to Flanagan though, "Democratic dispositions—to be open-minded, to trust others, to be committed to finding common ground that transcends differences—do not happen by default. People are not born with democratic dispositions" (Flanagan, 2013, p. 163). How can children and youth develop the competencies they need to cure the democracy deficit disorder? Adults need to get actively, deliberately, and continuously involved. "In order to achieve more equitable representation, adult allies need to help young people develop the skills, habits, knowledge and motivations that will increase their participation" (Levine & Higgins-D'Alessandro, 2010).

These competencies assume that the target is engaged in challenging the democracy deficit throughout society. The following traits, capacities, skills, dispositions, and abilities can make the difference between youth and adults who talk about democracy and those who actually *do* the work of democracy (Nagda et al., 2003, p. 166). These are personal traits of young people and adults that can determine what they can do, who they can be, and where adults and young people can go together to cure the democracy deficit disorder.

Humility is perhaps the first trait of adults who seek to build democracy with young people. This humility is apparent in actions, thoughts, and outcomes. Adults develop and maintain a modest view of their own importance in public and personal perspectives regarding their efforts in building democracy with young people. Despite all the things they may have accomplished in the past, adults who genuinely seek to support young people are constantly aware that there are challenges ahead. They work to show respect toward children and youth and when they celebrate successes, they are not arrogant or boastful in ways that adults can be. Adult allies of young people believe in a quiet confidence because in the long run character will speak for itself to children and youth. Young people learn humility because they want to learn. As Paulo Freire said, "Humility is an important virtue for a teacher, the quality of recognizing—without any kind of suffering—our limits of knowledge concerning what we can and cannot do through education. Humility accepts the need we have to learn and relearn again and again, the humility to know with those whom we help to know... The teacher has to be free to say to students 'You convinced me'" (Freire, 1985).

Learning to be ourselves and truly embracing the inner voice and knowledge each person possesses within themselves is a central characteristic of democracy that is called authenticity. Being authentic means that individuals know within themselves who they are and share outside of themselves what they truly feel, believe, question, and experience. Being authentic requires young people and adults eliminating the unnecessary and oppressive filters imposed and assumed within themselves so that they can freely express themselves in all ways.

Adults who support young people curing democracy deficit disorder have a learner mind that shows intellectual humility both personally and professionally. Each person sees the differences between being stuck in a rut and moving through a groove. Alert to the reality that everyone has more potential than they ever realize, the learner mind enables intellectual humility and encourages open mindedness. Constantly working to unlock potential, adult allies are in a perpetual state of growth and development. Knowing they will never "get it right" is a reality they gladly accept. Working to solve new problems that arise is embraced by adult allies by learning and growing personally and meeting challenges head-on.

Courage is the key to developing, sustaining, challenging, reimagining, and transforming democracy. As Maya Angelou said, "Without courage we cannot practice any other virtue with consistency. We cannot be kind, true, merciful, generous, or honest" (USA Today, 1988, p. 1). Young people and adults are genuinely empowered by courage, enabling themselves to reach higher and achieve more than they had anticipated. Facing all the challenges posed to democracy today, courage is an absolute necessity.

To cure the democracy deficit disorder, adult allies have to be able to foster, facilitate, and sustain collaboration and teamwork. Rather than hoarding power and authority, adults work with young people to build and sustain the necessary group and cross-group cohesion and operations needed to maintain success, whether at home, in school, throughout the community, or beyond. Collaboration and teamwork can happen online, in person, and with intimate, small groups as well as in large groups and communities.

Change management encourages adults and young people to identify, secure, use, sustain, and restore resources throughout democratic action and living. People who build democracy successfully move people, leadership, and constituents through transitions and times of change. They navigate change as a tool and see its value as an opportunity for learning and growth, instead of seeing it as an oppressive force for intolerance and inability.

Conflict management is being able to guide, direct, manage, and otherwise navigate conflict in powerful ways and is a key capacity of people to build democracy. Young people and adults identify and successfully navigate conflicts and problems from an operational, day-to-day perspective, as well as a systems-scale, whole earth perspective.

People who are curing the democracy deficit disorder are transparent, acting like open books who are available, accessible, and honest in word and deed. Young people and adults who are available and appropriately vulnerable can foster strong relationships built on trust and courage. Young people and adults can use these strong relationships to accomplish so much more than others can otherwise. Striving to act with integrity, young people and adults seek to be compassionate and loyal and try to be good listeners. As the old adage goes, at the end of the day it is not what anyone says or does, but how they make people feel that matters the most. In a democracy, each person cares about others, both personally and professionally. Peeling away the layers, both young people and adults strive to be open and transparent.

To foster democracy, people must have passion. What keeps young people and adults going? It is a genuine passion for engaging people. People building democracy are inspired because they believe in what they are doing and where they are going—even when people do not know where that is. People do not take "that will never work" for an answer. Passion gives people the determination that accompanies democracy, and with open eyes they are inspired by the people, places, and events around them.

Being able to make decisions is a key capacity for democracy. Young people and adults discern how, when, where, and why to make decisions, and how to help others make decisions, both on a micro- and meta-level scale.

People who are fostering democracy build community, not just colleagues. Working together, people of all ages serve the community by removing obstacles and enabling people to succeed on their own terms. The best decisions and ideas are made by people who take action, and each person wants to foster action among people. Children and youth collaborate with adults and vice versa, addressing the challenges in their own lives and beyond. Beyond that, people who are curing the democracy deficit disorder keep a conscientious eye open for the community they are in, and they actively care for others. Working together and playing together, the community lives democracy in many ways because bonds go beyond typical relationships.

Understanding diversity and being competent in others' realities is a necessary capacity to cure the disorder. Young people and adults acknowledge, embrace, and enable all sorts of differences as powerful motivators and assets.

Amazement is a tool of people who challenge the disorder, too. To amaze, young people and adults differentiate themselves by doing things in an unconventional and innovative way. People routinely go above and beyond the average level of action to create an emotional impact on people and organizations and to give them a positive story they can take with them the rest of their lives. They also see the amazing parts of other people, acknowledge the exception to circumstances and events, and embrace the potential of every moment possible.

Coaching others is essential in times when confusion, uncertainty, and apathy seem endemic to the world. People who foster democracy consciously guide, transition, and mentor others through their daily professional and personal challenges without attempting to teach or lead them. Coaching does not mean adults know the answers or have solved the problems, and it does not mean children and youth do not have any answers ever; it means everyone of any age can help others find the answers for themselves.

Curing democracy deficit disorder can require boldness—not unfettered recklessness, but the gritty, determined kind of action that marks true change. Young people and adults are not afraid to make mistakes because they boldly know that is one way people learn. Taking appropriate risks and encouraging others to take appropriate risks too, building democracy requires boldness to actively learn to make better decisions. Learning to believe in science, young people and adults also trust deliberate choices and respect differences.

Motivating and empowering others is a necessary capacity for people who are striving to build democracy. Young people and adults constantly seek to engage others in consistent, substantive, and sustainable ways that are motivating, empowering, and sustainable.

Having a sense of purpose, fostering passion, and knowing they are capable beyond individual beliefs is the key to determination. Young people and adults must have this capacity to foster democracy. Whether they are counselors, youth workers, parents, teachers, or others, people who build democracy constantly change and embrace positive, powerful democratic change with open arms. Never accepting the status quo requires always thinking of ways to change processes, perspectives, and opinions, hopefully for the better. Without change, young people and adults cannot continue to be useful to themselves or other people.

Personal and collective goals are absolutely essential for democracy. Persisting, empowering, and engaging others to achieve, young people and adults must foster goals as much as possible. When they are working together to cure the democracy deficit disorder, every child, youth, and adult must recognize individual and collective goals and their relevance to actions, and help others do the same.

Democracy requires open-heartedness. Help is a keyword for people who are committed to this work, and this means that young people and adults both offer it and ask for it often. Often, people cannot do everything required in a project, so in a large part, part of democracy building is helping others take successful action. Neither adults nor young people are expected to know all the answers, but everyone knows where they can go to find them, and everyone shares that with others.

Knowledge management is a key to curing the disorder. Using diverse ways of identifying, developing, sharing, and effectively using the knowledge of communities, young people, and adults work to expand the knowledge of individuals and organizations. Learning how to organize, implement, challenge, and recreate the knowledge, ideas, thoughts, and wisdom behind democracy is essential to curing the disorder.

Democracy can require a sense of humor. Young people and adults who are working to foster democracy know it is good to laugh at themselves frequently and to see the levity in every moment, especially the heaviest ones. Living should not be drudgery or toil. Young people and adults have fun and can be goofy even when there is work to get done, and everyone gets lots done. Being a little goofy requires being a little innovative, and each person who is committed to democracy is always looking for a chance to fully engage in life by bringing out the fun and goofy side of it.

People who want to foster democracy must have problem-solving capacities. Working together as partners, young people and adults effectively, consistently, and realistically identifies, addresses, critiques, and re-imagine challenges. Working in groups, young people and adults empower each other to solve problems in creative, appropriate, and powerful ways that make the world a better place for everyone.

If people want to build democracy, they must take action. Democracy requires living in action and doing risky things. Young people and adults learn to make note of ideas and turn them into actions, and that is why everyone is always encouraged to share their voice, whether it is children's voice, youth voice, or adults' voice. If everyone thinks an idea is compelling, they go after it as a team. Taking pointed, determined action is the key to curing the democracy deficit disorder.

Democracy can require simplicity. Since everyone who is building democracy seeks to turn ideas into action, both young people and adults want to share them as effectively as possible. Each person can do this by being simple. It takes more mental space for creators of all kinds to make something simple or communicate something complicated in basic terms, but ultimately, that is what people want. Young people or adults do not inherently need to explain everything the first time around. Everyone needs to facilitate the best tailored learning experience for themselves and their organization or community. Everyone always needs to break down knowledge into easily digestible, clear statements and actions.

People who want to foster democracy have communication skills. Young people and adults engage each other with words and language in effective, empowering, and meaningful ways that reflect their own hopes and desires. In turn, they strive to make the ways they communicate even better all of the time, whether online or in print, with their language or through their actions.

Curing the democracy deficit disorder requires personal engagement. When consciously building democracy, children, youth, and adults are encouraged to foster their own connection to the actions they are taking, maintain that connection, and sustain the relevance of the work they are doing throughout their own lives, as well as help others do the same. When people learn to find meaning in everything people do, they learn the power and possibility of democracy.

People who are curing this disorder focus on democracy, no matter what they are doing. Nobody looks for fame or fortune, and each person rejects greed and deceit. Instead, young people and adults constantly look for opportunities to serve others and share that energy and efforts as often as they can. Encouraged to see the ripple effect in everything people do, and not just the flashy or huge things, can heighten the abilities of young people and adults to focus. If people do not see the ripples directly, they learn to trust the waves are working. They know every action in their lives can set off an entire cascade of responses whose overall impact is huge, and each person knows this is true for every other person, too.

Democracy requires compassion. Working together to develop their ability to establish and foster empathy with people and places outside of their own personal or professional sphere, children, youth, and adults develop compassion. When everyone is compassionate, young people and adults learn to accept, understand, or at least hear the perspectives and possibilities of everyone, everywhere, all of the time.

People who build democracy know how to listen. In democracy, young people and adults speak by listening. Instead of rushing to come up with a quick reaction to what someone has said or done, both young people and adults take time to listen to each other and themselves. When the time is right, each person responds with knowledge. Lots of people assume that the world is interested in them, so they spend most of their time talking. That leaves a lot of people under-informed because people share whatever they think, try to be clever, and think about what they are going to say instead of listening to what someone else is saying to them. Children, youth, and adults can learn to slow themselves down and engage rather than debate. In democracy, it takes time to really listen to what people say, and young people and adults can try to learn from everything everyone says.

Understanding both informal and formal systems through systems thinking is an important capacity for people who cure the democracy deficit disorder. Young people and adults see how small things that seem separated can create big things through complicated interactions. Everyone understands that systems are multifaceted and show clear, understandable, and meaningful ways to make change.

Curing the democracy deficit disorder requires knowing how to facilitate people in a variety of ways. Young people and adults can provide appropriate support to learners. Adapting and contrasting, modifying, and transforming experiences in classrooms, workshops, and beyond, all people are capable of teaching others given the right training and experiences. In democracy, each person encourages each other to learn through questions and activities that build confidence, stretch understanding, and foster engagement in learning. Young people and adults successfully identify and meet the needs of each other through group training and individual learning. Facilitation is neither easy nor inherent. Everyone consciously works to improve skills and build abilities to teach, facilitate, support, and improve themselves and other people.

The characteristic of culture is a key to curing the democracy deficit disorder, and young people should be actively, meaningfully, and substantially engaged in all aspects of it. This includes creating, consuming, critiquing, and recreating all aspects of culture, including art, music, language, writing, and other forms of interactions and communication, as well as perpetuating, transmitting, and transforming culture. Understanding that they have multiple roles throughout culture is vital to democracy, as it reinforces the self-perception of being an active agent who does many things rather than a passive recipient who is subjected to others' perspectives of culture.

Democracy requires patience and consideration through deliberation. Learning to regularly stop and check their intentions and affirm their actions, young people and adults reflect about their intentions. If a young person is not aware of why adults do what they do, they can become disconnected from what matters to adults. The opposite is true, too. If young people and older people are disconnected from each other, they are ineffective at democracy. Deliberately staying aware of the intentions, outcomes, and actions of people involved in democracy and being deliberate in each person's actions allows each person to guide their own efforts with purpose and challenge others accordingly when it is time.

Challenge is a key capacity in democracy. When people get too attached to the way things are, they lose the greatest freedom of all: the freedom to fail. Without feeling like a failure, young people and adults do not have to assume that a slight misstep is a deep plunge into the abyss. Instead, everyone steps forward to challenges and sees them each as an opportunity to innovate using a smart idea or strategic thinking. When they step up to challenges, people working to cure the democracy deficit disorder accept that failure is going to happen where growth happens. Ultimately, young people and adults do not become better at democracy because of how everyone responds to success, but instead, what each person does with failure. Being challenged allows all of us to learn and grow together.

Applying these competencies in practical, actionable ways is essential to meeting the challenges of these times. Faced with myriad challenges to democracy, everyone can start by protecting what is public, shared, and democratic right now—at least in concept, if not in practice. Young people and adults can then proceed to build their personal capacity by focusing on these competencies while taking practical, purposeful action to cure the disorder this book focuses on.

Groups Can Cure the Democracy Deficit Disorder

While seeing that individuals can positively affect democracy, it is also essential to also recognize the necessary actions of groups and how they can affect democracy. Scanning the field of positive youth development provides context, both internationally (Koller et al., 2016; Dimitrova & Wiium, 2021) and within the United States specifically (Lerner & Silbereisen, 2007; Schulman, 2006; Garcia & Philip, 2018). Throughout that field there is a readily accessible vernacular that already applies to understanding the roles of young people in groups (see Appendix I). When applied to curing the democracy deficit disorder, this vernacular can reveal categories and competencies to serve as applicable waypoints for young people through society, since positive youth development inherently would not happen outside of the democratic operation of society. However, young people in these circumstances are treated through adultist viewpoints though, and as such cannot experience positive youth development in its fullest possibilities. That does not mean that democracy ensures the defeat of adultism; however, democracy does allow the possibility of defeating bias toward adults like no other organizing vehicle of its magnitude in society today.

An Array of Democratic Action

Many "shades" of youth engagement have been identified by researchers and practitioners in the past. Sometimes used as a synonym, sometimes used as gradient terms, these terms include youth participation (Checkoway, 2010, p. 341), youth involvement (Association of Alaska School Boards, 2001), and youth leadership (Dollar, 1975, p. 6). Presented as spectra, continua, and in other linear pathways, they represent a largely Eurocentric perspective of young people progressing along specific avenues toward deliberate goals. This decontextualizes young people though, isolating the highlights of young peoples' abilities without demonstrating any effects on the larger world around them.

Rather than continuing to harp on traditional civic engagement, it can be essential to acknowledge the array of democratic actions taken by anyone. This can validate the unexpected and vibrant ways young people are essential to democracy. Throughout this array there are categorizations of group processes that children and youth experience. Based on early findings by Arnstein (1969) and a later elaboration by Hart (1994), this array allows the exploration of what democratic action looks like from the viewpoint of children and youth today. Based on findings from Fletcher (2005, 2017), this array shows that democratic action is first present through democratic participation, then democratic voice, democratic engagement, democratic involvement, and finally democratic infusion. While these categories may appear to be similar to the point of overlapping, each actually has distinguishing features that demonstrate their value to any project seeking to cure the democracy deficit disorder. According to Fletcher (2006, 2014a), there are three aspects present throughout each of these categories that make the action democratic: empowerment, partnerships, and equity. Different forms and some examples of each of these categories are summarized below and are presented throughout the remainder of this book.

Democratic participation is the smallest form of democracy action. Happening when young people show up in active ways throughout their own lives and in the larger communities around them, it offers the first reflections of empowerment, partnerships, and equity in democratic action. While they are not necessarily substantiated with roles or encumbered with responsibilities, the mere attendance of young people is tantamount to acknowledging democracy exists and that they want to be part of it. This is true whether it happens in family settings, community organizations, K-12 schools, government activities, and beyond. While democratic participation is often the high bar for some adults' visions for young people in democracy, it is actually just the starting point on empowering children and youth in democracy.

Democratic youth voice may be best understood as any conscious or unconscious expression of any young person anywhere at any time for any reason (Fletcher, 2007, 2014c). While it is constantly present, in the context of curing the democracy deficit disorder, voice is second on the spectrum of youth in democracy because it inherently means more than just showing up. Instead, it means sharing the wisdom, opinions, ideas, actions, and creations of children and youth. Not necessarily verbal, voice is not contingent on adult invitation, acceptance, rejection, or denial. Instead, it is constantly happening in countless ways throughout life. For young people who are highly impacted by developmental disabilities, democratic voice is present solely in their behavior; for other children and youth who get into fights or scream at adults in the community, their actions also constitute democratic voice. The young person who puts on a formal dress or suit and presents against curfews at city council, or the child who organizes a neighborhood protest closing a park are also sharing their voice. There is no qualification for what constitutes democratic voice because it is simply any expression of any young person about anything, anywhere, at any time, for any reason. Acknowledging the power, depth, and potential of voice is what places it on the spectrum of youth in democracy, because seeing the personal, social, and political potential of these expressions is inherently liberatory (Hipolito-Delgado et al., 2022).

Democratic involvement is any deliberate effort that centers on young peoples' ongoing attendance in personal, social, institutional, cultural, and other forms of structural action throughout society. Involvement is generally formal, often including specific positions, education, and outcomes. For more than fifty years this concept has been promoted as an avenue for organizational reform that makes space for young people, particularly in nonprofits, government agencies, and community groups that seek to serve children and youth effectively (Wikipedia, 2022h). Through democratic involvement, adults generally create specific opportunities for young people to impact the places serving them. This involvement might be situational or isolated from an entity's entire operation, or may be seasonal or temporary because of the ages of the young people involved, or the altering roles of the adults who champion the activities to begin with (Fletcher & Vavrus, 2006).

When young people sustain their connection toward a particular thing, whether an idea, person, activity, place, or outcome, it is called democratic engagement (Fletcher, 2014a). Simply said, children and youth are choosing the same thing over and over again. That sustained connection can be social, emotional, educational, spiritual, sentimental, or otherwise, so long as it is sustained. This notion can provide a powerful mechanism for democracy because it moves the presence of young people beyond force, manipulation, compliance, and placation and toward personal choice. Acknowledging the roles of democratic engagement at home and throughout communities can be empowering because it positions young people as responsible for their choices and allows them to make them deliberately rather than coincidentally.

The final category on the spectrum of youth in democracy is democratic infusion. This term, coined by Wendy Lesko in the 1990s (Lesko, 2001; Lesko, Dec 2001), refers to "the fundamental goal to integrate youth and young adults into all spheres of community life and to ensure that their voice and action are valued and utilized in efforts aimed at social or community change" (Zeldin et al., 2000, p. 3). Of the countless decisions made about young people throughout society, few of them are made with them. The concept of democratic infusion seeks nothing less than the entire, holistic, and complete acknowledgment, empowerment, and belonging of young people throughout all of those decisions. This approach to participatory democracy may seem radical at the outset, however when examined beyond adultist lenses it might provide the most complete way to cure the democracy deficit disorder. Working together with adults as equitable partners, democratic infusion "achieves this vision by partnering with youth-serving organizations to create a participatory culture that fosters sustained youth-adult engagement and intergenerational change" (Perkins et al., 2003).

The three traits present through each of these categories are empowerment, partnerships, and equity. The following paragraphs describe each of these traits.

Empowerment is an attitudinal, structural, and cultural process whereby young people gain the ability, authority, and agency to make decisions and implement change in their own lives and the lives of other people, including youth and adults (Fletcher & Vavrus, 2006). Youth empowerment occurs on a spectrum because of its varying applications throughout the lives of all young people regardless of their identities, positions, or outcomes in life. Every single young person can experience youth empowerment, whether it happens on the hyperpersonal level or the meta-universal level, affecting simple, singular choices within the day or participating in the policy-making processes of the United Nations, and everything in between.

Partnerships happen when young people are fully equal with adults while they are involved in a given activity. This is a 50/50 split of authority, obligation, and commitment. One of the realities of this is that there is no recognition for the specific developmental needs or representation opportunities for children and youth. However, one of the advantages is that it ensures the presence of a supportive adult in the activities of young people. Closer to ideal though is youth equity.

Equity is the pro-active rebalancing of relationships between youth and adults to allow for appropriately empowered roles between youth and adults. It allows for a 40/60 split of authority or other percentage while everyone involved—young and older—are recognized for their impact in the activity, and each has ownership of the outcomes.

The categories and traits on the spectrum of young people in democracy represent the most distinct competencies any group can present in order to cure the democracy deficit disorder. They provide a starting point for further analysis of the issues and actions currently being taken by young people, and a launching point for establishing the active, sustained, and transformative repositioning of young people throughout society as well.

Group Characteristics to Foster Democracy

Reconsidering their approaches to working with children and youth in order to cure the democracy deficit disorder may cause many institutions to reconsider how learning, teaching, leadership, and other activities happen throughout their organization, whether it is at home, in schools, nonprofits, government agencies, or elsewhere. Following are group characteristics that form a new vision for young people throughout society. They show what is present in environments where democracy thrives, young people succeed, and communities grow in powerful, new ways. These characteristics were adapted from the findings of Fletcher, who wrote about the presence of them through Meaningful Student Involvement throughout education (2005).

The first group characteristic is organization-wide approaches to democracy. This means that all young people of all ages are meaningfully involved throughout their democracy as much as possible. All community reform measures include opportunities for young people of all ages to become engaged in democracy. It looks like young people being involved in system-wide planning, research, teaching, evaluation, decision-making, and advocacy, or any other activities they know will improve democracy. Democracy building starts before kindergarten and extends well beyond graduation and throughout adulthood. Everyone in an organization knows there are a variety of opportunities throughout each young peoples' individual learning experience. There are also a variety of opportunities for young people in the learning experiences of their peers, within their community, throughout their districts, and across their states. There are a variety of opportunities for democracy in organizational management, interactions with peers and adults throughout the community, and ongoing throughout their lives beyond youthhood. Finally, there are opportunities for Student/Adult Partnerships in learning communities, child- and youth-specific roles in building leadership, and intentional programs designed to increase young peoples' efficacy as partners in community improvement.

The second characteristic of groups working to cure the democracy deficit disorder is high levels of young peoples' authority through democratic action. This is apparent in the ways children and youth speak, talk, interact, and express themselves to each other and to the adults who support them. The knowledge, opinions, and experiences of young people in communities and regarding democracy are actively sought and substantiated by adults throughout the organization. Adults' acknowledgment of young people's ability to improve democracy is validated and authorized. Children and youth are deliberately taught about learning. They are taught the democracy system. They learn about children's voices and youth voice in democracy. They learn about community improvement. Organizations' commitment to democracy is obvious through sustainable activities, comprehensive planning and effective assessments, and those assessments measure shared and individual perceptions and outcomes of democracy.

Interrelated strategies to integrate democracy is the third characteristic of groups. That means that young people are incorporated into ongoing, sustainable community reform activities. There are deliberate opportunities for learning, teaching, and leadership for all children and youth throughout the community. In individual activities this can mean integrating children's voices and youth voice into leadership practices; giving young people opportunities to design, facilitate, and evaluate activities; or facilitating young peoples' learning about community systems. In the adult leader's office, it can mean young people having equitable opportunities to participate with adults in formal organizational or community improvement activities. On the local, state, and national levels it can include children and youth having full voting rights, and equal representation to adults. Whatever the opportunities are, ultimately it means all young people and adults recognize they are bound together in equitable relationships with the intention of improving democracy all the time. Every community should be in a continuous mode of democracy building; every single improvement effort should seek nothing less than to engage as many young people in as many substantive ways as possible. Doors should be opened constantly through policy, training, budgets, and other supports for adults. Each of these strategies should be integrated with an organization improvement plan or a community improvement plan, and each of these strategies should be obvious within regular policies and procedures in organizations, districts, and/or state agencies.

The fourth group characteristic is sustainable structures of support for curing the democracy deficit disorder. This includes policies and procedures created and amended to promote democracy throughout organizations. It includes creating specific funding opportunities that support children's voices and youth voice, as well as young people's engagement throughout every activity, entity, and outcome possible. It also includes facilitating ongoing professional development for adults focused on democracy. Young people should be engaged as fully integrated and infused members of organizations, including activities, committees and other standing entities, leadership, operational procedures, and policy-making and enforcement at every level. Curing the democracy deficit disorder engenders new cultures throughout communities that constantly focus on young people by constantly fostering democracy. With a constant focus on sustaining democracy within groups, children, youth, and adults actively co-observe, co-examine, co-critique, and co-challenge culture, structure, and outcomes. Structures of support include child and youth action centers that train young people and provide information to youth/adult partners. Structures also include activities specifically designed to teach young people about democracy and the roles of children and youth throughout it. There should also be fully funded, ongoing programs that support democracy at every step of the way.

Personal commitment to democracy is the fifth characteristic of groups. Personal commitment is apparent when young people and adults all acknowledge their mutual investment, dedication, and benefit. Acknowledgment is visible in every element of action, including learning, relationships, practices, policies, community culture, and many other ways, and it shows that democracy is not just about young people themselves. Instead, it insists that all adults, including administrators, volunteers, staff, parents, counselors, and others see young people as substantive, powerful, and significant partners in all the different machinations of organizations, as well. When they have this commitment, every person will actively seek nothing other than to fully integrate young people at every turn. Children and youth who were previously seen as "the other" are no longer viewed as different and separate, both in intention and action. Particular emphasis is placed on engaging low-income children and youth, young people of color and low-achieving young people in groups and communities where predominately white, upper-income and/or high achieving young people have been perceived as having greater value or more importance than other children and youth. Finally, personal commitment to democracy in groups looks like sharing and re-affirming personal commitments to democracy as a cultural norm within the environment where action is happening.

The sixth characteristic of groups are strong learning connections throughout democratic actions. This means that learning and young people's involvement are connected by learning and acknowledgment, ensuring relevance for adults and significance to young people. These deliberate connections tie together the roles for children and youth with the purpose of democracy. It also substantiates Student/Adult Partnerships and signifies the intention of adults to continue transforming groups as children and youth themselves evolve. Because of this characteristic, democracy should not be an "add-on" strategy for groups—it should be integrated throughout their regular activities. Adults should acknowledge exceptional involvement by children and youth with credit or other forms of acknowledgment.

Other group characteristics matter too. It is also important for groups to consider appropriateness. Young people have far more wisdom than many adults might think. At the youngest ages, they are capable of expressing their views in simple and powerful ways. Appropriateness includes involvement that is developmentally, age and stage, individuality and culturally appropriate. Respect is a vital element of groups. Democracy is founded on respectful relationships between young people and adults throughout group activities, leadership, and outcomes. Giving the floor to young people does not take away from adult responsibilities, and one of the most important things adults can do is ensure a safe and supportive environment where democracy can flourish for children, youth, and adults together. In groups, mutuality matters. That means that reciprocity is essential to democracy and includes developing a common understanding about why and how young people are being involved, what the purpose is, and how young people can contribute to shaping the way activities occur. Reciprocity cannot just happen at the beginning of activities, either—it needs to be monitored and honed as groups unfold.

Curing the democracy deficit disorder through groups requires acknowledging power relationships. Power is a key consideration in democracy because society is built on it. From the youngest ages children are taught adults count more than they do. Be mindful of power differences between young people and adults and do not put words into the mouths of the people they are trying to engage. Power dynamics can also occur among children and youth. When working with young people in a group setting, being sensitive to these dynamics and creating opportunities for everyone to be involved can be essential. Small social groups can work best; integration and infusion can too.

Acknowledging the ethical imperative of democracy can be vital. Adults in any group throughout all of the community have an ethical imperative to meaningfully involve young people when appropriate. It is essential to respect and honor the ethical rights of young people, the identities they have, the places they come from and the communities where they belong. Ways of doing this include providing clear information about what children and youth might do in your group and seeking their genuine interest in becoming involved before automatically assigning them.

Make an agreement with young people that if they choose not to become involved there will be no negative consequences for that decision; voluntary involvement can be the key. Even if young people agree to take part, they should have the freedom to withdraw at any time without penalty. Young people also have the right to privacy and confidentiality. This includes seeking their explicit permission for any material arising from their involvement being published. Finally, young people have the right to be assured that their involvement will be worthwhile and enjoyable.

These group characteristics can provide all people in organizations, young and adult, with opportunities to collaborate in exciting new ways while securing powerful new outcomes for everyone involved, most importantly young people themselves.

Part II
Fighting Democracy Deficit Disorder

Young people around the world are fighting apathy, indifference, and resistance to democracy. Working for the benefit of the entire world around them, these children and youth are activists, researchers, teachers, evaluators, researchers, decision-makers, and advocates for issues much larger than themselves. This section examines their efforts to challenge democracy deficit disorder.

8

Issues That Matter

This chapter examines the various issues young people are addressing in communities around the world. Since the 1990s, there has been an increasing groundswell of youth engagement globally that seeks the healing power of democracy (Lesko & Tsourounis, 1998; Kim et al., 2002; Fletcher & Vavrus, 2006; Checkoway & Gutiérrez, 2012; Cammarota et al., 2013). International youth-led movements like the Arab Spring and the Hong Kong protest and American youth-led movements like Parkland's March for Our Lives #NeverAgain and Black Lives Matter #BlackLivesMatter have burst into the public consciousness, with millions of young people taking action. Recently, climate activism has spurned more youth engagement, enlightening and empowering more young people to make a difference. This is a groundswell that foreshadows massive social change toward curing the democracy deficit disorder.

Before addressing the breadth of issues young people are looking to solve through positive, powerful democratic action, it can be important to identify what they are not doing. Children and youth who have embarked to make a difference are not addressing things that only affect themselves. The myth of so-called youth issues is pervasive throughout the consumption-oriented consumerist culture that dominates and perpetuates the democracy deficit disorder. Since young people are routinely segregated from adults throughout society, including mainstream decision-making, problem-solving and policy choices, addressing this head-on before understanding anything else is vital. Among youth-serving organizations and within K-12 schools, there is a frequent temptation to pigeon-hole children and youth by focusing on issues that affect children and youth specifically.

Luckily, young people will not have any part of this. Children and youth activists are not fooled anymore by adults' frequent insistence that they need to focus on what adults think they should. Instead, they are addressing hundreds of inconvenient truths facing the world today in immeasurable ways. As Giroux says, "…it should now be evident to all Americans that young people bear a significant portion of the burden of a multi-trillion dollar deficit, disappearing social safety nets, stagnant job growth, and decrepit educational institutions at all levels while the current leadership of the United States maintains a collision course headed relentlessly toward the destruction of future generations" (2015, p. 122). These realities and many more are evident to young people right now.

Following is an examination of issues and actions taken by young people to cure the democracy deficit disorder. Eriksen (2018) translated three types of action from European literature that quickly categorize the following issues and actions. The first is *liberalistic democracy*, which is personally oriented and places the individual freedoms of children and youth highly enough for young people to have control free from adults. The second is *majority democracy* that values young people serving the community above their personal freedoms by making majority rule the operating norm. The third type of action is *deliberative democracy* that shows young people how their personal participation in communication, empathy, and consensus can make the community stronger. Each of these types is reflection.

Issues and Actions in Education

Planning the winter dance, setting the price for Valentine's Day candies, and deciding the new school colors are decisions some schools call democratic. However, challenging the democracy deficit disorder requires much more than this. There are literally countless issues throughout the education system where young people can be partners with educators and demonstrate they can be crucial for success (Fletcher, 2017).

Right now children and youth are working in schools as well as those working for school change from outside schools. Focused on challenging the democracy deficit disorder, Student/Adult Partnerships can transform education in sustainable ways. The following are some of the ways these relationships are being enacted right now throughout the education system.

Funding Priorities. Young people have been working with adults to challenge the continuous under-funding of public education in recent decades. Funding basic education is a key to dismantling democracy deficit disorder. Working together with adults, many children and youth are demanding better teaching resources, healthier school buildings, and more to that goal. Additionally, they are calling for increased teacher pay. Teachers often purchase supplies out of their own pockets, or simply go without in schools that are underfunded. In affluent school districts young people generally have access to better materials and teachers get paid high salaries, affording those students better educations. In turn, this reinforces the academic achievement gap that separates many students. This is the democracy deficit disorder in full effect. Through Student/Adult Partnerships, calls for equitable funding equity are frequent.

School-to-Prison Pipeline. The school-to-prison pipeline is a social and economic practice unfairly targeting low-income young people and students of color that uses school rules, curriculum, and teaching methods to jettison young people out of schools and into incarceration for the benefit of private prisons and elected officials who claim they are tough on crime. Running directly from early childhood learning through whichever point students are pushed out of schools and into the waiting clutches of incarceration, the school-to-prison pipeline is a tangible injustice affecting schools and students today (Giroux, 2015b, p. 105). Driven by practices including traditional classroom management and zero tolerance policies, both unfairly target these specific populations. In-school suspensions, out-of-school suspensions, expulsions, and school arrests are all markers affecting the youngest students straight through graduation. Working together, youth and adults can disrupt this pipeline by transforming learning, teaching, and leadership to focus on democracy building in systemic, structured, and strategic ways.

Special Education. Democracy deficit is obvious within special education through the labeling of young people, under-funding the support services that special education students receive, and the absence of mainstreaming special education students throughout the school population. Disproportionate representation of males and students of color as special education students, as well as equal access to support for such learners ails democracy, also. Charter schools and other schools of choice are sometimes criticized for weeding out special education students since they have more leeway in which students they accept. Young people—particularly young people involved in special education—are challenging this reality. By doing so, they are challenging democracy deficit and engaging in the important work of educating democracy beyond themselves.

Education Technology. The issue of schools maintaining their relevance in the face of technological developments is not new. In the 1950s the US became engulfed with the Cold War, and schools were forced to innovate their educational goals with the supposed purpose of keeping America competitive with the Soviet Union. Today the issue of how to teach about and with technology continues, as some schools limit access to the Internet, raising concerns about free speech, while other schools are increasing their use of technology in the classroom (Garcia & Philip, 2018). Virtual schools and online classes are becoming more and more common, and many educators believe the future of education is found in technology. Young people are challenging the non-democratic nature of technology in schools by empowering themselves and other students with tech knowledge, as well as working with adults to ensure more children and youth have more access to the tools they need to build democracy (Posnick, 2020). They are also taking actions to change the situation from outside the education system, transforming their own usage while challenging schools to respond too (Dalgaard, 2021).

Teacher Quality. Teacher quality was one of the biggest issues being discussed now by teachers unions, politicians, and teachers themselves. Long before the COVID-19 pandemic, conservatives and neoliberals were dominating the education debates in many ways, including saying that schools needed to determine who is a good teacher and who is a bad teacher (New York Times, 2015). What some are saying is that when young people are not succeeding in schools at sufficient rates, it must be the teachers' fault. While teachers certainly have an impact on their students, outside factors are also a big issue, including poverty, home life, and the outside community. Getting rid of teacher tenure (which gives teachers extra support from being fired) and firing low-performing teachers based on student test scores is the new approach taken by districts around the country. This entire line of thinking may have contributed to extreme stress on both teachers and students themselves, forcing the apparently catastrophic mass resignation after the pandemic (Will, 2022).

Teacher Development. Addressing what teachers learn and how they learn can make schools work better. The idea is that more and better opportunities for support, mentorship, and professional development for teachers will lead to better teaching and improved teacher quality. In some countries, teachers have far less teaching time than in the United States and have more time to plan with other teachers and observe the teaching of others. Half of all teachers leave teaching within their first five years, and new teachers have a steep learning curve.

Class and School Size. The number of students to teachers, called "student/teacher ratios," has been shown to affect how well young people learn. Many advocates call for smaller class size, while others claim size makes little difference. School consolidation, where small schools in local communities are merged into a single large school for a large surrounding area, has been happening since the 1940s. Now many of those larger schools are being closed, such as in New York City, to create smaller schools.

Charter Schools. In most states that have them, charter schools are schools that are publicly funded and privately operated (outside of the typical school district), and which students and parents can choose to attend instead of the local public school. Charter schools are all different; some are experimental and innovative, while others are very traditional but with longer hours. Studies are mixed about the benefit of charters, but the issue is becoming one that dominates education today. Many political leaders are supporting the creation of more and more charter schools, while those opposed believe charter schools take the most engaged parents and students, leaving the least engaged to stay in the regular public schools.

Curriculum. The question of who decides the curriculum in schools has a big impact on what goes on in schools. With influences ranging from textbook companies to politicians, and from school boards to businesses and more, schools and teachers somehow have to sort this out and provide a meaningful learning experience for students.

Voice and Engagement. The question of who has control and authority in schools has long been answered with "leave it to the professionals," meaning administrators and policy-makers. However, as more people push for participatory structures throughout the government, there are also efforts toward more participation throughout the educational system. Creating opportunities for meaningful involvement for students, teachers, and parents is growing in many communities, while the federal government is increasingly asking how and where nontraditional voices can be engaged in decision-making. Businesses, community organizations, mayors, and others want roles, too. This is a topic that many people can rally around.

Time in School. The length of the school day has been a popular topic for decades, especially in recent years. Recent brain research has shown youth have different sleep needs than adults, while it has been popular to say that students in the US have less seat time than students around the world (as a matter of fact, this is incorrect: while students in some countries have more days of school than the US, most of those countries have shorter school days that results in less seat time). The length of the school year is also a consideration, as some advocates are determined to add more seat time by replacing traditional summer breaks with more frequent shorter breaks throughout the year. The number of years a student needs to attend school is also an issue, as more public education leaders consider a "P16" system essential: pre-kindergarten through college graduation. These decisions can directly affect how youth consider the timing of democracy, how it affects them and what it means to others as well.

Scheduling. Seriously considering the physiological and psychological effects in the lives of young people can demonstrate to them whether they are considered serious members of a democratic society. The schedule of a school often drives the learning and curriculum in the school. The traditional 45-minute period of high schools, for instance, means that projects and activities are harder to do and fit within that time, as is traveling outside of the school for field trips or connecting with the community. Block schedules often have 1.5- or 2-hour blocks of time for classes, which provides some of these opportunities. Other schools provide classes for part of the time and give students self-directed learning time to pursue projects that earn them credit.

School Processes. Everything that is not governed by formal school policies is controlled by formal and informal processes and procedures. Issues such as what students do when arriving at school, riding school buses, school lockers, activities in the cafeteria, absences and truancies, student illnesses, school material usage, qualifications for participation in extracurricular programs, cell phone usage, and many more activities exclude youth. Engaging youth in these activities includes positioning them as problem-solvers and decision-makers, planners and evaluators. That is democracy in action.

School Planning. Democratic action with young people can include in school planning that equitably partners them with adults to create school culture, plan school activities and operations, promote school improvement, and design the physical building. All education processes and procedures that teach students with intention and purpose can exemplify meaningful involvement.

School Climate. The way a school is physically built and looks affects school climate as much as the interactions among students and between students and teachers. Engaging students as partners in school climate does not mean handing over the schools to students for them to learn on their own. Instead, it means acknowledging they are already leading building climate, whether adults admit it or not. Educators can move from passively allowing students to lead school culture to actively encouraging them to take responsibility for it through learning opportunities focused on their roles. While doing that, schools can challenge democracy deficit disorder by substantially enhancing individual and building-wide culture.

Education in the Media. It is increasingly popular to quote students in education articles. Engaging youth in the news can challenge authoritarian, anti-democratic portrayals of students as incapable. Other tools can include student-created articles for mainstream websites and newspapers, student-led video, student school twitter feeds, and other news distribution channels.

Out of School Time. Offering activities after school, in the evenings, on the weekends, and throughout the summer are common in some schools, while other schools do not provide them at all. Tutoring and mentoring, sports and extra-curricular clubs, and other learning or social experiences are out of the norm for many students, as their families or their schools are fiscally incapable of participating. Schools and communities could come together to devise creative ways to offer these opportunities to all students, regardless of income.

Classroom Management. Partnering with students to make classroom guidelines, school policies, and district regulations is how adults can foster democracy in discipline. Student courts are another approach, as is having students lead remediation and conflict resolution. Simple activities designed to prevent, intervene, or respond to challenging student behavior can give appropriate and necessary credence to students as partners. Doing this can make learners essential contributors to substantive activities within the normal learning environment of the classroom. In turn, this allows them to understand themselves as essential actors, which allows their transition from passive recipients of adult-led education toward Student/Adult Partnerships promoting learning, teaching, and leadership for all.

Community Connections. Democratic action can substantiate community connections throughout the education system. Place-based learning happens in classroom activities rooted in local things, including the unique history, environment, culture, economy, literature, and art of a specific place. Because of their knowledge and familiarity with the places they live, place-based learning is an ideal avenue for engaging students as partners. This can include methodologies such as service learning and adventure education. Serving as more than mere puppets of well-meaning adults, students who are engaged as partners can serve as true liaisons between the school and the community. This allows schools to genuinely benefit from all of any communities' inherent assets, apparent or hidden.

Teaching and Learning Issues. When students are meaningfully involved in teaching, they have opportunities to teach other students through facilitating learning, curriculum planning, evaluation, and other means. They can teach each other, they can teach younger students, they can teach teachers, and they can teach school administrators. For example, youth organizers from the Baltimore Algebra Project in Baltimore, Maryland helped organize the Free Minds Free People Conference in their city in 2018. The Baltimore Algebra Project works to ensure that all students have access to quality, 21st century education which includes learning and mastering advanced math. The organization's staff is entirely under the age of 25 and work as tutors, organizers, leaders, and executives for the organization. All decisions are taken democratically by the whole group, and their objective is to foster true democracy so that everyone gets their voices heard. With the belief that education is a constitutional right, they educate themselves and those around them. About the conference, the youth organizers learned that planning and hosting the event was a formative experience that opened the door for many opportunities to grow. They also found out that tapping their personal and financial resources was exhausting and found the need to strike balance in their work on the conference with their life journeys (Gillen, 2014).

Professional Development. When students teach teachers about youth culture, student rights, learning styles, and other topics important to them in schools, democracy can be present in teacher training. Students can also co-facilitate learning opportunities for adults focused on the critical study of power, language, culture, and history as they fight democracy deficit disorder, ultimately and appropriately teaching teachers to value that their experiences and contributions to education.

Class Evaluation. When students evaluate themselves, their teachers, their peers, the curriculum, physical classroom, or other parts of the school, they are building democracy. Evaluations that are designed, facilitated, implemented, and studied by students are an avenue for meaningful involvement to happen. Facilitating student learning, action, and reflection on the process of conducting student evaluations can help ensure meaningfulness.

School Research. Students who research their schools examine learning, behavior, funding, policies, and more for efficacy and purpose. By both sharing and collecting student voice, engaging children and youth as partners in school research can help identify gaps and secure data in ways that many adult researchers cannot. They can also reveal the biases implicit throughout education in ways that adults do not, including racial, gender, socio-economic, and other factors that drive curriculum, teaching practices, assessment, and more every day

(Cammarota & Fine, 2010, p. 51). It can also be a powerful opportunity to teach students about the practical application of research in schools.

Curriculum Planning. Curriculum planning can be made richer and more effective with democratic youth engagement. By participating as partners, students can help decide topic areas, curricular approaches, teaching methods, and other essential parts of the process. Equal partnerships through regular curriculum committees, as well as individual teacher planning can all challenge democracy deficit disorder.

Democracy Issues for Young People

The issues young people are engaged in right now are as diverse as young people themselves. That means that every identity child and youth can have is engaged in issues that address the democracy deficit disorder. This includes all socio-economic statuses; all gender identities; all intellectual and emotional capacities; and racial assignments of all sorts; as well as every other identity that can be imagined.

There is a lot of democratic action happening across the United States and around the world that is driven by young people. These activities challenge democracy deficit disorder and propel the world into deliberate, intentional action that is creating positive, powerful changes in homes, communities, nations, and worldwide (Stoneman, 2002). Substantial scholarship and writing have been focused on young people transforming democracy, including hundreds of stories of child-led and youth-led action. Barret wrote a significantly accessible summary of dozens of stories (Barrett, 2015), while historically a book called *Student Power, Participation and Revolution* compiled a number of essays written by young people about contemporary youth-led action from the 1960s and 1970s (Erlich & Erlich, 1971), while the turn of the millennium saw the emergence of scholar/ activists writing about young people and democracy. One work touting itself "the first and only comprehensive resource on youth organizing and activism in the US, featuring analysis of the movement" compiled the stories of more than 100 youth-led organizations (Kim et al., 2002), while a decade later, academics including Shawn Ginwright (Cammarota et al., 2013) and Barry Checkoway (Checkoway & Gutiérrez, 2012) made their findings known through significant storytelling.

Through the contributions of early online resources including What Kids Can Do (whatkidscando.org) and the Freechild Institute for Youth Engagement (freechild.org) were made available, the importance of the Funders Collaborative for Youth Organizing (fcyo.org) cannot be overstated for storytelling and other purposes. Each of these websites has offered reports, guides, and other tools unavailable before their existence. In addition to these reports, websites, books, and studies, media has covered the topic of youth building democracy in various ways, too. Sometimes highlighting the human interest angles, sometimes emphasizing the issues, and sometimes dismissing the effects, it seems that mainstream media, explicitly politicized media, and social media have all shown various angles on the issues and actions young people have taken throughout society to cure the democracy deficit disorder.

It is obvious to say that no single issue can engage all youth everywhere all the time; however, there is no young person who does not have a single issue they engage in. Instead, these issues and actions overlap and interface constantly with the identities and intersections of every part of the lives of children and youth. Even if their concern, interest, investment, and ownership is extremely hard to identify, every young person can be engaged.

Given their multi-faceted identities, belonging, and determination, it is important to recognize that despite how they are explored on the coming pages, young people are not fixated on singular issues either. Indeed, many have a transformational perspective of the interrelated reality of humankind, seeing wholistically what many adults try to singularize and uniting what others are seeing as disparate. That said, the following issues are shared to begin to identify some of the multiplicity.

These are just some of the ways young people are engaged in around the world right now and throughout history.

Water is a democracy issue for young people. Engaging children and youth in the surface cover of 72% of Earth includes swimming, drinking, and protecting it. Having access to clean, healthy water is a basic human right that enables democratic function, including democracy within personal lives as well as democratic governance. With increasingly widespread limitations and accessibility, water democracy is an increasingly important and obvious way to engage young people (Feldblum, 2019). As an example, Fionn Ferreira saw the damage caused by microplastic pollution on the environment as he was growing up near the ocean in southern Ireland. Determined to make a difference, early in high school he invented a process for extracting microplastics from the ocean. When he was 17, his method won the 2019 Google Science Fair competition for his process (Jacobo, 2019). Another story comes from Canada, where one young person has been on the international stage since they were eight years old. Autumn Peltier has been an activist for clean water rights. As a member of the Eagle Clan

Anishinaabekwe from the Wiikwemkoong First Nation in Ontario, Canada, she has been raising awareness that First Nation communities across North America cannot drink their water because of pollution from industry and oil. When she was 14 years old, the Anishinabek Nation named her Chief Water Commissioner for forty First Nations in Ontario. In this role at 15, she visited reserves, met with community leaders regularly and spoke internationally about indigenous and water rights (CBC, 2019).

The issue of beauty matters. Teaching young people about the deliberation of beauty, the potential of different perspectives, and the aesthetic potential of the world around them can help foster deep democratic desires (Park, 2020) Becoming engaged in beautiful things can mean a lot to young people. This does not necessarily mean superficial beauty either. Instead, it can be an ethereal, spiritual beauty that is resonant and present within and throughout everything. Democracy is harbored in the imagination and grows through creativity, and beauty can foster both. Youth beauty pageant participants in South Africa became involved in Youth Month as a form of activism. These leaders in the Miss Teen SA competition used the experience to celebrate the 1976 Youth Movement in South Africa which helped end apartheid (SABC News, 2021).

Intentional breathing leading to relaxation and calm matters to children and youth today. Young people are becoming consciously engaged in the moment-by-moment function of living with purpose. Mindfulness, meditation, and calming strategies are learned and innate within children and youth, and giving them space and supporting adults in engaging with them can cure the democracy deficit disorder. Children and youth are also struggling to transform the environmental racism that has made breathing toxic, homes sickening, neighborhoods depressed, and people held back for centuries. In Baltimore, youth organizers spent more than a decade challenging environmental racism in their community by conducting participatory action research, leading protests, and challenging political, social, business, and educational leaders to transform the situations which had kept generations diseased because of what they were breathing and more (Fabricant, 2022).

Another issue that matters to children and youth today is abortion. Young people have been on the frontlines of the pro-choice movement since the 1973 Roe v. Wade decision by the Supreme Court. Their activism has often occurred parallel but not in conjunction with other social justice organizing (Rosen & Conner, 2016), and has often included middle class white young women, which other youth movements were missing during the last 50 years (Cammarota et al., 2013). However, their involvement continues to grow because of increased pressure to repeal abortion rights nationwide (CIRCLE, 2022). With the leaked draft of a Supreme Court opinion ending Roe v. Wade, young people across the country organized in droves. Originally very active in building support for the 1973 opinion, in 2022 young people from youth-driven organizations nationwide became active in fighting for federal abortion rights, including March for Our Lives and the Sunrise Movement. "This Supreme Court does not represent Gen Z or the future we imagine for our country," said Voters of Tomorrow, a youth-led nonprofit involved in organizing resistance. These youth are rallying, leading sophisticated campaigns, and working with adults to ensure abortion rights continue (Lehrer, 2022).

Self-empowerment is an important issue for children and youth in democracy today. Young people can build democracy within themselves and discover the roles they have in the world through self-empowerment (Broumas, 2017). This is not an easy or simple call for personal development, but a practical and purposeful pursuit of new possibilities and fulfillment of potential for children and youth, whatever their situation. Whether they are building their minds, improving their physical conditions, or increasing their resiliency, self-empowerment means they are pursuing more ability and capacity on purpose. Teaching people how to empower themselves is essential. One of the ways they do this is through the practice of unschooling. Many young people who unschool are gaining the knowledge and skills they want to by actively determining what they want to do with their time, how they want to do it, where they want to spend their energy, and who they surround themselves with (Hern, 1996). At the 2017 European Democratic Education Community Conference there was a lively debate on whether unschooling and democratic education are competing approaches to learning. Participants in the conference were said to debate the issue, but final consensus suggested a compromise in that the highly self-motivated unschooling students and the democratic education students were both benefiting from self-empowerment for the larger community's benefit (Fisher & Sudbury, 2017).

The issues of gender, gender identification, and sexuality matter to young people today. Identifying as lesbian, gay, bisexual, transsexual, transgender, queer, questioning, and intersex (LGBTTQQI) can offer children and youth essential perspectives for curing the disorder. Their empowered self-identities combined with practical, daily expressions of their voices might provide these young people with particularly effective ways to impact change in their own lives and throughout the world around them. In Olympia, Washington, a twenty-plus-year-old organization called Stonewall Youth focuses on client-led services, with a nineteen-year-old youth designing the organization's outreach activities, two high school aged youth as full members of the board of directors, hiring committees that are mostly youth, and by paying youth employees the same hourly wage as adult staff. Through a variety of services the organization serves young people in southwest Washington and beyond, including support group activities, social services resources, leadership development, and peer support. They have a youth speaker's bureau, a Queer Rock Camp summer camp, a yearly Drag Show and many other activities as well (Stonewall Youth, n.d.).

Globalization matters to children and youth today. Engaging young people in enriching world perspectives and uniting cultures through democracy is a point for youth engagement in globalization (Welton & Wolf, 2001). This does not mean they are crass consumers mindlessly attempting to buy their way to happiness; instead, it means they are conscious citizens of the world who honor and uplift themselves and others through connectivity and do not seek isolation. Young people involved in these activities focus on "global justice, fair trade, debt relief, and sustainable development" and more (United Nations For Youth, n.d.). For instance, it was the 1999 anti-globalization protests in Seattle, Washington, that saw thousands of young people leading the march against the World Trade Organization. More than a North American response, this effort was part of an international campaign with roots in Indonesia, Europe, and Africa (Moraitis, 2006).

STEAM—Science, Technology, Engineering, Arts, and Math—matters to children and youth today. Young people are learning the practical functions of the most important subjects in many schools when they engage in STEAM. In turn, this reinforces their abilities to engage in critical thinking, social change, and self-empowerment, which are all necessary to curing the democracy deficit disorder. Rather than simply positioning adults to drive STEAM, student-driven learning positions them strongly to build their democratic dispositions and practical actions to transform the world they live in.

Another important issue is hiking. Walking, climbing, and otherwise traveling by foot can be a very engaging way for young people to experience democracy. Democracy relies on connectedness with nature, and actively engaging young people in interacting with the outdoors through hiking is one avenue to enrich their lives, improve their advocacy and responsibility for the outdoors, and maintain their conscious interdependence with the natural world around them (Louv, 2008). A youth-led hiking club in Cape Town, South Africa called @hikingclub. cpt creates safe spaces for young people to socialize and connect with nature (Earth Edition, 2022).

Dating violence matters to young people in democracy today. Young people build democracy through fighting negative physical, emotional, and psychological assumptions about dating and relationships while addressing patriarchy, gender bias, homophobia, and more. Their commitment to ending dating violence can translate to increased family, civic, and cultural engagement while moving toward active and purposeful lifelong roles in democracy (Istvan, 2018).

The issue of white supremacy, anti-racism, and Black Lives Matter matters tremendously to children and youth. Compelled to action by a generation of frequent police shootings of unarmed Black people, a national movement for Black lives emerged in the United States in 2013. "[A] decentralized political and social movement that seeks to highlight racism, discrimination, and inequality experienced by black people" (Wikipedia, 2022j), the Black Lives Matter movement has been driven by young people across the nation and expanded beyond to Western countries around the world. Fighting for social, political, and economic justice has been moored in efforts by children and youth to propel this work forward in many ways. Starting in 2013, the Black Lives Matters movement was founded after the police killing of African American youth Michael Brown near St. Louis, Missouri. Organizing against the violence of police against Black people, protesters across the United States led dozens of campaigns and have had a massive impact on the national conversation about racism and white supremacy. Many of the organizers since then have been under 18 years old and have continued campaigns into adulthood (Bort & Aleah, 2020). Nupol Kiazolu was 17 years old when she founded Vote 2000. When she was 18, she became the president of the Youth Coalition for Black Lives Matter of Greater New York. Named one of Teen Vogue's 21 Under 21 in 2018, she organizes campaigns against white supremacy in the city and beyond (DoSomething.org, n.d.). In another example of youth of color challenging white supremacy, Native American youth with the American Indian Movement (AIM) organized a 500-mile "Run for Survival" from Minneapolis, Minnesota, to Lawrence, Kansas, in 1978 (Peters & Strauss, 2009).

Art matters to young people. Engaging children and youth in art can mean creating it, viewing it, critiquing it, and more. Whether it is validating an infant's playful creations, substantiating a young person' graffiti, or otherwise embracing the act of designing and composing artistic works, all artistic creation is a form of voice. This voice implicitly enhances democracy by giving expression to those who do not have it, and "invites viewers into perspectives and ways of life different from their own—and with that, helps foster a sense of empathy required for democracy" (TED Talks, n.d.). One example comes from Bali. Cruz Erdmann is a 14-year-old who was born and raised in Bali. Since he was 10, Cruz has logged more than 160 dives and has been an underwater photographer since he was

12. The Natural History Museum in London named him the Young Wildlife Photographer of the Year in 2019 (New Zealand Herald, 2020).

Young people are deeply committed to farming today. Growing food and consuming local farm food can deeply engage children and youth in democracy. Not only does food provide nutrients to sustain life, it also has deep political and cultural value around the world. Young people engaged in farming can move from consumption to production, selection, education and advocacy and beyond, thereby building democracy and curing the disorder.

Police reform matters to young people. With the militaristic transformation of policing and increasing amounts of police brutality happening worldwide from the 1990s through today, it became routine for police forces worldwide to use increasingly hostile techniques to subdue the populace, including children and youth. Whether it is acknowledging their place in the school-to-prison pipeline or recognizing the abrasive, anti-democratic techniques used in policing, engaging young people to become key agents in police reform can lead to curing the democracy deficit disorder.

Young people care about homelessness in democracy. When they experience substantive connections with people who live without a permanent home, young people can become deeply compassionate and engaged in the myriad causes of homelessness. Visible homelessness can engender feelings of "otherness" along with separation, alienation, and differentiation. Joining in the struggle to end homelessness empowers democracy among young people by showing them their actions can empathetically impact others, particularly when they succeed in transforming social structures or cultural norms that accept such injustice.

Gun control matters to children and youth today. With hundreds of mass shootings yearly, the rampant and out-of-control gun rights movement in the United States is toppling the safety of children and youth across the nation. Youth activists are working hand-in-hand with adult organizers nationwide to overcome the power of the control lobby by organizing sophisticated campaigns to encourage politicians to curtail the murders, innocent deaths, and accidents of young people caused by guns every day. Students who survived the 2018 Stoneman Douglas High School shooting in Parkland, Florida, continue their anti-gun violence campaign with policy advocacy, public awareness, and educational activities (Wikipedia, 2022d). They have been attributed with completely transforming youth activism in the United States since that time (Barrett, 2019). In 2019, 13-year-old Naomi Wadler led a walk-out at her school in Virginia to mark the one-month anniversary of the school shooting in Florida, and she wants people to join her in remembering the many African American girls lost to gun violence (World Economic Forum, 2020).

Young people are committed to fighting racism and segregation. White people have a history of segregating different races for the benefit of white people. Around the world, young people have been challenging segregation and white supremacy for decades, which inherently builds democracy and defeats the racism underlying much of the democracy deficit disorder. For instance, South African high school students began a peaceful march in 1960 that turned deadly when the police attacked the protesters. Marching against a law enforcing white supremacy, their movement led to the international divestment campaign against apartheid. The broad government cruelty was exposed and eventually Apartheid ended because of the youth activism (Ndlovu & Peterson, 2016, p. 36). A more recent example is a result of the so-called War on Terror. When he was 12 years old, Ziad Ahmed established a youth-focused international social justice organization called *redefy*. Placed on the TSA no-fly list as a youth inspired him to help young people combat racial prejudice. Today, redefy offers stories by student journalists and shares resources with young activists internationally (Redefy, n.d.).

Children and youth care about emergency relief. When places cannot get enough of what they need, it is engaging for young people to provide relief. This can happen in the form of food, clothing, education, or public health; it can also happen through social-emotional support and the end of trauma. Relief between friends and relief between nations may appear massively different because of scale, but it is essentially the same thing by helping others get the things they need to survive and thrive despite challenges. When children and youth are engaged in relief efforts, they actively cure the disorder.

Challenging political corruption in democracy matters to children and youth. Throughout the centuries young people have led many campaigns about the corruption, despotism, authoritarianism, and totalitarianism that upends, represses, or otherwise defeats democracy (Hoose, 2001; Barrett, 2015). In the past twenty-five years this pace has accelerated and mushroomed into a global phenomenon, where the pace of social media has collided with the possibilities of democracy to inspire youth activists to struggle for freedom against political corruption and more. For instance, in 2000, hundreds of thousands of Filipino young people protested and ultimately toppled the government they perceived as corrupt (Moraitis, 2006). In the 2011 Arab Spring uprisings across the Middle East, youth are attributed with central roles in overthrowing corrupt regimes in Egypt and Tunisia. Their ability to mobilize in large numbers, achieve political consensus quickly via technology and motivate older people to action were cited in the success of their efforts (Schwartz, 2011). From 2006 to 2015, young people in Chile actively protested the quality and access in the nation's school system. Struggling against high levels of inequality between classes, students demanded an end to corruption that stopped government approaches to education reform from benefiting low-income people (Guzman-Concha, 2012; Wikipedia 2022m). These are just some of the examples from around the world of youth working to cure democracy deficit.

Young people create, transmit, consume, critique, and transform culture every day. There are a growing number of children and youth who are doing those things to the benefit of democracy throughout society. One example of this is from the United States, where more than 300 youth and elders throughout Helena, Montana, enjoyed the March 2019 Round Dance facilitated by the Helena Indian Alliance All Nations Youth Council. Led by youth, the event focused on commercial tobacco, diabetes prevention, and other issues. Health food, singers, and a hand drum contest were enjoyed by (Inter-Tribal Council of Michigan, Inc., 2019, p. 109).

Being engaged in athletic play, competition, or achievement can be essential for the democratic growth of children and youth. Jens Sejer Andersen, director of an international NGO called Play the Game, once wrote, "If you think that a ball game is merely a game about a ball, you may have got it wrong. Sport and our movement culture broadly speaking is an intense, never-ending battlefield about the values and norms that guide our lives" (Andersen, 2017). Learning competitive norms, exploring personal connections to athletics, keeping one's physical, mental and emotional well-being in focus, and experiencing the practical implementation of democracy within the sports setting can build, challenge, and grow the practice in every generation.

Challenging adult reticence, reluctance, and indifference to the global climate catastrophe through advocacy and direct action, young people around the world are leading action right now. This is evident through a story from Puerto Rico. After a massive hurricane in 2017 threatened to take out Puerto Rico's electricity for at least a year, 17-year-old Salvador Gómez-Colón created the "Light and Hope for Puerto Rico" campaign. Through it he found and shared more than 3,100 solar-powered lamps and hand-powered washing machines for families across the nation. Salvador continues to support the implementation of smart energy systems in Puerto Rico and has launched a similar program in the Bahamas (TIME, 2017). It is also obvious in the story of Greta Thunberg. A homeschooler all her life, when 17-year-old Greta learned about the climate crisis she stopped eating, stopped speaking, and fell into depression. Becoming determined to take action, Greta studied climate change and its causes and began changing her own habits and challenging her family. She began protesting outside the Swedish parliament during school hours in 2018 and kept striking there every week for more than a year. Her personal activism has grown into a global movement since. Her action has inspired people in her generation around the world to make a difference, too (Kraemer, 2021). Seventeen-year-old Ayakha Melithafa organized youth and adults in South Africa to advocate for low-impact growth and a just energy transition where she lives. In 2019, she joined a group of youth activists as part of the African Climate Alliance in a call to world's leading economic powers accountable for stalling on the climate crisis (World Economic Forum, 2020).

There are many other issues that matter to young people. They include peace, which is fostering nonviolence in the lives of young people and the lives of others which can be very engaging for children and youth. Friendships and developing short- or long-term connections with people they choose matters. Wildlife conservation matters, with children and youth surveying animals, studying birds, and participating in sustainable fishing and hunting.

Young people care about nutrition and learning about healthy eating, food knowledge, and diverse food sourcing. They also are challenging illegal drugs, defeating the perception of youth as addictive, mindless drug users through education, advocacy, and social justice campaigns against manufacturers and weak government responses. Young people care about history, where children and youth can become engaged in the heritage of their culture, neighborhood, family, or other identities, as well as their interdependence with others' histories. They are fighting against disconnection, where young people are engaged in fostering healthy connection and bridging new engagements.

Economics that engage children and youth in personal, community, organizational, or cultural economics matter to them. So do politics, which can develop lasting connections between young people and the formal and informal structures of influence and power. Young people care about weather emergencies during which young people can engage with others to immediately and deeply impact those around them. They are fighting censorship, where children and youth examine, challenge, advocate, test, and change censorship in print, online, in music, and otherwise. Trees matter to young people who are examining, learning, reforesting, planting, preserving, or caring for them and their histories, roles, and places throughout communities. They care about fun and the intentional engagement of children and youth in creating, becoming part of, or expanding fun in their own life or with others.

Other issues include engaging children and youth in rights, including examining what rights are, what they are not and how to have them respected. Languages matter to young people, including listening, speaking, or exploring communication in its myriad forms. Children and youth are challenging white supremacy, fighting the hateful notion that people of European descent should dominate culture, economics, politics, and more around the world. They care about solar power and connecting children and youth deeply with alternative energy to cure democracy deficit disorder around the world and within themselves. They also care about identity and belonging, including fostering and exploring connectivity between and within identities.

Whether or not adults care, young people care about fashion and appearance and establishing deep connections with others and their own clothing needs by making, critiquing, and distributing clothes, fashion, and more. They also care about public health and healthcare, and engaging young people in making sure everyone can access healthcare and knowledge about staying healthy is important. Youth care about personal engagement and recognizing the ways they are engaged within themselves can be essential for young people. They also challenge inequality in order to bridge social, cultural, economic, and structural differences and build democracy.

Other issues that young people are building democracy through include music, when children and youth listen, share, create, dream, sleep, and breathe music, they become engaged in the democracy of life. Place-based connections matter to young people, whether living rural, urban, online or in-person, or beyond any of that can cure democracy with young people when done intentionally. The are using poetry and engaging people in the feelings, motions, ideas, and thoughts of others and themselves can happen through rhyme, meter, tradition, and innovation; cooking for children and youth to engage with the foods and meal-making that sustain people throughout their lifetimes. Young people also care about refugee support, where people who escape from oppression or suffering can engage each other and non-refugees for exchange, enlightenment, and empowerment.

These issues expand on the possibilities of curing the democracy deficit disorder, and in many cases have gone a long way toward ensuring it has continued to exist around the world. However, there are many, many other issues young people are actively engaged in right now that are transforming myopic or anemic democracies right now and encouraging healthy democracies to continue evolving through time. That is one of the essential roles of children and youth in democracy, to ensure change. Luckily, that is a duty that is inherent to the station of all young people throughout society.

9

Adults as Allies

Several authors have written about the failures of adults in the past century, lambasting them for their bias against children and youth and much more (Freire, 2004, 2015; Neill, 1990; Holt, 1974; Gatto, 2017; Giroux, 1981, 1999, 2008). One of the things each reiterates is that many adults today believe children and youth are subhuman and inferior to adults in nearly every way possible. They consistently lambast educators, youth workers, parents, and others for inadequate, antiquarian, opportunistic, and oppressive behaviors, attitudes, perspectives, and actions. These arguments are nearly constant in the literature.

What is not as obvious is the compassion necessary to relate to these adults in order to overcome their ignorance and inabilities. The simple reality is that adults today have lived with a democracy deficit for their entire lives; adults today often never knew democracy as young people; adults today are products of the environments in which they were raised; and *en masse*, adults have little or no civic imagination that would allow them to reconceptualize roles for young people throughout society.

At the same time this compassion is missing, the overwhelmingly oppressive forces that are eroding the democracies in which young people are growing up today are becoming more powerful. As Giroux states, "Collective supports and rights for young people are disappearing as the family, school, social state, and various civic institutions abdicate their former guardianship and no longer serve as the primary forces shaping children's lives" (2009, p. 28). This is true of every station for children and youth throughout society.

Examining the world in which they grew up can help people today understand the democracy deficit disorder in adults today. In the years between 1950 and now, the roles of youth were situated throughout global society, shaped by politics, technology, war, economics, and education. Worldwide, the manufactured segregation was the product of earlier generations which confined young people to schools in order to end child labor and broadcast economic mobility through schooling and later, out-of-school time programs (Jenks, 1996, p. 18, 57; Taft, 2019, p. 111; Gatto, 2017, p. 118). Adherence to this formula was systematized through government regulation, social programs, philanthropy, and popular media, and allowed both conservative and neoliberals to enforce their agendas for social compliance and profiteering (Hayden, 2001, p. 73; Giroux, 1999). Sociologist Mike Males (1999) observed that in the 1980s and 1990s, today's adults were also painted as criminalized "superpredators" who were supposedly destroying America, while crime rates were actually falling nationally.

It is against that backdrop of hyperconsumerism, superpredator-ization, and age-based segregation that the adultist anti-democratic opinions and actions of adults today have to be examined. From that perspective it can be easier to compassionately relate to the lenses many adults view children and youth through, including an absence of imagination, the negation of hope, and overall generational despair, as well as civic malaise toward the world in which young people co-occupy with adults today.

Reliant on hierarchies, command and control authority, absolutist thinking, and totalitarian ways of being, the disorder in democracy today is well-suited for fascist dictatorships. It is not suited for democratic republic nations, democratic socialist countries, or global institutions perpetuating freedom and justice. We can apply Gillen's summary of public schools to every scale of young peoples' realities, from the hyper-local to the transnational and global: "The great majority of citizens in our 'democracy' have not begun to imagine that workplaces or schools could be democratic. Even the adults in schools accept the absolute authority of the principal and follow the 'mandates' that they themselves had no role or representation in formulating... The idea that high-school students should see themselves as peers of teachers or administrators is even more outlandish. Even at eighteen...'the students' relation to school authority is still entirely dependent and subordinate" (Gillen, 2014, p. 114).

Meanwhile, many adults are indifferent and apathetic, recalcitrant and even indignant about the expanding roles of young people in society beyond that of passive recipients. Frustrated by their own inability to participate in democracy in meaningful ways, there are parents, teachers, social workers, counselors, and others who fight against integrating young people into democratic society in democratic ways. Instead, they are wholly vested in maintaining power structures and even expanding the authority of adults, whether online or in-person. Refusing to acknowledge the potential of succeeding generations, many of these adults condemn children and youth to toiling in vain against the problems facing the world today. Antagonizing the young, they openly mock youth activists and advocates in the media, classrooms, public forums, online, and elsewhere, while advocating their own opinions, ideas, actions, and experiences above those of young people.

Defeating the democratic deficit disorder today insists on vigilance by even the most well-meaning adults though. Not only must they confront the oppressive behaviors and attitudes of fellow adults, they must also stay aware of their own internalized adultism and the temptation to succumb to cynicism and self-defeat. It can be said that that "Great Resignation" of 2022 afflicting education and youth work of all kinds is partially the outcome of these realities (Patten, 2022; Johnston, 2021). While parents are not reported to be quitting their duties in kind, there are still anecdotal reports of them struggling through this period of time, too.

All of this amounts to a challenging vision for children and youth today. Given the toil of adults throughout previous generations and their subsequent projections onto young people today, it might seem inevitable that adultism continues to project the democracy deficit disorder.

However, in the previous fifty years a lot has changed for the benefit of engaging children and youth worldwide in democracy, starting with the advent of the Convention on the Rights of the Child and the subsequent national and state laws created in response (United Nations, 1990). The rights of young people in the United States, a non-signatory to the UNCRC, can be said to have expanded in a variety of ways, too (Guggenheim, 2007). Following is a recitation of many of those rights from around the world.

The Rights of Young People

Any conversation about the rights of young people needs to begin with the understanding that the world keeps changing. More young people are gaining more access to more information than ever before. Communities continue to be reliant on children and youth for their subsistence, and combined with more information, young people are demanding more justice, access, and abilities than ever before. In the absence of those demands being fulfilled, many children and youth are creating opportunities for themselves like never before. Unlike the past though, young people are included and leading themselves as never before, too. Democracy is spreading.

With the emergence of media youth activist stars, more adults than ever before have been engaged in an ongoing conversation with young people and adults around the world focused on the question, "What can children and youth do to change the world?" The answer is that there is no limit. That makes it essential for adults to recognize that young people are assuming more responsibility for democracy than ever before. They are doing this by improving schools, helping the environment, promoting positive community development, challenging apathy, and promoting civic action like no other generation. Unfortunately, cultures around the world have had oppressive attitudes toward young people for hundreds or thousands of years. Adults seemingly everywhere have routinely and systematically segregated children and youth from adults; made them into the chattel of adults; eliminated their economic livelihoods; fought their attempts to restore balance to social perspectives of their capabilities. There is another way, starting with acknowledging the rights of young people.

There are certain things that everyone should be able to experience, do, and have in their lives. They should be able to do those things simply because they are human beings. Nobody should have to earn these opportunities, or rights. The Universal Declaration of Human Rights was the first international statement to use the term "human rights" (United Nations General Assembly, 1948). It is short, and worth reading the whole document. There are many rights included in the document including the right to equality, freedom from discrimination, the right to life, liberty, and personal security, freedom from slavery, freedom from torture and degrading treatment, and the right to recognition as a person before the law.

The European Convention on Human Rights was the first international document to give people the right to take the government to court based on human rights abuses (Council of Europe, 1950). In the United States, rights are named and protected by the Constitution and the Bill of Rights. The legal system in the United States was designed to protect, enforce, and uphold those rights, but with questionable application according to racial, gender, socio-economic, and other identities. Most nations have legal mechanisms like a Bill of Rights that make rights available for certain people.

Never in history has there been a universal agreement on who youth are. Some people say that youth is more a state of mind than a time of life, like former United States Attorney General Robert Kennedy, who famously said, "This world demands the qualities of youth; not a time of life but a state of mind, a temper of the will, a quality of the imagination, a predominance of courage over timidity, of the appetite for adventure over the life of ease" (Kennedy, 1966). However, many government agencies, nonprofit programs and media outlets define youth as a distinct period of time in life and name ages for when it begins and when it ends (Fletcher, 2016). In some instances, youth begins at 8 years old; in others, it starts at 16. The same ambiguity exists when naming when youth ends, since for some it happens at 18, 21, or 25 years old. Legal systems around the world skirt the issue by using terms like adolescent, juvenile, and teenager to describe this age range. Sometimes, this is to provide a distinct boundary for when people can begin voting or serving in the military; other times, it is to allow a person to be executed or taken from their families. The age ranges of youth are generally defined in law to meet political objectives, rather than for the genuine wellbeing of young people or society at large.

Children's rights are specific opportunities endowed to people under the age of 12 simply because they are children. Youth rights are the specific freedoms every person has between the ages of 12 and 18 years old, including opportunities, freedoms, rights, and responsibilities. They are distinct from the general human rights identified earlier because they are young. They are different from children's rights because they acknowledge the evolving capacities of youth, as well as the evolving nature of the society we all share. For more than a century, some youth and some of their adult allies have been advocating for youth rights.

These rights have generally fallen into three categories: provision, which is protecting young peoples' access to particular things like food, clothes, shelter, education, and so forth; protection, which is making sure that young people are safe from abuses, including physical, mental, and psychological abuse; and participation, which is giving young people the opportunity to make, direct, evaluate, and critique decisions that affect them throughout society.

The Background of the Rights of Children and Youth

Throughout the course of the last century awareness was raised worldwide that children and youth were not sufficiently protected by the general human rights documents. Worse still, young people themselves believed they were protected but still had their rights routinely violated and relinquished by governments at all levels (Holt, 1974; Epstein, 2010). Because of this awareness, different entities have created a variety of documents to expand the rights of children and youth. When Ban Ki-moon was Secretary-General of the United Nations he said, "Let us acknowledge and celebrate what youth can do to build a safer, more just world. Let us strengthen our efforts to include young people in policies, programmes and decision-making processes that benefit their futures and ours" (United Nations, 2010). The ambition of his statement is reflected in one main document today.

Perhaps the most powerful statement ever supporting the notion that young people have specific rights is the United Nations Convention on the Rights of the Child (CRC) (United Nations General Assembly Resolution 44/25, 1990). Combining all three categories of rights mentioned earlier (provision, protection, participation), this document is the most-widely ratified treaty in the world, with every single nation on the planet except the United States signing on. In the United States, conservative Republicans do not agree with the function or objectives of the document. Since the UNCRC focuses on "every human being below the age of 18 years unless under the law applicable under the child majority is attained earlier," it includes the rights of both children and youth.

Some of the rights guaranteed by the UNCRC include protection from discrimination; the best interests of the child; the child's right not be separated from his or her parents against the child's will; the child's right to maintain contact with both parents if they separate; the child's right to be heard in any judicial and administrative proceedings; the child's right to freedom of thought; the child's right to privacy; the child's right to information from national and international mass media. Through the UNCRC, children placed in physical or mental health care settings have the right to a periodic review of their circumstances and treatment; the child's right to a standard of living adequate to the child's physical, mental, spiritual, moral, and social development; the child's right to rest, leisure, and recreational activities; and state obligations to protect children from all other forms of exploitation that are prejudiced against the child's welfare.

Children and youth never waited for this document or other adult acknowledgment of their rights though. As early as the 1860s, young people began protesting for more rights around the world. Working hard and earning meager wages, children and youth in Western nations demanded higher pay, fewer hours, and access to more services. Later, as more adults became allies in children's rights and youth rights struggles around the world, young people fought for universal education, health care, and more (Hoose, 2001).

In the 1930s, an organization called the American Youth Congress produced a Declaration of Rights of American Youth, which they presented in front of the U.S. Congress. This was the first recorded effort by youth for youth to push a concise youth-focused policy agenda on the federal level in the United States. While they succeeded through the creation of the federal National Youth Administration, their efforts were ultimately dismissed because of the political affiliations of their membership (Wikipedia, 2021a).

During the 1950s and 1960s, the Civil Rights Movement included a lot of seemingly brash youth leadership. Claudette Colvin was 15 when she refused to give up her seat for a white woman, 9 months before Rosa Parks' famous launch of the modern movement (Hoose, 2010). In 1960, three young men—Ezell Blair Jr., 18, Franklin McCain, 19, Joseph McNeil, 17, and David Richmond, 18, all students at a nearby university—took action where others had failed. Refusing to leave the segregated lunch counter where they wanted to eat, they took a stand against segregation that had massive effects. Later called the Greensboro Four, they started a national sit-in movement in the United States that spread to more than 50 cities. Because of their activism, lunch counters across the country rapidly desegregated (Nittle, 2020). The Birmingham Campaign, focused on challenging the cultural, political, economic, educational, and social discrimination Black people faced in that Alabama city, was most successful when adult organizers actively engaged child protesters in calling for their rights (Franklin, 2021). These were youth rights-specific campaigns and part of a successful civil rights movement that continues to inspire today.

In the 1960s and 1970s, a youth liberation movement emerged around the idea that young people of any age could and should have the full and complete rights of all adults, and not just the limited ideas that were pushed around by well-meaning adults. According to those activists, children and youth of all ages should be allowed to vote, work, drive, own property, travel, have legal and financial responsibility, control their own learning, and have a guaranteed income (Hefner, 1970). There were even more far-out elements of this platform that called for all young people to be able to use drugs and have sex without restraint (Gross & Gross, 1977).

In the mid-1990s a youth rights movement emerged on the Internet calling for society to pay attention to several parts of this platform. In other arenas, youth-led organizing has expanded toward completely youth-led campaigns in cities across the United States and around the world (National Youth Rights Association, n.d.A). At the same time, work in the United Kingdom and across Europe led to particular expansions of youth rights, including increased opportunities for civic engagement and voting rights being lowered in several nations (Wall, 2021).

Since the beginning of the new millennium, youth rights advocates have been active around the world. In 2011, young people in Chile took over the nation's school systems in order to have more rights in schools (Guzman-Concha, 2012). In 2014, youth in Scotland played a vital role in their nation's referendum to stay part of the United Kingdom (Breeze et al., 2017, p. 754). A marked uptick in community organizing led by youth in the United States has shown remarkable returns in social justice movements across the nation (Paterson, 2021), and in Hong Kong, youth are leaders in the pro-democracy movement (CNBC, 2019). The youth-led climate crisis movement is gripping the globe right now and incensing a generation of youth activists worldwide. They are demanding their right to live in an environmentally sustainable world, and claiming their right to the future right now, while they are young (UNICEF, n.d.). The #BlackLivesMatter movement is credited with engaging youth of color today in social action across the United States and worldwide, demanding for their rights to live free of white supremacy, racism, and discrimination (Bort & Aleah, 2020). For more than 50 years, children in Peru have led a movement showing that "kids can—and should be—respected as equal partners in economic, social, and political life" (Taft, 2019). The list goes on.

As these examples show, there is no single agenda for children's and youth rights everywhere, all of the time. Instead, the movement is made of many agendas reflecting the diversity of young people around the world today. Following are some of the children's and youth rights issues being addressed today.

Growing Traditional Rights for Children and Youth

Any conversation about democracy must include the inalienable rights of the individuals throughout society. Following are some of the traditional rights for children and youth that people have granted to them before, or that have been advocated for across the last hundred years (Wikipedia, 2022k). While commonly agreed on as "children's rights," it should be emphasized that the following summarizes children's and youth rights around the world. Taken from many of the leading documents cited previously, the following is an amalgam of issues from many places.

The traditional rights for children and youth include the right to abuse-free living, which acknowledges that all young people have the right to live free from all types of abuse, including emotional, physical, and psychological abuse. They should live free from economic, social, cultural, religious, and personal exploitation. They have the right to know peace and nonviolence throughout their lives. The right to creativity means that without excuses, all young people have the freedom to creativity in speech, expression, and action. This includes physical, spiritual, intellectual, and emotional creativity which can be shared without harming another person's wellbeing or freedom to creativity. The right to education means that whether through informal or formal avenues, all young people have the right to free and universal education. This education should cover everything essential for democratic participation throughout society. The right to employment includes the ability of all youth everywhere to be free to choose work that fulfills their objectives as young people. Reasonable limits focused on safety and health should be considered and taught to young people rather than mandated without their consent. Youth also have the right to fair pay and benefits for their labor. Food access rights include the right to healthy, sustainable, and essential food is the right of all young people everywhere in order to ensure their health. The right to healthcare includes mental, physical, and spiritual health, and should not be limited according to a young person's income. It also includes recreation through informal or formal avenues. Time and physical space should be guaranteed with both structured and unstructured opportunities to relax, have fun, and socialize. The right to shelter means that youth have the right to safe, secure, and sustained shelter, whether with their family of origin or in other situations they find suitable. Shelter should not be provided contingent on adult approval or through manipulation. Movement is a right and should not be restricted. This means they can walk, bicycle, or otherwise transport themselves, and should not be restricted from accessing public transportation the same way as other members of society. The right to vote means that children and youth have a right to political representation in elected bodies, as well as the right to establish or relinquish laws affecting them and the larger society they are members of. This happens through voting and political participation.

There are current laws in the United States and around the world that prohibit or ban things that are done to children and youth. Other laws exclude young people, including physical and psychological maltreatment or neglect; illegal labor, endangerment and infanticide; parental actions including youth maltreatment;

gender identity and/or sexual orientation; sexual abuse/exploitation; neglect or abuse; sexual or labor trafficking; disabilities; familial migration; unaccompanied children in a situation of migration. Other laws protect young people without parental care or who are in alternative care; police custody or detention; homeless youth; parents in prison or custody; court or other judicial proceedings; custody disputes, including parental child abduction; racial discrimination; discrimination against minority ethnic groups; female genital mutilation; forced marriage; young people who are not in compulsory education or training or working children below the legal age for work; and bullying or cyberbullying against youth.

Expanding the Rights of Young People in Community

In the past 50 years, a number of efforts have been made to gain additional rights for young people beyond those cited above. Organizations and individuals have worked to defeat adultism. Young people have asserted the right to live without being discriminated against because of their age. These rights have been conferred upon by advocacy organizations and academics; legal mechanisms have been created internationally, nationally, and locally around the world that have established codified rights for children and youth. The outcomes of these opportunities vary, but as Wall (2021) suggests, "Democracies would be incentivized to deconstruct their own adultist biases and reconstruct themselves from childist points of view" (p. 134) with the onset of voting rights and more.

Expanding the rights of young people throughout communities includes seeking to have a right to live without arbitrary confines based on time. In the presence of curfews based on age, it is said that young people cannot express themselves, take work, or fulfill their right to free movement whenever they want. In the absence of being able to choose what is best for their own health and wellbeing, children and youth have been sent to behavior modification camps, effectively losing all their rights. Behavior modification camps inherently discriminate against every part of a young person's identity. The right to vote, run for political office, and campaign freely for themselves or other people belongs to all young people because of civic youth engagement. Being able to complete other civic activities is a right of youth too, including volunteering and participating in community groups. Portraying all young people as castaways to mainstream society, the media and police often criminalize children and youth, essentially casting young people as criminals by virtue of being young. Youth also have the right to not be associated with crime.

According to advocates, more young people want the freedom to earn money, save money, and invest their time and energy how they choose. The right to economics includes the right to use economic institutions at their own volition, and to be represented for the taxes they pay. The right to learn should not be sacrificed to adults who do not know how to engage young people as partners in schools. In education reform young people have the right to transform education as equal and meaningful partners throughout the education system (Frost & Roberts, 2011). There are young people who want emancipation from their guardians. The right to become independent of parents or guardians for legal purposes is important for the safety, wellbeing, and health of youth. Access to entertainment and the creation of media for themselves and other people to consume is a right all young people have. The ability to choose for themselves what they want to consume, what they want to produce and whether they want to participate should be determined by their capacity to choose, rather than their age. Children and youth have the right to equal and fair treatment in law enforcement and throughout the eyes of the law, whether through traditional trial by peers or restorative justice. Punishment, retribution, and other forms of justice should be made with attention to equity, and anyone who committed a crime should be rehabilitated and educated. Other consequences should reflect their personal growth and abilities, and not be generalized across all young people. Being portrayed unfairly due to their age is not justice for anyone, and because of this all young people have the right to be represented through fair media representation. They should not be typecast or stereotyped because of their age, race, socio-economic status, educational level, or other perspectives either.

Expanding the Rights of Students in Schools

As distinct environments where young people spend the majority of their waking hours, schools affect children and youth in very specific ways. From the 1960s through today, young people around the world have been advocating for their rights to be acknowledged in schools, challenging schools to expand on their rights and working for more rights to emerge throughout the education system (Erlich, 1971; Collins, 2019, p. 9). Sometimes these attempts have worked; sometimes they have failed. For several years, the National Youth Rights Association in conjunction with the Freechild Institute hosted an online website called YouthRights.net for more than 10,000 contributors to brainstorm what rights students should have in schools. In the process, the project identified the most comprehensive list of student rights in schools (YouthRights.net, 2012). Following is a summary of that list.

According to the people who contributed to that project, all young people in schools have the undeniable right to the freedom of existence and belief in every imaginable area including, but not limited to, sexual orientation, political, moral, and spiritual beliefs, and the freedom to express such beliefs without fear or influence from schools, as long as no one's property or person is physically damaged or violated by said beliefs. Students have the right to expression, including wearing any clothing they want, when they want, how they want, without codes of appearance hindering their free expression in schools. Clothes should not materially, substantively, and/or directly disrupt the educational process (to be judged by young people and adults).

On YouthRights.net, contributors believed children and youth have the right to freedom of speech, freedom of press, and freedom to organize protests or petitions of grievances to any employee in the educational system, which includes the school, district, state, or federal staff, and all elected, appointed, official, or unofficial leadership. All students have the right to self-control, self-management, and self-leadership, no matter what their ages. They should also be able to select which classes he or she wishes to participate in, without pressure from parents, teachers, guidance, and administration.

All students have the right to the acknowledgment of their skills, according to that project. Students should be certified in their skills and education regardless of arbitrary requirements imposed by school administrators, the government, or parents. To fulfill this, certificates of completion and class transcripts for a given course should be awarded by schools for each course they teach. Students have the right to choose which form of diploma they may pursue, be it individual class, vocational or career-specific, college preparatory, or state awarded. From this it follows that all young people have the right for their certificates of academic preparation to be equally evaluated by any future school, college, or university to which they may apply; and students who choose to pursue diplomas other than a standard high school diploma have the right to have their individual courses evaluated as a measure of their academic achievement.

Contributors to YouthRights.net believed that all students have the right to deny self-incrimination. No youth can be forced, under threat of punishment or otherwise, into signing any documents that state that they confess to having done something against school policy. All students have the right to refuse assistance in school, specifically help in the form of special education curriculum and instruction, medication, or psychiatric help. No public school may expel children or youth who refuse these or other services. A student may also reserve the right to petition the school for these services if he or she feels that they would help in some way. All students have the right to view on their own accord their school records and to request a copy of the specified documents. No school policies, such as zero tolerance, can punish a youth for having educational tools, such as scissors or a compass, or a medication that is useful or needed.

Students have rights to physical health, according to the YouthRights.net project. If a faculty member thinks a questionable object is unfit for school it can be confiscated (as long as it is returned in a timely manner) without punishment, but no one can deny a student a needed medication. If a young person is found with a medication considered unfit to be on their person, a faculty member may take them to the nurse's office but cannot personally confiscate it. Young people have the right to refuse medication on a given day or altogether if they so choose.

Similarly, all students have the right to be free from harassment, assault, or bullying, and require every form of physical safety and support adults can provide, including freedom from school shootings, bullying, fighting, and physical pain inflicted by adults. To that extent, all children and youth have the right to be free from all forms of corporal punishment, including but not limited to paddling, i.e., beating the youth's buttocks with a wooden board. Schools need to be entirely free from all forms of corporal punishment and the sexualized and sadistic hostile environment they impart to all students and staff. All students are entitled to immediate medical care if needed. The nurse's office should not refuse any students who express that they feel that they might vomit, have a seizure, become unconscious, or any other function that may lead them to be a danger to themselves and other youth in the classroom setting. Anyone who needs medical care is to be first priority.

Contributors to YouthRights.net wrote that students have the right to use the school facilities as needed, including restrooms, technology, hallways, and student-focused spaces. All youth who are the victims of harassment, physical, sexual, or otherwise, assault, or bullying, both verbal and physical, have the right to have their grievances dealt with in a proper manner, including an investigation into said incident, and proper punishment of the culprit, and determent of any act of vengeance. This includes harassment, assault, and bullying by teachers, staff, deans, guidance counselors, head principals, and vice principals. No youth is required to go to a specific person to report such incidences. Furthermore, any staff member who witnesses such acts is obligated to report them. Any youth or staff member who reports such incidences has the right to confidentiality. All children and youth have the right to keep school and community separate or together, including the rights to organize, promote, and participate in organizations of their choice on or off school property, so long as they are law abiding. They can also seek sponsorships for their organizations from outside sources such as private businesses, church groups, and community centers. This right extends to sports teams, clubs organizations, and to music and art departments. This is to ensure that youth are able to enjoy activities of their choice without having to worry about funding being cut partially or completely from the school's budget. Unless the school has strong suspicion of abuse (sexual, physical, and/or psychological), neglect, and/or endangerment, they may not question a youth about his or her home life. If the school has evidence of abuse, they are to report it immediately to the authorities.

All children and youth in schools or beyond have the right to deny participation in any activity that is self-revealing, according to YouthRights.net contributors. They believed that any scholastic activity that requires communication in any form about family finances, home life, and/or the occupation of the young person's parents should not be obligatory. Money should never be an issue in schools. All youth have the right to privacy, including expression, and the right to refuse drug testing unless there is a court ordered warrant for it. Refusal to take a drug test is not to be considered sufficient reason for a warrant. All students have the right to refuse searches of their person and personal belongings such as purses, book bags, and lockers unless there is a court ordered warrant for it. Refusal to allow a search is not to be considered sufficient reason for a warrant. Furthermore, all youth have the right to have a purse or bookbag in their possession, and also the right to the temporary ownership of any available locker.

In the YouthRights.net project, contributors believed all young people have the right to be provided an adequate and well-balanced education regarding the topics of drugs, alcohol, and human sexuality. Youth and only the youth are to decide whether they want to learn these topics. A parent may not withhold their child's education if the youth is willing and wants to learn. Likewise, a parent cannot force their child if the youth does not want to learn, and nor can the school, unless it is considered necessary for a degree in a particular subject. All students should have the right to an uninterrupted education. No school will refuse to enroll a youth or deny a youth their education because of their living arrangements or home situation. A parent may not un-enroll their child from school if the youth want to continue to attend. No law shall be passed or enforced that directly or indirectly denies a youth their right to an education. Students should have the right to a quality education that covers the disciplines, including music and the arts, and is fair and balanced. Teachers have the right to teach and cover more material than what the school administration has prescribed, so long as it is within the limits of the law and all the required material is covered.

According to contributors, all students have the right to formally and informally evaluate their concerns and complaints regarding a teacher's or staff member's performance, their knowledge about curriculum and classes, and their opinions about school culture and climate. Their evaluations should be taken into consideration for planning and other processes affecting them. All children and youth have the right to participate throughout their school and the education system. This includes the right to representation, participation, and meaningful involvement as education planners, evaluators, teachers, researchers, advocates, and as community organizers focusing on education. All students should have the right and responsibility for being involved in educational decision-making at all levels, including decision-making affecting them personally, in their classrooms, local schools, and at the district, state, and federal levels. Also, students should have the right to full participation in all forms of formalized education decision-making, including committees, site councils, school boards, and other venues. Youth must be allowed, encouraged, and able to participate fully, including voting on school boards, budget referendums, and other activities, and in all areas of education, including budgets, personnel, and curricula.

All students have the right to youth courts according to the YouthRights. net project, and to the privacy and effectiveness they offer. Adults should not directly or indirectly impede or influence their ability, authority, and sustainability without permission of the youth governing body. All youth have the right to participate in any school sponsored activity. Because of this, no school may deny any youth the right to participate in any sport based on their grades, performance in said sport, or membership in any youth-based group. No school may deny any youth the right to participate in any sport on the basis of gender if the sport is not offered for both males and females. No school may deny any youth participation in school athletics if they are involved in a community athletics team. All students have the right to knowledge about student rights and the values, perspectives, and knowledge of them. No school has the right to keep children and youth ignorant about their freedoms within, or any other document that contains information such as rules or rights the students have. No employee of a school should lie to a student about their rights either.

While this list might appear bloated or over-explanatory, it is important to understand that in a total institution as severely adultist as schools it can be vital to expound on every single situation students face within that environment. This list is not even wholly comprehensive. There are extremely segregated spaces within the education system that entirely prohibit and ultimately ban students' involvement, especially within the administration of schools at all levels of the education system. However, naming the rights as the YouthRights.net project did is essential for starting a serious conversation about defeating the democracy deficit disorder within schools.

The Movements for New Rights

In addition to new thinking, critical engagement, and theoretical equity between young people and adults, defeating the democracy deficit disorder requires pragmatic, visible, and effective action. The movements for children's rights and youth rights continues today with varying agendas and purposes (Collins, 2019, p. 8).

Although they are rarely acknowledged within academia and popular media, there are several extant organizations and programs committed to the conviction that young people have the right to live free of adult oppression. These organizations want free speech, sexual education and safety, foster youth rights, youth involvement, and much, much more. Perhaps the foremost organization, since 1999 the National Youth Rights Association has heralded this movement in the United States by organizing chapters, providing educational materials, and promoting activism focused on expanding youth rights (National Youth Rights Association, n.d.B). An emerging entity is the Children's Voting Colloquium, a cadre of international advocates and academics who are working to lower or eliminate the voting age (Children's Voting Colloquium, 2023).

Activists around the world are challenging discrimination against youth by holding protests, producing publications, going to court, and creating pro-youth climates in a variety of communities and institutions. For instance, 18-year-old Natasha Mwansa of Zambia advocates against child marriage. She is a journalist who also acts as a monitor for various health organizations and tracks the rights of women and girls throughout her country. Today, she is also a member of the African Union Commission's Youth Advisory Board (World Economic Forum, 2020).

The gulf between the intent and activities of the youth rights movement and the children's rights movement continues to grow. Traditional children's rights advocacy organizations continue adult-driven, adult-centric change focused on benefiting children's basic human rights; youth rights organizations are generally focused on expanding the current civil rights of youth and challenging discrimination against youth. Young people themselves, as well as adults who were youth rights activists, are winning court cases, taking influential jobs, and serving their communities in a variety of ways that continue to promote youth rights agendas, all without the multi-million-dollar budgets and high influence of the people involved in the children's rights movement.

Adults Taking Action to Support Youth

In 1963, Dr. Martin Luther King, Jr. was speaking about a strike in Nashville, Tennessee, when he explained, "At the heart of all that civilization has meant and developed is 'community'—the mutually cooperative and voluntary venture of man to assume a semblance of responsibility for his brother." This conception of democracy reflects King's belief in "total connectedness and a network of reciprocity" (Jahanbegloo, 2018, p. 44). It is with this same sense that adults should assume responsibility for engaging every young person throughout democracy. Instilling, imbuing, and otherwise setting up all children and youth to co-create and inherit the ongoing sense of responsibility for democracy is essential to the successful functioning of democracy.

This means that parents, teachers, youth workers, counselors, politicians, neighbors, business owners, and every other responsible adult in the life of any young person is inherently bound to uphold, educate, challenge, transform, and reinvent democracy with those young people. This is a large charge that requires identifying how this responsibility is exercised in daily life. The Convention on the Rights of the Child spells out these duties by saying adults have responsibilities to,

> … in a manner consistent with the evolving capacities of the child, appropriate direction and guidance in the exercise by the child of the rights recognized in the present Convention. (United Nations, 1990)

Little prepares adults for these responsibilities today. As Giroux identified about teachers, "Instead of learning to raise questions about the principles underlying different classroom methods, research techniques and theories of education, students are often preoccupied with learning the "how to," with "what works," or with mastering the best way to teach a given body of knowledge. For example, the mandatory field-practice seminars often consist of students sharing with each other the techniques they have used in managing and controlling classroom discipline, organizing a day's activities, and learning how to work within specific time tables" (1981, p. 95). The same can be said of other professions that serve children and youth, including social service workers, government program employees, mental health counselors, and many others who can support young people curing the democracy deficit disorder.

Adult roles in this work are neither to be passive backseat riders in these efforts nor the main drivers. Instead, the responsibility is to become an adult ally. This is generally not a named position, but an identifiable trait of someone who does support children and youth in word, action, and outcomes in visible, tangible, transparent, and transformative ways. Parents, teachers, and anyone relating to young people can be an adult ally. Adults are allies to these efforts to cure the democracy deficit disorder because these activities, approaches, and avenues for action are youth-led, community-focused, and purpose-driven. No matter what their roles, adults' responsibilities are to engage them however possible. The Young Wisdom Project of the Movement Strategy Center reported (2004) that,

> A youth-led organization or project is one in which the youth constituents decide what gets done and how it gets done. Youth led does not necessarily mean 'no adult involvement or role.' 'Youth led' is a specific relationship between youth and adults where adults are supporting youth to gain the skills, information and capacity to make decisions about the organizations in which they find themselves. Adults play the roles of coaches, trainers, and advisors to young people who are the decision makers. Youth leadership promotes the notion that adult allies should not do for youth what young people can do for themselves. (Young Wisdom Project, 2004)

Once adults grasp what their responsibilities in these efforts are, it is vital for adults to check their own assumptions, beliefs, ideals, and values, and to see how they may impact their roles.

Checking Mindsets

A lot has been said about mindsets in the last decades. Extensive scholarship about adults learning about the concept, and teaching students about the idea has been coupled with professional development for educators. Elaborating on the role of growth mindsets for engaging young people in democracy building is important. Carol Dweck started studying growth mindsets in the 1990s and reported that the concept is centered on students' perceptions of failure (Dweck, 2007, p. 23). Dweck found that some students came back quickly from failure and some students were devastated by failure (p. 25). By studying their perceptions of failure, Dweck identified that the difference was that some students had a growth mindset and believed they could get smarter, while others had a fixed mindset and thought they would never succeed (p. 154). Testing whether those mindsets could be changed for the positive, Dweck and other researchers discovered that fixed mindsets could be changed with specific interventions (Dweck et al., 2015).

Applying Dweck's concept of mindsets with the adults in schools, communities, and beyond, one can find that adults' mindsets often determine which youth are engaged in activities or events, which young people are meaningfully involved in schools or programs, and which youth are focused on democracy building activities. These subjective perceptions about young people can be routinely informed by youth identities and behaviors and are far from the equity that many adults say they aspire to.

Young peoples' involvement in democracy building activities, such as volunteering and other civic engagement activities, is often predicated on whether adults thought the children and youth who were involved *deserved* to be involved (Cockburn, 2007, p. 448; Checkoway, 1996). If they *deserve* it, adults let these young people know. This type of gatekeeping allows certain young people to be involved while establishing and maintaining roles for adults as gatekeepers. Gatekeepers routinely decide which young people can be involved according to various spoken and unspoken factors, including academic achievement, likeability, and compliance with adult expectations. Although it is less likely to be acknowledged, factors including race, gender identity, sexual orientation, and socio-economic background are used to determine who has access to these democracy building activities, too.

These "gates" are predicated on bias, allowing and excluding or denying some young people from being valued while other children and youth are wholly silenced, dismissed, or ignored. It is the adults' mindset or the joint mindsets of several adults that permits, accepts, and sustains this bias. This fixed mindset about young people believes that children and youth have to deserve or earn the right to be engaged in democracy; only certain young people selected by adults should be heard and other children and youth should not be heard; there is a "perfect" or "right" type of youth engagement in democracy; and every other young person is imperfect or is not right, and that they are not "okay." These same adults frequently believe young people should simply reproduce the opinions, actions, beliefs, and knowledge of adults, and that only certain children and youth have innate abilities to be democratically active, while others do not have this ability.

When adults have a growth mindset about young people, they allow and encourage all children and youth to experience democracy throughout their lives whether or not adults accept them. Adults see that all young people have the capacity to become vital to democracy, and all young people understand they deserve to be involved—not because they are particularly special, but because they are members of a democracy, and all people should be heard, seen, acknowledged, and empowered within and throughout democracy.

When adults have growth mindsets about young people, they believe every young person deserves to be heard. They make space for children and youth to share what they want to, rather than just what adults want them to share, and they work to deliberately engage every single young person every single day in every single way possible. Adults with growth mindsets about young people teach them to focus on improving how they build democracy, not which young person shares or what they share. They focus on why children and youth matter and why young people share how they do. They believe in increasing other adults' capacities to meaningfully involve young people in democracy, too.

Decades ago, Dweck and her colleagues showed that teacher mindsets directly and deeply impact student mindsets (Dweck et al., 2015). One of the informal findings has been that when adults think young people are capable of positively transforming democracy, children and youth learn to think they are positively capable of transforming democracy. While their actions are (luckily) not contingent on adults believing in them, more young people are going to become more active in democratic transformation when adults learn to check themselves.

Adults Taking Policy Action

Stakeholders in the issues touched upon here include children and youth, parents, law enforcement, classroom teachers, community educators, public health workers, social workers, childcare providers, government officials, school leaders, mental health providers elected representatives, youth workers, business owners, healthcare providers, nonprofit organization leaders, community advocates, mental health counselors, and others. In order for each person to cure the disorder, everyone has to take practical action.

There are policymakers who could make laws to engage young people in democracy and defeat the democracy deficit disorder. These individuals have control and legislate or otherwise represent all people in democratic societies, including children and youth. Every day they make, enforce, modify, or otherwise affect youth in countless ways, and they are elected officials who can be essential to defeating the democracy deficit disorder.

They include local elected officials such as mayors, county commissioners, city councilmembers and aldermen, school board members, utility or hospital district commission members, local judges, and justices of the peace. On the local level, they can also include elected county and city attorneys, elected law enforcement individuals include police, marshals, sheriffs, constables, and others, as well as elected registrars of deeds, tax collectors and assessors, and members of elected advisory boards and committees.

Similarly, on the national level, in many countries there is a president or prime minister as well as a vice president, a Congress or Parliament, or another democratically elected official who can prevent youth discrimination and fight the democracy deficit. In many states or provinces there is a premier, a governor, a secretary of state, or a member of a legislative body such as a state legislature can affect youth discrimination. Each of these individuals can directly affect the democracy deficit disorder, and the people who elect them can hold them accountable to do as much.

There is a lot of action to be taken in policy development, reform, transformation, and implementation. Working across every level of communities, in some situations young people are not waiting for adults, instead opting to lead action to change policies on their own. This is the case demonstrated in Taft's 2019 book entitled *The Kids Are in Charge: Activism and Power in Peru's Movement of Working Children*. It details how, since 1976, children and youth in Peru have been lobbying for themselves as working children have lobbied for "more horizontal intergenerational relationships" that remove the stigma of child laborers by acknowledging the need for their existence in the flawed capitalist system (Institute of Development Studies, 2022).

Each of these political mechanisms, including elected officials, government lawmaking bodies, and the judiciary are responsible for the miserable condition democracy is in today. Each is also capable of making changes needed to change the tides driving the disorder. Similarly, the secondary and tertiary elements of the democratic system, including the education system, the social service sector, and the systems of care affecting youth most directly in some situations are essential to curing the state society is in today. When these systems fail to live up to their obligations to democracy, it becomes essential for young people and adults to work together to challenge them. As Baldwin wrote, "I love America more than any other country in the world and, exactly for this reason, I insist on the right to criticize her perpetually" (Baldwin, 2017). The next step is where youth and their allies make this criticism palpable.

Part III

Learning to Challenge Democracy Deficit Disorder

10

Youth Facilitating Democracy

Social change led by and with young people provides individual children and youth with important opportunities to experience and impact democracy first-hand and allows adults the chance to relax and learn from young people by work-ing with them, instead of for them and it gives communities hope by developing lifelong expectations and opportunities for everyone. One of those expectations is that there are communities worth living in for everyone, including youth. One of those opportunities is that democracy needs to be constantly reinvigorated through social change.

In his last book before he was assassinated, Dr. Martin Luther King, Jr. (2010) wrote,

> One of the great liabilities of history is that all too many people fail to remain awake through great periods of social change. Every society has its protectors of status quo and its fraternities of the indifferent who are notorious for sleep-ing through revolutions. Today, our very survival depends on our ability to stay awake, to adjust to new ideas, to remain vigilant and to face the challenge of change.

Activists, educators, youth workers, young people, and all people around the world must stay awake and vigilant to the challenges facing society today. The need to strengthen democracy has never been greater, and the resources have never been so limited. Communities can no longer afford to ignore the power of children and youth, either morally or fiscally. As Giroux (2011) insists, "[N]ot only do young people need to have a passion for public values, social responsibility, and participation in society, but they also need access to those public spaces that guarantee the rights of free speech, dissent, a quality education, and critical dialogue." The following chapter illustrates how this happens right now in practical, meaningful terms.

How to Take Action

Within the last decade, there has been a groundswell of youth engagement around the world. International youth-led movements like the Arab Spring and the Hong Kong democracy protests and American youth-led movements like Parkland's March for Our Lives and Black Lives Matter have burst into the public consciousness, with millions of young people taking action. Recently, climate activism has spurned more youth engagement, enlightening and empowering more young people to make a difference. This is a groundswell that foreshadows massive social change whose time is at hand.

Taking action to stop the democracy deficit disorder includes all kinds of youth activism and youth leadership, including some actions adults like and other actions adults frequently dismiss. It also includes all the issues addressed throughout this book.

Stopping democracy deficit disorder happens when more young people are choosing to become active in more activities addressing more issues than ever before. It makes adults in society pay attention to issues they would otherwise neglect or deny, i.e., drug use, sex, vaping, or gangs. This is also true within the family structure when individual youth become engaged in sports, romantic relationships or video gaming. In recent years, this work has happened in the issues mentioned above, including pro-democracy movements, public health crises, and racial justice. Historical peak youth engagement has been seen around these topics, and others too, including anti-war activism and economic reform. Society has yet to see peak youth engagement in issues like school reform and lowering the voting age, and only time will show what comes next. That is hard to anticipate.

For better or worse, and perhaps more than any time in the past 25 years, the media, politicians, community leaders, academics, and others are hyping the power of young people to change the world. There are many, many local, regional, national, and international organizations that say they support youth engagement, especially with the youth they specifically serve and the issues they particularly care about.

Advocates to stop the democracy deficit disorder must address widespread adultism. Whether it is a *Washington Post* article screaming, "A youth revolt grows up when it reaches beyond its beginnings" (Meyer, 2018) or a 1960s youth activist in his senior years lambasting youth activists today (Gitlin, 2003), there is now-normal posturing from well-meaning but poorly informed adults who embody bias toward other adults and routinely discriminate against youth—even those trying to build democracy. This type of adultism is cynical at best; belittling and demeaning, it assumes young people are not capable of finding the strategies and approaches that matter most to them. Adultism pervades the popular response to youth engagement in its myriad forms. Democracy invites these hyperbolic and ineffectual responses though, and with the power of youth intact, these criticisms fall to the side.

Soon, the social change at hand will see challenges to democracy deficit disorder reach massive proportions across all populations around the world. More adults than ever will come to support young people in active and empowering ways, and all kinds of transformations will take place. Aside from meeting basic human rights and the values enshrined in the United Nations Convention on the Rights of the Child, the emerging peak youth engagement will ensure global transformation.

Transformations throughout society that will cure today's democracy deficit disorder and build democracy in successive generations range from the broad and ambitious to the specific and focused. Broadly speaking, we need to change the individual attitudes of children, youth, and adults everywhere; the shared cultures of organizations, communities, nations, and the world; and the institutional structures that frame activities and the outcomes from them.

In individual attitudes, young people and adults must confront adultism first. As this book identified earlier, the deeply ingrained assumption that the world needs to be biased toward adults everywhere, all of the time is toxic at best. It is essential to understand the intersections of adultism with racism, sexism, homophobia, classism, and other forms of oppression, too. With discrimination against children and youth at the core of every young person's reality, it is apparent that the unnecessary and often irrelevant cultural bias toward adults throughout families, organizations, communities, and the world is an animating force for further oppression because of other identities beyond age, also. Finally, since it is expressed in parenting, education, social services, government programs, the legal system, healthcare, mental health, and so many other systems in society, it is essential to confront the systemic nature of adultism, too.

Individuals need educational opportunities to learn to challenge themselves and others to face internalized adultism. Doing this can allow for self-care and healing that stems from generations of discrimination against young people that adults might be unconsciously perpetuating toward today's children and youth. In addition, mental health counseling in group and individual settings might be useful, youth mentoring adults can provide poignant witness, and fiction books can provide alternative narratives to confront adultist attitudes, ideas, and actions.

There needs to be social awareness campaigns designed to confront cultural adultism and to encourage people to address it when it occurs. These can include social media and print efforts, as well as information designed for individuals and organizations to consume. Through media and social action, organizations and governments can teach parents and guardians to eradicate adultism. Additionally, they can teach teachers to confront adultism in schools, politicians to challenge adultism in government, and so on. Social action can bring activism to the forefront to address adultism in public places, social interactions, and other activities.

Taking systems approaches to facing adultism can provide the most obvious and immediate solution for adultism. Changing policies can provide sustainable ways to cure the democracy deficit disorder. This can address many issues, such as youth suffrage. Governments everywhere can eliminate voting ages entirely to eradicate the tyranny of adultism. Funding streams, evaluation mechanisms, and other avenues reflect a commitment to addressing systems promoting adultism. Finally, as part of the structural, systemic transformation for these institutions, education systems can confront the hierarchies in teaching and learning throughout schools. This can happen by establishing assessments for adultism, adopting anti-adultism curriculums, providing professional development for educators against adultism, and restructuring teacher training programs in higher education in order to ensure future generations of educators do not fall back on adultist training and assumptions, but actually personalize and individualize learning with anti-adultist, pro-democracy activities and outcomes.

The value of each of these approaches has been studied in their given contexts. For instance, worldwide practitioners in the arena of youth suffrage have identified the philosophical and theoretical instances for the end of voting ages (Holt, 1974; Jahns, n.d.; Epstein, 2010); the biological and psychosocial development of voters (Peto, 2020); and the practical implications, challenges, and applications of eliminating the voting age (Sarkar & Mendoza, 2005; Taft, 2019). Similar studies have been conducted in many of the fields described prior, demonstrating the viability of these radical-appearing yet practical approaches to curing the democracy deficit disorder.

Exploring which specific activities can cure the democracy deficit disorder can inspire practical action that young people, adults, organizations, communities, and ultimately, the world can benefit from immediately.

Types of Activities to Cure Democracy Deficit

There are many ways young people learn to become engaged in democracy (Stoneman, 2002). Howard Gardner's multiple intelligence theory (Gardner, 1983; Gardner, 2008) espoused that there is a multiplicity of ways learners become intelligent. A compelling proposition that allowed generations of educators to expand on their teaching practices, this theory still allows for divergent thinking about intelligence. Expanding on Gardner's theory of multiple intelligences (Gardner, 2008) it is possible to illustrate how holistic youth development can look in the lives of children and youth. A holistic approach to democracy in the lives of young people is an all-inclusive, whole child concept (Hendrick, 1992). It means recognizing that there are many areas within the lives of children and youth, and that young people are part of everything going on around them (Fletcher, 2014b).

Within this concept of holistic youth development, there are different types of activities that are more likely to foster further development of democratic mindsets, skills, and knowledge for specific learners. They include the following thirteen different types of activities that can be used to defeat the democracy deficit disorder.

The first type are intellectual activities. Understanding the roles of democracy in the mental lives of young people is essential. This includes engaging democratically with the thoughts, mindsets, ideas, knowledge, and intellect of children and youth. As people have intuitively known for generations, this space is the most fertile ground for planting and growing democratic self-conception. However, with current research and practices into psychological aspects of young people, there is now evidence that the brain is both a fascinating and primary foundation for the democratic lives of everyone in society (Lilleker & Ozgul, 2021). There is research from the neuroscientific community that says children and youth are too physiologically immature for democratic participation like voting. Psychological evidence shows otherwise by suggesting that young peoples' capacities for reasoning and their cognitive control of those capacities are significant enough to warrant inclusion in democracy (Peto, 2020, p. 62). The tensions in those find-ings are riveting, but as the rest of this book shows, the latter is reinforced by experience rather than inference. The former is used by critics who too consis-tently rely on anecdotes and conjecture. The mental lives of young people are rife for defeating the democracy deficit disorder.

Interpersonal activities are the second type. Young people who become engaged through interpersonal activities focus on understanding and dealing with other people. They are very social, often trying to understand peoples' motives and feelings. Engaging them in democracy can focus on communication and give children and youth opportunities to organize their peers, their families, and their communities for social justice and more. Interactions and exchanges between young people are key to supporting democracy. In these private, per-sonal relationships at home, school, and throughout the community, children and youth learn how to act and think in ways that embrace freedom and enhance liberty by engaging them with intention. The interpersonal lives of young people might include relationships with their peers, their younger siblings and neighbor-hoods, older children and youth, parents and adult family members, extended adult family members, adult neighbors, in-school and out-of-school educators, and many other people. Each of these relationships has the capacity to reinforce the democracy deficit disorder, and in many ways many of these relationships already do that in the vast majority of relationships young people have around the world today. However, the same interpersonal relationships can reinforce and expand on democracy in the lives of individual young people, as well as all young people as a whole. They can do this through direct interactions that are both implicitly and explicitly democratic in their nature; they can also do this through indirect relationships affecting all young people every day.

The third type of activities are intrapersonal. Engaging children and youth through intrapersonal activities means focusing young people on understanding themselves to foster self-sufficiency, confidence, and informed opinion-making, and to do things on their own. Empowering young people by giving them more control of their surroundings and through self-driven activities is a key to build-ing democracy with these young people.

Emotional and feelings-oriented are the fourth type of activities. The interior lives of young people are complex, and often mis-portrayed, misunderstood, and maligned by even the most well-meaning adults in their lives, including parents, educators, and others. While their physical plant might be under-developed to successfully navigate and manage their emotions in many situations, it is rou-tine for adults to minimize, underestimate, and otherwise infantilize children and youth when it comes to their emotional lives. Instead of simply seeing their expressions as irresponsibly responsive to the direct situations they are in, it becomes vital to understand the behavior of young people as an expression of emotions. Similarly, these emotional realities are real to the people experiencing them, no matter what their age. Because of this, the emotional lives of young people are essential for the development of democracy in their lives. Securing, ensuring, and embracing the freedom of feeling can allow young people of all ages to know democracy directly, and to see the ways that democracy can sustain their own personal emotional health, as well as their physical safety.

Visual-spatial are the fifth type of activities. Being within their bodies and within themselves, young peoples' physical lives include the literal world including home, schools, and places. More importantly though, it involves their physical treatment, reactions, and responses to their physical selves. Young people who become engaged through spatial awareness focus on shapes, locations and distances and are democracy builders. They are good designers and builders, as well as physical re-arrangers and spatial manipulators. Democracy building with them can focus on community planning, building design and creating charts and maps. It can also focus on anything exterior to the young person affecting the young person.

Recreational activities are the sixth type. There are many young people for whom having fun, being entertained, and relaxing are central to their experiences of democracy. These young people choose activities different from others and do them for different reasons than those in those specifically predominant areas: They surrender the activities to having fun rather than for engaging in those specific types of activities. This often allows people in those activity types to "hide" behind the purpose of their democracy building engagement, claiming to have fun when they are emotionally, socially, or otherwise stimulated by those specific types of activities. However, young people who are drawn to recreational activities can often genuinely need this type of apparent downtime in order to substantiate their experiences of democracy building. For instance, the young person who plays video games and talks to other players via the Internet may be deeply committed to having fun. Simultaneously though, they are voting on group decision-making, choosing the themes of the adventures they are participating in, and otherwise actively practicing democracy in a variety of ways. This type of democracy building activity is just as valid as every other type.

The seventh type of activities are best addressed as existential. Young people who are deeply spiritually engaged or understand the world best through a connection with all other things are focused on existentialism. They are deeply spiritual, frequently seeing the interconnections of man and nature, looking for purpose and passion in activities, ideas, and outcomes. Democracy building with those activities can empower youth by enabling their deeper understanding and giving them space to practice their style.

Cultural activities are the eighth type. These combine capacities and qualities within individuals to show empathy, compassion, and connectivity among people. Engaging in the values of the people who are involved, cultural activities can challenge assumptions about people, places, cultures, and discrimination. Ultimately, cultural activities can build bridges through language, music, dance, art, and much more.

The ninth type of activities are language-oriented. Young people who become engaged through speaking, talking, and sharing their linguistic abilities focus on language and how it is used. They might remember names, places, and dates easily and spell words quickly. Democracy building activities focused on verbal engagement can focus on words, sounds, and meanings and spend a lot of time reading and writing.

Music is the tenth type of activities. Becoming engaged in democracy through music can focus on harmonies, rhythm, and pitch. There are young people who experience engagement best through music. They concentrate more when music is played, sing to themselves a lot, or make up songs to remember details. Building democracy with these children and youth can include making music, analyzing music, and teaching other people music.

The eleventh type of activities are logical-mathematical. Engaging children and youth through logic and math can focus on patterns, numbers, and logical relationships. These young people are good at math problems, puzzles, and mental challenges, and approaches to engage them in democracy can use computers, graphic design, and logic activities, as well as logic games, technical activities, and sometimes even conversations focused on Socratic methods.

Bodily-kinesthetic activities are the twelfth type. Engaging children and youth through physical action focuses on physical skills and movement through games, projects, and other doing-oriented activities. Young people engaged this way are good actors, athletes, and craftspeople who do not like to sit still. Activities to teach democracy with these young people focus on constant activity, with reflection and critical examination built throughout.

The last type are naturalistic activities. These children and youth engage best in their natural surroundings. This can include doing natural projects with animals and plants, learning about different species, or simply sitting in or walking through the outdoors. It can also focus on challenging the climate crisis, volunteering for native habitat restoration, or challenging environmental racism. Their innate democratic tendencies make these young people sensitive and ethical, and wanting to understand the holistic ways the world works, as well as its complexities—including the role of humanity within the greater ecosphere.

None of these activities are meant to be a value judgment about what is better or worse. Instead, they are simply different ways of viewing how to cure the democracy deficit disorder. Deliberately engaging children and youth in learning, teaching, and leadership throughout communities and beyond with these activities can provide an impetus for transformative thinking, learning, and creation. Through these, new methods, structures, and outcomes can reveal the truest possibilities of democracy today and in the future.

11

Beyond Activities, toward Strategies

Democracy can and should happen through each of these activities, all the time. A review of the literature has shown different conceptions of democracy appearing in each of these activities; however, there are few or no comprehensive examinations of democracy throughout each of these parts of the lives of children and youth today. The reality is that the individual rule, self-governance, and freedom experienced by adults throughout society should be recognized as having roles within individual conceptions of the self, and the roles everyone establishes for themselves in the world. The physio-psycho-social place where everyone forms that conception is in childhood; it is tested, reinforced, and expanded upon in youth (Jenks, 1996, p. 32). The need to recognize this and consciously and constantly recognize and grow this should be imperative to anyone who is committed to democracy, let alone to healthy children and youth within democratic societies.

Unfortunately, the lack of awareness and actions betray the true intentions of many adults. Rather than engendering democratic thinking and substantiating the roles of everyone throughout democratic society, we—both consciously and unconsciously—reinforce the passivity, indifference, and inability of everyone by dismissing the children and youth in this way. Many people recognize the areas of young peoples' lives listed above, and some even work to teach democracy in those parts. A mental health practitioner may teach young people about self-determination and conscientious decision-making in order to foster democratic self-governance within youth. In a similar way, a nature teacher might teach children about the interconnectedness of ecosystems and the role of humans in the climate crisis, therefore nurturing a child's understanding of themselves within the world around them. However, by treating young people as if they are just one side of themselves at a time, adults inadvertently teach them to betray their whole selves, which is to say, they learn to see themselves as dissected humans, simply as parts of themselves instead of as whole people. This dissection is the antithesis of democracy, which is reliant on people seeing the larger world around themselves.

It is not as if the areas listed above are wholly responsible for this dissection though. Instead, popular media negates the whole personhood of children by teaching them discriminatory, paternalistic, and predatory self-conceptions. Depictions of children as consumers (Giroux, 1999), youth as predatory (Delgado, 2019), and young people as incapable are routine throughout popular culture, including movies, music, television, and more. The overwhelming effects of this media *can* be overwhelming and inadvertently reinforced by the very people society charges with the responsibility of countering them, including parents, teachers, youth workers, and others.

This makes the challenge of all schools, afterschool programs, summer camps, and even businesses to stop parsing out the parts of young people as if they were puzzle pieces missing a whole picture. Instead, it is contingent upon any person committed to overcoming the democracy deficit disorder to start treating all children and youth everywhere as whole people who are more capable, more thoughtful, and more caring than adults typically see and treat them. These are not simply the democratic actors of the future; they are the democracy in action today; if the adults who support young people procrastinate taking a holistic approach now, they are undoing the future and the present, too.

Writing about Paulo Freire's take on education transformation, Aronowitz wrote that democracy schools must be "'deformalized,' debureaucratized, a measure that entrails democratizing schools so that 'the community' elects the school director, and there is direct accountability. This means the director can be removed at any time by the base, but also that curriculum and other decisions are broadly shared" (Aronowitz, 2015, p. 74). Such concepts in this strategic approach must be attributed to Freire, including accountability, transparency and accessibility. This same reality must be applied to any project seeking to cure democracy's ills including deformalizing, debureaucratizing, and fostering accountability, transparency, and accessibility through all activities with children, youth, and adults.

The only way to accomplish such thorough and tall orders is by strategizing and deliberating on an overarching theory of transformation with everyone involved.

There are a number of specific strategies that can be used to cure the democracy deficit disorder with young people. These strategies provide overarching theories of change devised over time throughout the fields of youth development, education, civic governance, and other areas. However, their considerations as instruments for democratization in the daily lives of children and youth needs to be further explored. Following are five specific strategies including youth-led community organizing, youth infusion, community youth development, Meaningful Student Involvement, and youth mainstreaming. Meaningful Student Involvement is "the process of engaging students as partners in every facet of the education system for the purpose of strengthening their commitment to education, community and democracy" (Fletcher, 2017).

Youth-led community organizing "empowers young people while simultaneously enabling them to make substantive contributions to their communities" (Delgado & Zhou, 2008). Focused on challenging, contesting, uplifting, and otherwise demanding change, this strategy can entail research, advocacy, education, evaluation, and many other specific activities underneath a wide umbrella of social change (Fletcher & Vavrus, 2006). This action "typically involves a critical analysis of social, political, and economic power, often uses participatory action methods, and emphasizes collective concerns identified by young people to improve their daily lives" (Flanagan, 2013, p. 31). Working in highly equitable relationships with adult allies or on their own, young people engaging in leading this work are engaged in a variety of activities for the sake of fostering, sustaining, and transforming society through culture, economics, education, healthcare, by stopping white supremacy, and more. Often tasked with addressing the hottest button issues in the lives of young people, it is often youth of color, low-income youth, youth in violent schools, and other young people who are highly impacted by the failures of democracy who lead community organizing campaigns (Cammarota et al., 2013; Checkoway & Gutiérrez, 2012; Kim et al., 2002).

Youth infusion seeks to foster "intergenerational partnerships with *every* young person in every community throughout every opportunity in order to make the world a better place" (Lesko, 2001). This is an overarching strategy which unifies approaches to youth voice by integrating roles for young people throughout the entirety of an organization, including the operation, leadership, implementation, and outcomes. This is done for the sake of the organization and the community it serves, as well as young people involved. Children and youth in these activities are treated equitably and engaged in an array of specific activities that allude to the wider goal of organizational transformation (Fletcher & Lesko, 2021).

Community youth development offers an adult-driven strategy for engaging children and youth in democracy. Organizations address the needs of their local community by intentionally developing the skills, knowledge, and positive outcomes of youth through relationships, programs and partnerships that fulfill local demands (Borden et al., 2003). It positions young people as recipients of adult-driven programs, yet often manages to embody broad social awareness, and can foster the individual and collective consciousness of young people.

Meaningful Student Involvement is a strategy combining a variety of approaches to fostering student voice, student engagement, student leadership, student-led action, and Student/Adult Partnerships throughout education (Fletcher, 2005). Providing practical frameworks for collective action by students of all ages working with adults in equitable partnerships, Meaningful Student Involvement positions strategic approaches to collective action for all learners and leaders to work together to transform schools (Fletcher, 2017).

The last strategy to mention here is youth mainstreaming. Focused on integrating youth into every aspect of organizations and communities, youth mainstreaming includes the individual perspectives, shared cultures, and system-wide structures affecting young people every day (Freechild Institute for Youth Engagement, 2016). This approach begins with "acknowledging the implications of intergenerational relations among youth and adults, and young people's unique developmental rights and evolving capacities in conceiving and delivering policies and plans for them" (Commonwealth Secretariat, 2017, p. xxviii). From this perspective, youth mainstreaming can offer a holistic approach to engaging young people in democracy.

These five strategies provide overarching thematic avenues for action to engage young people in curing the democracy deficit disorder. They are necessary to consider because of the potential for activism without learning. Freire wrote, "Critical reflection on practice is a requirement of the relationship between theory and practice. Otherwise, theory becomes simply 'blah, blah, blah,' and practice, pure activism" (Freire, 1998, p. 30). Each of the strategies above moves beyond pure activism and toward democratic learning through its abilities to foster intentionality, critical thinking and reflection, and practical action for social change.

Recognizing the substantial roles of young people in each of the areas listed above is essential. That means teaching, fostering, supporting, encouraging, challenging, and transforming young peoples' conceptions and practices of freedom of speech and expression, freedom of religion and conscience, freedom of assembly, and the right to equal protection *within* themselves as well as throughout the world they live in every single day. Let us examine each of the areas listed at the beginning of this chapter as they relate to democracy in the lives of children and youth.

Locations for Democracy with Young People

Curing the democracy deficit disorder begins with belonging. Considering where children and youth belong is a challenging task in a society that is prone to erase, silence, and deny their very existence at many turns. If it is true that there is nothing more frightening than looking in the mirror and not seeing yourself, many young people must constantly live in fear from not seeing themselves throughout this supposedly democratic society. Where can children and youth see themselves in the mirror of democracy?

The number of places where young people can become engaged in democracy are countless. They include local, state, national, and international nonprofit organizations. No matter what issue they serve, children and youth can be engaged all the time in nonprofit organizations through their programs and operations. Research institutions including universities, public education institutions, or others, can offer ways for young people to co-research any number of issues, whether it relates to themselves, a program topic, their communities, physical spaces, intellectual subjects, or otherwise. Young people who research their communities examine learning, behavior, funding, policies, and more for effectiveness and purpose. Both sharing and collecting young peoples' perspectives, engaging young people as community researchers can help identify gaps and secure data in ways that many older adult researchers cannot. Nonprofit boardrooms offer another place for young people to be present, present ideas, share concerns, and sit with adults as allies to cure the democracy deficit disorder. This is most effective when boards have full roles for young people rather than tokenizing them as representatives only.

Local planning agencies can foster unique opportunities for children and youth to co-create community culture, plan community development and operations, promote diversity, equity and inclusion, and otherwise facilitate community improvement to build democracy. Similarly, public spaces can provide powerful ways for young people to engage in democracy. Whether a young person creates an intricate graffiti mural on the wall, facilitates a youth-designed chautauqua, or speaks regularly at town halls, they may be engaged in curing the disorder. So might young people who are loitering, walking in groups, and sharing regular public spaces with adults and families. Youth are actively involved informally throughout communities all the time, with or without adult supervision and/or approval, and by doing so they help cure democracy. This can be facilitated with intention.

Particularly powerful places for young people to build democracy are community protests. Youth-led advocacy and community organizing can include picketing, research, presentations, teaching, and more. When adults do not engage young people in meaningful ways, young people may feel compelled to force adults to hear them. Policy-making agencies can engage children and youth in making formal decisions at the local community, states, national settings and international levels. Young people can create, critique, evaluate, re-create, and otherwise direct and guide policy-making in many ways. Community improvement organizations can provide a role for children and youth to improve democracy in the places where they live, work, and play every day. Taking action in their communities in creative and strategic ways can happen when young people have substantive roles through researching, planning, advocating, implementation, and evaluating public structures, activities, and outcomes. Young people can be powerfully engaged in curing the democracy deficit disorder through out-of-school time programs. Both educational and recreational afterschool and summertime activities can engage young people in a variety of ways, whether educational, recreational, cultural, or social justice oriented. Fraternal organizations and social clubs offer particularly interesting places for young people to build democracy. Fused together with support throughout the organization, children and youth can help these organizations sustain their purposes not only with their presence, but also with reinvigorating their missions, activities, and impact. There are refugee camps worldwide that have engaged young people in democracy building, too, as well as former war zones. For instance, Mohamad Al Jounde fled for Lebanon from Syria when he was a child. When he was 12, Mohamad built a school in a refugee camp. In 2020, at the age of 18, as many as 200 students come to his school daily to heal, learn, and have fun with games and photography (Guilbert, 2017).

Schools can provide a powerful avenue for engaging children and youth in democracy (Frost & Roberts, 2011; Mitra & Serriere, 2015). This means positioning young people in a variety of opportunities through Meaningful Student Involvement (Fletcher 2017). Their roles in planning, teaching, evaluation, and decision-making should be infused with learning and built into the daily life of the school, rather than behave as separate, unrelated activities. Executive offices for executive directors, principals, mayor's offices, or other leaders can give young people important roles in decision-making on the personal and community level. They can inform, advise, direct, and lead democracy from these places in a variety of ways. The media provides interesting avenues for engaging children and youth in the news, culture, and popular education of the public. Young people can write articles for mainstream websites and newspapers, create videos, host social media feeds, and generate information and more for news distribution channels. Finally, standing committees can provide children and youth with ways to sustainably impact their communities, organizations, businesses, and other places in order to build democracy. In these roles, young people can participate as full partners in policy-making, program selection, staff hiring, and more.

At first blush, the geography of children and youth curing the democracy deficit can appear astounding. International efforts, many driven by Article 12 of the UNCRC, abound. There is evidence of localized action outside that framework that highlights the roles of young people, with thorough studies from South America, including Peru (Taft, 2019), Chile (Guzman-Concha, 2012) and Brazil (Campus in Camps and Grupo Contrafilé, 2014), which is not generally acknowledged for their child participation and youth involvement campaigns; the United States, which is not a UNCRC signatory; and elsewhere. Young people leading and partnering with adults to lead democracy building is truly a global phenomenon.

These locations for young people can help cure the democracy deficit disorder. The activities they can do within them are even more compelling than the diversity of places where they can happen. However, one place stands above all others and has its own set of unique activities to implement there. This is the home.

Democracy Deficit Disorder at Home

Luckily, curing the democracy deficit disorder is not up to adults. On the whole, young people are highly capable of expressing themselves when, who, where, how, what, or why they want to. These expressions of children and youth are essential to the cure, and they exist everywhere, all of the time. Young people do not even have to strive to make themselves heard because they are always expressing themselves, either accidentally or on purpose. This shows the reality that it is not a question of whether youth are sharing their voices; it is whether adults are listening to what is being shared.

In most homes today, adults do not know what children's voices or youth voice is, what it means, how it is shared, or what to do with it. There is not a common understanding of the democracy deficit disorder either. Parents, guardians, and caregivers are not familiar with programs at school or throughout communities seeking to elevate the expressions of young people in positive ways in order to reinforce, sustain, and reinvent democracy. However, the thoughts, ideas, knowledge, wisdom, and actions of young people—all of which are voice—are valid and important at home, too.

Exploring the home setting can show us different ways to engage young people throughout democracy in new, vibrant, and vital ways. There are several types of children's voices or youth voice that adults can pay attention to. Following are some ways to engage children and youth in democracy at home.

Activities to Facilitate Democracy at Home

According to Flanagan, families can have a deep impact on young peoples' thinking about politics. She identifies four ways: "through the advantages to civic learning that accrue through parents' education; through family discussions of current events and politics; through the values that parents emphasize in their child rearing; and through parents' views about the world, about fellow human beings, and about the trustworthiness of society's institutions" (2013, p. 22). These become evident through the following activities.

There are two types of decision-making at home: personal and household. Household decisions affect everyone in the home; personal decisions only affect individual people. Children's voices or youth voice can be shared in decision-making in many ways. Household decisions include places to go together, family food, decorating, shared activities, and household budgets. Eating, clothing, and bathing are personal decisions. Since young people are members of homes, everything they do can affect every other person in the home, including seemingly personal decision-making.

Giving feedback does not just happen from adults-to-children; instead, it happens from children-to-adults and children-to-children. It happens all the time too, whether or not adults are listening or even want to hear it. Voice can be shared in feedback given about any subject or activity at home.

Young people are constantly creative, whether they are in their own space being personally creative or creating out loud for everyone around them to see, hear, feel, taste or touch. Creativity shows children's voices or youth voice within homes in all kinds of ways, including music, painting, poetry or knitting, as well as moving furniture, making meals or other expressions.

Children and youth are teaching and learning all the time at home. The subjects and the issues they are learning about vary and include things unique to their home like family history, making food, and constructing walls; as well as things they share with young people around the world, like gaming and tech, creative writing, or academic subjects. Young people also learn through teaching their siblings and their parents. Children's voices or youth voice comes through learning in all these ways and many more.

When faced with challenges affecting the whole family, children and youth can be partners with adults in the home to solve problems. Creating opportunities for that collaboration can foster family cohesion and positive belonging for everyone involved. Voice can come through problem-solving at home in many ways, especially in day-to-day activities as well as long-term.

The way people in a house think and feel affects how they treat each other. This treatment sets the household tone and culture and is a visible factor to anyone within the home. The energy of the house is reflected in the language, attitudes, beliefs, and ideals within and among the people who live there.

As young people have fun, relaxation and recreation is essential to daily living. Whether it is gaming or reading, dancing, or bicycling, there are many ways recreation happens. Recreation can share children's voices or youth voice in many ways, including making decisions and the tone of the recreation, the choice of activities and the people who are chosen to participate.

Household consumption is a choice everyone makes all the time, and those choices are a type of children's voices or youth voice. Whether young people are consuming food, electricity, or otherwise, they can make their decisions about consumption on their own, help others in the household make their choices, and partner with adults at home to choose how to consume things.

The styles of communication in a household reflect children's voices or youth voice indirectly and very directly. Whether it is communication between adults and children or from child-to-child all communication in a household is an expression of countless factors. These expressions can happen through spoken words and unspoken body language, actions by a person as well as inaction, and many other ways. Voice is shared in the ways young people express themselves; the topics and subjects expressed about; the timing of expressions; who they are expressed toward and with; and where they are expressed.

A person's health, including their mental, physical, and spiritual realities, includes their sleep, food, exercise, surroundings, activities, and much more. Children's voices or youth voice is expressed through health in all ways, because ultimately every way a person treats themselves reflects their thoughts, knowledge, feelings, ideas, and wisdom.

The mindset is a mental framework every person approaches the world with. Children's voices or youth voice reflects mindsets, and mindsets reflect voice. Young people share their core beliefs, personal assumptions, cultural wisdom, and much more through their mindsets.

Looking over these activities in the home, it can be important to consider how they affect democracy directly and indirectly. Each type identifies specific ways to take action to apply democracy at home as well as in work and throughout communities. There are significant differences apparent throughout the home environment that can affect how democracy is enacted, taught, and received both by adults and young people. Those differences can be as glaring as whether or not a child or youth has a physical home or experiences living with people they are related to; they can also include a household's income, race, education, economic ability, gender identity, or religion. These realities can cause us to question whether every child and youth experience can share their voices everywhere, all of the time. However, seeing the potential in the activities above shows us a clear answer. Perhaps the most important question is whether adults at home are genuinely open to children and youth building democracy, and authentically able to engage young people as partners in curing the democracy deficit disorder. If they are, then home can provide a solid foundation to start doing this work.

Building Democracy on the Internet

Research shows children and youth are using the Internet and social media more than ever right now (YPulse, 2020; Moyer, 2022). This usage is complex and sophisticated, and can build democracy in nearly countless ways. This section explores how young people are using the Internet right now to cure the democracy deficit disorder. It also looks at where this is happening and why it is happening. Since the COVID-19 pandemic sent young people online worldwide, it has become more important than ever to understand how democracy can be fostered on the Internet. This means understanding which young people are engaged in democracy online, how it happens, why it matters, when it occurs online, and what it means to cure the democracy deficit disorder on the Internet.

Adults' concerns for young people often reveal distrust and disrespect for children and youth. Parents, teachers, counselors, youth workers, and others seemingly assume the worst of young people participating in many spaces. Relying on cold data and calculated statistics, programs and classes appear to assume young people are doing the worst possible things they can be until adults correct their course of action. Unfortunately, this is true online too. With sensational headlines and screaming pronouncements adults decide learners are not learning, leaders are not leading, and children and youth are going to hell in a handbasket whether they are playing video games, chatting with friends, or otherwise not doing what adults want them to, where they want it done, in ways they can predict.

To defeat these worst projections, adults should understand the value of young people being engaged on the Internet. The following section shows there are four factors important for examining the roles of young people curing the democracy deficit disorder on the Internet. These factors are: Expressions of young people on the Internet; aspects of children and youth engaging online; types of children's voices and youth voice on the Internet; and the continuum of young people engaging online.

Expressions of Young People on the Internet

This analysis begins by understanding youth voice as any expression of any young person anywhere, about anything, any time, in any way, for any reason at all (Freechild Institute for Youth Engagement, 2016). This definition reflects the wide-ranging intentions, forms, and outcomes of youth voice. It is meant to deny the necessity of adults in approving youth voice, and instead affirms the most authentic forms of youth voice. Young people do not need adult permission, activities, or acceptance to share youth voice; it is already shared wherever children and youth are all of the time. The question is not whether young people are sharing their voices; it is whether adults are willing and able to hear what is being said.

Expanding on what and how adults think about democracy can happen on the Internet. Curing democracy deficit disorder through action, in research and at home requires adult allies to look for a plurality of ways young people currently express themselves, including their thoughts, ideas, attitudes, knowledge, tone, feelings, beliefs, opinions, ideas, wisdom, and moods. It also requires paying attention to the idiom that "behavior is language," particularly when young people do not have the ability to express themselves via spoken language. Behavior can include actions and mannerisms and more, as well as things that are created, including websites, circumstances, the arts, construction, social media, music, memes, gaming, and more. That is not a complete list of different expressions of youth voice, either. However, it can begin to alert adult allies to the various ways young people make themselves heard on the Internet already.

Since youth voice can be expressed in virtually countless ways online, examining different aspects of online democratic engagements is vital. One way is by observing the ways democracy online is personal, and the ways youth voice online is public. Understandings of Internet usage have long been separated into two camps, one focused on personal usage that is private, and the other is public usage, which is shared (Gruzd & Hernández-García, 2018, p. 421). It can help to understand young peoples' usage for curing the democracy deficit disorder this way, too. The difference between these two can be seen as follows.

Personal democracy can be transient, fluctuating, isolated, direct, and immediate. In different types of personal democracy, the expressions of young people can appear and disappear quickly. They are targeted toward certain people, frequently their peers. They are also often intimate, personal, and emotional, whether funny, depressing, angry, or just blah. It is most often shared alone, between just two people, or within a small group of people. Personal democracy fluctuates and reveals the differentiating nature of young people, changing according to their increasing knowledge, skills, and abilities. Finally, it is immediate and sudden, often reflecting critical analysis, but also showing wit, style, and perception at the same time.

Public democracy can be more permanent, steady, expansive, indirect, and gradual. When young people are engaging with adults in large online group settings, working together with their peers to lead movements or make large-scale statements, building online strategies and creating massive social change, they are sharing public democracy. Public democracy typifies young people because it can seem like these expressions freeze children's voices and youth voice in a single place and time, making it appear as a steady, regular phenomenon. With countless issues it can be expressed toward, public democracy can seem very broad too, and with its apparent permanency public democracy can seem to make a gradual appearance, as if it comes from a logical, intentional, and strategic place.

The Internet provides a unique avenue for engaging children and youth in democracy because it is public and personal at the same time. When children and youth build democracy online, they can be hyper-conscious of these different aspects. For instance, in the traditional types of young peoples' engagement on the Internet, children, and youth create public artifacts for the masses to consume on the web. This includes commenting, web design, blogging, video-making, and conference calls. These are all static ways the Internet has been used for a long time, if not throughout its entire existence.

In current types of online democracy, the Internet is used in personal ways, including emails, private chat, texting, and messaging. These are all transient ways that can and often do completely disappear after they are consumed. Examples of this technology include TikTok, Snapchat, iMessages, Discord, and more. Video game chats and social media messaging fall into this category, too. Hashtags can represent both personal (transient) and public (static) types of democracy built online, too.

Continuum of Young People Engaging Online

Understanding why children and youth express themselves online is not rocket science, but it is not always clear, either. It can be useful to understand all democratic engagement with young people online on continuum with three "C's": Creation, Consumption, and Criticism. These three C's can help us engage young people in democracy via the Internet more effectively. We can ask, are children and youth creating the Internet by producing content and communicating, including chatting, blogging, creating websites, PDFs, infographics, photos, videos, and so forth? Are children and youth consuming the Internet by reading, buying, watching, listening, playing, and otherwise intaking different content already produced on the Internet? And, are children and youth criticizing the Internet and its content with critical thinking and interacting with other web users through conversation, commenting, recreating, and remixing the Internet and its content?

When considering these factors, understanding that curing the democracy deficit disorder with young people online is never simply one thing for all children and youth, everywhere, all the time. It is not simply online either, but also at home, throughout the community, and beyond. Democracy building on the Internet is a broad, dynamic, and constantly shifting reality. It can be an avenue for social engagement and culture building, as well as critical pedagogy and social justice. However, it can just as easily be weaponized to implement fascism and enforce the will of tyrants. Adult allies can help teach the difference to ensure authentic youth engagement.

12

Praxis Matters

After the decades of reports on youth civic engagement, civics education, and community youth development little has been done to affect an actual cure for democracy deficit disorder. More so, any logical analysis of the last presidential term, the insurrection at the U.S. Capitol, and the ongoing domestic terrorism plaguing the country demonstrates the outcomes of this disorder run unchecked. This book is meant to highlight practical considerations, share thoughtful analysis, and provide initial explorations into the work that needs to be done.

It is essential for young people and adults to establish praxis, which is the mutual understanding of the problems, potentials, resources, activities, learning, and more that arises in any authentic attempt to challenge the democracy deficit disorder. As Paulo Freire wrote, "The revolutionary effort to transform these structures radically cannot designate its leaders as its thinkers and the oppressed as mere doers" (Freire, 2004, p. 94). This means that adults cannot simply lead action and young people cannot simply do what is demanded; instead, it is essential to consider the mutual roles that everyone has in the action.

Praxis can appear as a grandiose vision for idealists; however, modern schools and youth programs have found great potential in establishing this approach to learning, teaching, and leadership throughout society. Young people of all ages and stations in life rise above adult expectations and reach unpredictable heights because the process was honored, and adults were not merely fixated on the outcomes. The following sections explore how praxis happens in order to defeat the democracy deficit disorder.

Roles for Young People in Praxis

There is identifiable praxis young people are establishing with adults right now to lead their communities in order to reinforce democracy, including traditional and transformative approaches (Freechild Institute for Youth Engagement, n.d.A). Youth building democracy is not just a good idea. Instead, it is actionable praxis that uses tangible, teachable and pragmatic activities, methodologies, and outcomes for all kinds of young people. It can build critical thinking, foster habits and traits, and demonstrate the outcomes of democratic action that benefit children, youth, and communities. The following activities can facilitate learning and powerful, positive democratic action that changes schools, communities, and the world. Indeed, they fulfill Dewey's charge that, "The very idea of democracy, the meaning of democracy, must be continually explored afresh; it has to be constantly discovered, and rediscovered, remade and reorganized; while the political and economic institutions and social institutions in which it is embodied have to be remade and reorganized to meet the changes that are going on in the development of new needs on the part of human beings and the new resources for satisfying these needs" (Dewey, 1987, p. 182).

In 1995, Golarz and Golarz wrote about integrating democracy in schools and found,

> To confer decision-making power upon a small number of people... reduces community involvement to an advisory status. Little has changed as others come to understand their participation carries no more weight than it did before, and that all-inclusive community involvement in developing and carrying out a mission statement is mostly an illusion... 'Our schools' will once again become the responsibility of others; they will remain 'their schools.' (Golarz & Golarz, 1995, p. 6)

What they found should be applied to the following activities as well. None of these are meant to be limiting, prohibitive, or restrictive in any sense. They are not stand alone activities intended to make student resumes shine, communities a little bit better, or adults feel good. They are not meant to show all that young people can do to build democracy, defend themselves, advocate for the communities or issues they care about, or otherwise suffer from the "pervasive literalism" that defines so many conversations about the roles of young people (Gillen, 2014, p. 19). Instead, they are intended to help reveal the potential for all kinds of action by children and youth right now.

These activities can offer the frameworks of social change, and when built upon and mixed together intentionally, they can cure the democracy deficit disorder. The following activities have been identified through an examination of current and historical rigorously researched works, including those by Kim et al. (2002), Hoose (2001), Welton & Wolf (2001), Delgado & Zhou (2008), Cammarota & Fine (2010), Cammarota et al. (2013), Checkoway & Gutiérrez (2012), Erlich & Erlich (1971), Fletcher & Vavrus (2006), Barrett (2015), Fletcher (2017), Terriquez et al. (2020), and Franklin (2021).

Child-led action and youth-led activism is an approach that intentionally trains young people in community organizing and advocacy. Youth-led activism can position children and youth in putting democratic skills into action. These actions can alter power relations and create meaningful change throughout communities. Through youth-led organizing, young people can employ activities such as political education and analysis, community research, campaign development, direct action, critical thinking, and membership recruitment.

Children's councils and youth action councils are groups of young people who develop group approaches to use their individual abilities collectively to solve serious social issues. In youth action councils, young people develop, implement, and evaluate actions through Student/Adult Partnerships that are democratically oriented. Hosted by nonprofits, K-12 schools, local/state/federal government agencies, school districts, community groups, international NGOs, and other organizations, the actions and outcomes of youth action councils can vary widely. Member ages, terms, numbers, issues, and actions vary according to organizational priorities, such as racial equity, children's voices or youth voice, truth and reconciliation, and other factors.

Children and youth as activity leaders in nonprofits, community organizations, and other areas includes young people facilitating, teaching, guiding, directing, and otherwise leading youth, adults, and children in a variety of ways. Positioning youth with responsibility and authority can be very democratic when done with transparency, intention, and meaningful outcomes. With young people as activity leaders, drivers and motivators of culture, heritage, and history, youth activity leaders can teach native languages, serve as historical tour guides or facilitate the development of youth culture. Through homework assistance, tutoring, community enrichment, or other activities, young people can drive and direct their own after school spaces. By identifying genuine interests and building their skills and abilities, youth activity leaders can facilitate social change.

Children and youth as advisors can coach adults by providing genuine knowledge, wisdom, and ideas to each other, adults, organizations, institutions, communities, and other locations and activities that affect them and their world at large. Engaging children and youth as advisors requires adults to move beyond simply treating youth like puppies to be trained! It means meaningfully, substantively, and truly engaging young people and adults in equitable partnerships that substantiate everyone's perspectives and actions.

Children and youth as advocates are realized when young people stand for their beliefs and understand the impact of their voices, they can represent their families and communities with pride, courage, and ability. Children and youth as advocates take action throughout communities and society already. When this is deliberately created as a strategy for social change, the world can change together.

Children and youth as artists provide substantial contributions to democracy when they create any kind of art, make any kind of art, or demonstrate any kind of art, allowing young people as artists to change the world. Child and youth artists can entertain people, share social messages, create momentum, and build support for changing the world, and otherwise transform their lives and the lives of others in countless ways.

Children and youth as board directors happens when healthy nonprofit organizations and government agencies consider their entire communities or populations when they are determining organizational leadership and stewards. Engaging young people as board directors can ensure relevance to the people being served and healthy relationships between young people and adults. Their roles should be full-voting, full-term opportunities with specific learning experiences designed to ensure the relevance and rigor of child director and youth director positions.

Children and youth as consumers can save democracy by recognizing anytime a person uses something, they are consuming it. This is especially true when money is used for goods and services. Young people as consumers do a lot with money, including paying for recreation, clothing, food, and a variety of services. Children and youth can learn to change the world by consuming responsibly.

Children and youth as decision makers happens through formal and informal decision-making. Young people as decision-makers are engaged in making powerful, meaningful, and substantive choices, decisions and determinations that affect themselves, their peers, their communities, and the world. A lot of child-focused and youth-focused activities, organizations, and programs are run by adults. However, anytime adults are charged with managing programs for children or youth they must take steps to engage children and youth in organizational decision-making in new and different ways. This is true in community organizations, schools, foundations, government agencies, and religious organizations, as well as at home and throughout communities.

Children and youth as designers occurs by engaging children and youth as designers to lead to more authentic learning, programming, and organizations. Young people participate in creating intentional, strategic plans for an array of activities, including curriculum, building construction, young peoples' and community programs, and more. Designing programs, organizations, communities, campaigns, art, and other activities are all powerful ways children and youth as designers can change the world.

Children and youth as entrepreneurs occurs when young people recognize a problem or challenge in the world. They can use entrepreneurship skills and knowledge to organize, create, and manage activities that change the world. Engaging children and youth as entrepreneurs can help build economic and cultural value as young people learn skills and develop knowledge that contributes to their communities in unique ways. Child entrepreneurs and youth entrepreneurs can specifically uplift and empower families and communities, too.

Children and youth as evaluators happens when young people are assessing and evaluating the effects of programs, classes, activities, and projects, and organizations involve young people in powerful ways. Young people can learn that their opinions are important, and their experiences are valid indicators of success. Adult evaluators may not be able to interpret data, examine findings and ensure effectiveness as well as youth evaluators.

Children and youth as facilitators happens when knowledge comes from study, experience, and reflection. Engaging young people as facilitators can engage both young and older learners in exciting ways. Whether facilitating for learning, communication or action, child facilitators and youth facilitators can lead groups in dynamic ways that are more effective for their peers, younger people, and adults.

Children and youth as farmers happens through gardening, farming, and otherwise raising food. It can be a powerful way for young people and adults to work together. Teaching essential lessons about sustainability, production, and hard work, communities can become healthier and more empowered through child-led and youth-led farming. Engaging children and youth as farmers can be an exciting way to change the world.

Children's forums and youth forums place children's voices and youth voice at the center of social change, providing an engaging, empowering way to develop consensus, discuss issues, and build community among youth in a community. As a structured, purposeful event, youth forums are meant to give youth an opportunity to express their ideas, opinions, and needs to adults or other youth. Youth forums can be youth-led or adult-led, and because the purpose of youth forums is to engage voices, young people should be prepared to share it. Rather than all talking, multiple engagement styles should be used. Youth do not need permission to share children's voices or youth voice or change the world—youth forums just make it easier for them to do both.

Children and youth as influencers happens because social media is repositioning young people from being passive recipients of information to becoming the directors, makers, promoters and propagators of information. This role, called "influencer" in popular culture, can be more than humorous or product promotion. Young influencers can drive popular awareness and promote activism for social justice, democracy and against adultism.

Children and youth as grant-makers happens by engaging young people in philanthropy, including them in identifying funding, distributing grants, evaluating effectiveness, and conducting other parts of the process involved in grant-making. When communities create opportunities for children and youth as grantmakers and youth as philanthropists, they create opportunities for authentic, impassioned, and powerful youth curing the democracy deficit disorder.

Children and youth as lobbyists happens when young people are influencing policy-makers, legislators, politicians, and the people who work for them. With their unique insights, passion and wisdom, young people can guide and influence the political process in ways that adults cannot, helping elected officials and others make informed decisions that benefit everyone affected.

Children and youth as makers and producers occurs when making, producing, developing, manufacturing, designing, redesigning, recreating, identifying, specifying, and otherwise creating anything, which is at the heart of the maker movement. Engaging young people as makers can mean empowering them with the resources to build what they want, what communities need, and what the world is calling for (Martinez & Steger, 2013).

Children and youth as media makers shows communities how to move forward and transforming the behavior of youth and adults, engaging youth media makers can lead to social change in a lot of ways. Youth can become change agents through television, zines, radio, social media, magazines, podcasts, and newspapers, together with the people and organizations involved in their production. Media making can include media deconstruction, too, where young people examine a variety of media sources for their political, economic, social, cultural and other biases.

Children and youth as mediators teaches young people to understand conflict within themselves and others. Discovering how they influence conflict, how to self-manage conflict, and how to identify strategies for calmness and clarity is enhanced by learning listening and speaking skills and how to understand other peoples' point of view. Youth mediators can help other youth, younger students, and adults to have important conversations in order to become clearer themselves, understand each other's perspectives, and make decisions about next steps. Youth can change the world as mediators when they apply these skills throughout their lives, including at home, in school, and throughout their communities.

Children and youth as mentors happens through non-hierarchical relationships between youth and adults, adults and youth, or among youth themselves, that helps facilitate learning and guidance for each participant. Roles for young people as mentors can position them as equitable partners with adults who work together to build skills, share knowledge, and transform communities in mutually engaging, intentional relationships.

Children and youth as organizers occurs through community organizing, which happens when leaders bring together everyone in a community in a role that fosters social change. Engaging young people as community organizers can focus on issues that affect them and their communities. They can also rally their peers, families, and community members for action.

Children and youth as planners happens in programs, operations, activities, and other events and activities where youth can benefit nonprofits, schools, their homes, and any other institution throughout society. Engaging young people as planners can provide resources for youth, adults, and others throughout the community. Planning is involved in everything every single person does. Either they plan their lives and their world, or someone else plans life for them. The more opportunities young people have to see all the different ways planning happens, the more they can create the future they want for themselves and for the world.

Children and youth as policy-makers happens when they research, plan, write, and evaluate rules, regulations, laws, and other policies, engaging young people as policy-makers can enrich, substantiate, enliven, and impact the outcomes of policies in many ways.

Children and youth as politicians means running for political office at the community, city, county, or state and provincial levels. Engaging young people as politicians should include being able to run for a variety of positions. While this practice is currently illegal in most places around the world, there are stand-out examples where young people have changed the world through engaging in government and politicians. As Michael Moore once said, "Democracy is not a spectator sport; it's a participator event. If we don't participate in it, it ceases to be a democracy" (Collette-White, 2009).

Children and youth facilitating popular education happens when young people are creating spaces for youth and popular education to support dynamic, powerful, and just opportunities for social justice, youth empowerment, and community engagement. Popular education is a way of facilitating learning that moves youth from being recipients toward becoming fully equal partners. Brazilian educator Paulo Freire taught that this approach can build learners' beliefs that they can change the world, by engaging them in the world instead of separating them from the world (Freire, 1998). It can also integrate youth throughout communities by positioning them as co-learners, co-leaders, and full members of society.

Children and youth as recruiters looks like youth building excitement, sharing motivation, or otherwise helping their communities or people to get involved, create change, or make all sorts of things happen. Engaging young people as recruiters must mean more than simply propping them up for some adult-led, adult-driven activities. Instead, it should be part of a larger process designed to engage young people as partners throughout their communities.

Children and youth as researchers includes identifying issues, surveying interests, studying situations, analyzing findings, and developing projects in response are all powerful avenues for young people as researchers. Youth researchers can provide analysis, study or research, examinations and facilitate discussions about social, economic, and similar problems that are uniquely their own, and that add to, enhance, challenge, or flip over the perspectives of adult researchers. These youth who are researchers are helping to reshape and build entire fields, including public health (Augsberger, 2022), education reform (Fletcher, 2015), and many other areas.

Children and youth as specialists could mean youth teaching youth, and that could be relatively easy. However, seeing new roles for youth to teach adults is more challenging. Young people as specialists bring expert knowledge about particular subjects to programs and organizations, enriching everyone's ability to be more effective.

Children's summits and youth summits are opportunities for young people to become engaged in positive, powerful and passionate action to change the world. They can create a short, safe time and space where youth and their adult allies can learn and grow, share children's voices and youth voice, and become engaged in what matters most to them. Also called youth conferences, youth summits should increase the inspiration, education, ability, and impact of empowerment-oriented action through Student/Adult Partnerships.

Children and youth as teachers includes facilitating learning for themselves, other youth, adults, or children. Youth can be teachers of small and large groups in all kinds of topics. Young people as teachers can facilitate learning, activities and reflection for their peers, children and adults of all ages on all sorts of topics.

Children and youth as trainers includes when they train adults, youth, children, and others. Young people can share their wisdom, ideas, knowledge, attitudes, actions, and processes in order to guide programs, nurture organization and community cultures, and change the world. Roles for young people as trainers can build Student/Adult Partnerships, engage diversity in practical ways, and build communities that everyone can benefit from beyond their ages.

Children and youth as volunteers happens when anyone gives their time to a cause they believe in. Without getting paid, engaging young people as volunteers can use natural talents, develop skills, share knowledge, and gain experience. They can also experience the joy that can come from making a real difference to other people's lives, as well as their own.

Engaging children and youth as voters may be the highest civic potential in any democratic society. That key tool is the highest ability of everyone, but unfortunately, in most democracies worldwide, extremely large minorities of residents are not allowed to vote: young people. Children and youth around the world are not allowed to share their voices and represent their own best interests through voting. Eliminating the voting age and granting suffrage to young people in every municipality, city, state, province, and country around the world could challenge that (Freechild Institute, n.d.B). Children's suffrage and youth suffrage is a key to engaging young people in democracy (Wall, 2021).

Children and youth as workers happens when organizations, businesses, agencies, and other groups hire youth, they can be staff members in programs for adults, other youth, children, or for the community at large. Engaging young people as workers can be an empowering opportunity for them, and an enriching activity in the workplace.

Curing the democracy deficit disorder will help classroom teachers, youth program workers, organization leaders, grantmakers, and others consciously and specifically develop the metrics they need to ensure success. It can show the rest of society where politics, culture, family, and community are going next.

A practical next step on this journey can be learning the history of youth activism. Young people have been making positive, powerful change for a long time. When they learn about that history, read stories, and ask older people and get connected, young people can successfully reach across the past in order to move forward.

Another step can be exploring power. In a world run by the powerful, groups can rise above being powerless. When children, youth and adults work together in community to make a difference, children, youth, and adults can create power and challenge those in power. Understanding, critiquing, and challenging power can be an ultimate step in curing the democracy deficit.

Defining the issue can be the next step. That can include exploring what young people want to change and researching what matters personally, exploring how to make a difference, and getting more information. Leading community building can be a positive step. The powerful want to cut off youth from each other and adults. Young people can challenge that by rallying friends, strangers, older and younger people, and people who are different from them. Democracy can be fostered by moving learning into action this way.

The next step can be networking. Children and youth who are invested in important issues can join with adult allies to build coalitions where everyone can share space, ideas, knowledge, and strengths. Mapping engagement can be a logical step. In order to build investment, young people can match action to issues, map out the steps to making a difference, name a communication strategy, and get to work.

The next step could be celebrating. Reaching out to the people, organizations, elected officials, and others who are allies, young people can also celebrate with people in their networks using social media and in-person contacts. Highlighting what is happening, children and youth can also gather ideas and support, and keep moving. Finally, they can reflect on what they have done. Looking back on what has happened, exploring what has been done and could be done, and planning next steps using new learning can be powerful ways for young people to cure the democracy deficit.

These activities can be useful throughout communities, including nonprofit organizations, community groups, government programs, and beyond. However, considering the specific places where curing the disorder is happening can be important. Toward that end, following are some considerations about schools specifically.

Educating to Cure Democracy Deficit in Schools

> Education is not just about empowering people, the practice of freedom, it is also in some ways about killing the imagination… We often see pedagogies that teach to the text, simply about accountability, objective standards, that are designed to undercut the possibility for students to be critical thinkers.—Henry Giroux (França, 2019)

Education that promotes social justice through critical thinking and practical re-imagining of the world that is possible is at the heart of curing the democracy deficit. When learning and involvement are connected by passion and purpose, they push back against the democracy deficit disorder. Right now, young people are facilitating substantial learning with the following methods that infuse meaningfulness into learning, teaching, and leadership. This learning challenges democracy to be responsive, engaging, and practical, which in turn challenges the disorder. Using these methods for teaching and learning can help all educators of all ages thoroughly foster substantial democracy. When shown to parents, communities, and the public in general this learning can signify the intentions and abilities of young people to continue transforming democracy.

Educators, writers, researchers, advocates, and others have identified repeatedly that no single classroom method, approach, style or ideology encapsulates democracy (Dewey, 1916; McDermott & Bird, 1999; Fielding, 2004; Mitra, 2014; Fletcher, 2019). Recent scholarship and field studies have shown us this is why young people use many different strategies, including those listed below and many others (Kim et al., 2002).

Used consistently and interwoven with each other, these different methods can be used to enhance, enrich, encourage, and enliven democracy throughout learning, teaching, and leadership. Ultimately, they can add up to classrooms and schools becoming more meaningful than ever before and can help cure the democracy deficit disorder.

Blended learning combines different ways of teaching and learning in lesson plans in order to teach students more effectively by enabling and empowering educators to adapt and transform their lessons to reach students. Focusing largely on technology and interactive learning approaches, including service learning, experiential education, and environmental education, as well as approaches such as Foxfire (McDermott and Smith, 2010) provide options. Young people can be at the heart of each of these approaches through planning, research, teaching, facilitation, evaluation, and decision-making. Blended learning embodies democracy because it is great for the practice of teaching; it increases students' access to knowledge; promotes social interactions between learners; develops personal agency in students; uses classroom resources more effective; and is highly adaptable (Osguthorpe & Graham, 2003).

Citizenship education provides opportunities for students to learn the values, ideals, actions, and outcomes of shared social, political, cultural, and economic lives. The elements of citizenship education include: Awareness, when youth are aware of the rights and responsibilities of shared society; Knowledge, when youth are informed about the world around them and learn about what matters to the people around them, too; Conscientiousness, with opportunities to grow their concern about the welfare of themselves and others for youth to develop their capacities for caring; Sharing, where youth develop their abilities to share their beliefs, knowledge, arguments, and ideas; Compelling, whereby exploring their knowledge and conscientiousness, youth expand their capacities to influence and change the world; Active, when youth can take deliberate actions to create change, make opportunities, and explore different ways of being throughout their communities; and Responsibility, including knowing and understanding their roles in society to allow youth to share their capacities in their families, neighborhoods, communities, and the world.

At the center of engaging citizenship education is student voice, which is any expression of any student about anything related to learning, teaching, and leadership. Student voice can drive each of the elements listed above and should be extensively entwined throughout all citizenship education activities (Fielding, 2004).

Student behavior and classroom management are consistently important issues to educators and students in democracy, although for different reasons. Classroom teachers often report they want to use democratic activities as an incentive to make students behave better; students often report that if they were democratically involved, classroom behavior would not be an issue. When considering the variety of issues that are tied together within student behavior, it may seem important to address it through school improvement approaches. However, what democracy in classrooms promotes is consideration and understanding of the contexts of challenges in schools. This includes the overall issue of student engagement and the different ways different youth are engaged throughout learning, teaching, and leadership. There are many issues to consider when thinking about student behavior, including: What makes student behavior right or wrong? Who determines what is right or wrong? What happens when youth behave well? What happens when they are not doing well? Should youth sacrifice their happiness for good behavior? When we expect youth to behave well, do we limit expectations for them in other ways? What informal rules do we expect youth to follow?

When educators use rules arbitrarily and without learning objectives, youth often see behavior as an artificial measure for their behavior. Similarly, when behavior is rewarded and made an example of, youth can see it as a measuring stick for their intelligence and ability. Democratic learning in action positions youth as co-learners with educators, allowing everyone in the classroom to learn and grow together. Engaging young people in all grade levels in curing the democracy deficit disorder should include exploring what is "good," whether everyone should behave "good," whether "good" behavior earn the outcome youth want or adults want, what outcomes can "bad" behavior get youth, what happens when two youth cannot be judged by the same standards, and can everyone learn their way to good behavior, or is it something each person either does or does not do? With this type of inquiry-based learning, classrooms and schools prove to be vibrant, vital, and ever relevant for learners of all types, including those who are historically disengaged. Democracy with young people can allow the traditionally static relationships between learners and teachers to become more elastic, and that sense of ability to change everyone's learning experiences, including youth who traditionally get "in trouble." Infusing democracy into classroom management has become a challenge in many classrooms. Mark Barnes, an author and the creator of the Results Only Learning Environment (ROLE) method (Barnes, 2013), shares three simple steps for teachers, which are to (1) create a workshop environment in the classroom that encourages the pursuit of learning and allows little time for disruption; (2) set the tone from the beginning of the school year by eliminating all discussion of rules and consequences by explaining that your learning space is built on mutual respect and the quest for knowledge; and (3) keep activities engaging and behavior will never be an issue.

By infusing democracy into student/adult relationships throughout the community, youth activities can foster healthy, successful community engagement. Community engagement is any sustained connection a community has with the larger community which it is a part of. Because of their knowledge and familiarity with the places they live, community engagement offers strong possibilities for Student/Adult Partnerships. This can include methodologies such as service learning and adventure education. Serving as more than mere puppets of well-meaning adults, youth who are engaged as partners can serve as true liaisons between the school and the community. This allows schools to genuinely benefit from all of any communities' inherent assets, apparent or hidden. Democratic action throughout the community can substantiate connections throughout the lives of young people and beyond. Place-based learning happens in classroom activities rooted in local things, including the unique history, environment, culture, economy, literature, and art of a particular place. Any learning that happens through community engagement, including service learning, outdoor education, and other approaches, can be enriched by the people who genuinely use the community on a regular basis—including adults and youth (McDermott & Smith, 2010). Beginning at the conception of the school/community relationship, community engagement can happen in a variety of ways. Planning activities can be conducted with youth as partners. Working with adult allies, youth can inform, drive, and sustain community engagement in ways adults cannot. Building connections and enriching school/community ties, youth can research education issues, actions, ideas, and outcomes in communities. Youth can facilitate learning activities within and throughout communities, representing their own perspectives as well as those of their peers, families, and neighborhoods. Developing and conducting evaluation activities, student/adult partners can determine what perceptions, ideals, and outcomes communities expect from schools. Participating as full members in decision-making activities, youth can develop, drive, and determine who, what, when, where, why, and how community engagement happens. Engaging as advocates throughout their educations, youth can connect with community allies, build community support, and drive community perceptions about schools.

Tailoring teaching to individual youth's needs happens through differentiated instruction. Teachers do this according to the individual learning needs and aspirations. Differentiated instruction can include self-led learning time, integrated technology usage, modified curriculum and assessments, or modified teaching approaches. It fosters democracy when it is infused with youth authority and children's voices throughout learning and teaching.

Formative assessment is process-driven which happens in the course of learning and teaching in order to explore how youth are performing. Through formal and informal procedures, formative assessments can provide teachers with information during the learning process to modify teaching and learning activities to improve student attainment. Democracy can be a key factor in formative assessments because it reflects, suggests, and sustains the learning trajectory throughout learning, teaching, and leadership. Formative assessments typically involve qualitative feedback (rather than scores) for both student and teacher. These focus on the details of content and performance instead of the outcomes of testing. Studies have shown that formative assessment practices that democratically involve youth can help all learners. The results are most dramatic with struggling or disengaged youth (Pinchok & Brandt, 2009).

By asking youth to discover knowledge on their own with guidance from their teachers, inquiry-based learning can be deeply integral to democracy, both in the classroom and throughout the education system. Working from the assumption that every teacher of every subject can share equal responsibility for teaching and evaluating skills, educators can infuse inquiry-based learning in schools today by creating performance rubrics focused on student competencies and by making skills-oriented growth 60% of their grade. Any classroom can be on the path to supporting inquiry-based learning, in turn nurturing democracy for every young person (Markham, 2013).

A professional learning community, or PLC, is a team that works together to become better at their jobs. By engaging with youth as partners, teachers can improve teaching and learning in schools through co-learning, co-examination, and genuine partnerships. Building and district-level PLCs can focus on teaching practices, curriculum, assessment, school climate and many other issues, and through democratic action everyone can take schools to powerful, positive new places. Giselle Martin-Kniep of Communities for Learning wrote that learning communities must involve learners as well as teachers, administrators, parents, and other adults, because "students have firsthand experiences that affect their learning and their thinking" (Martin-Kniep, 2008, p. 88). If they are organized by grade level, content area, or an entire teaching staff, PLCs can include students from the same grade level, multiple grade levels, and different learning abilities. Including diverse students as partners is essential to the success of democracy in PLCs. By fostering partnerships throughout education educators can foster learning communities between adults and youth, throughout their classrooms and throughout entire schools and districts. When they are facilitated effectively, there can be a lot of positive, powerful outcomes to democracy in PLCs. Just like every kind of democratic action, these outcomes are not just for youth; they are for teachers, administrators, parents, and systems, too.

Meaningful Student Involvement transforms education by empowering democracy in Student/Adult Partnerships to foster student engagement. Through a systems thinking orientation, this method focuses on engaging every student throughout schools in improving schools. Democracy can include student-led learning; student evaluations of lessons, teachers, curriculum, tech, and so forth; classroom climate; teaching hiring; curriculum planning; tech integration; service/project-based learning; and more. Ultimately infusing learning throughout every educational activity, this method can transform policies, practices, and outcomes throughout the entire education system.

A mindset is the way someone thinks about something. A growing body of research and literature has shown that youth mindsets determine educational effectiveness, school culture and much more. Mindsets affect democracy as well. By focusing on the intersection between mindset and strategy, educators can help youth learn a practical framework for identifying opportunities so they can proceed from promising ideas to practical actions in schools. Whether seeking to start a school improvement campaign or infuse a meaningful mindset into their current classrooms, youth should learn directly from the firsthand experience of youth who have experienced democracy throughout education while immersing them in school improvement activities that share knowledge, build skills, and launch youth into Student/Adult Partnerships that transform learning, teaching, and leadership and own their own education.

Engaging youth as researchers who examine teaching, learning, leadership, or anything to do with education is called participatory action research, or PAR. Student researchers actively work to transform education during and after their research and reflect throughout the process. Democracy happens when PAR emphasizes co-learning among youth and between youth and adults and embeds action with stated learning goals focused on youth experiencing and transforming schools in new ways. Youth with a nonprofit organization called Austin Voices for Education & Youth in Austin, Texas, research their schools to make their priorities heard during the ongoing school improvement process. Similarly, student researchers at North High School in Denver, Colorado, The North High School Report shared more than 700 youth perspectives on learning and teaching and school improvement efforts happening throughout their building. Youth in Oakland, California with a program called REAL HARD designed and collected 1,000 report card surveys evaluating teaching, counseling, school safety, and facilities at three Oakland high schools. The youth compiled their findings, analyzed the results, and made concrete recommendations to improve the schools in the Student Voices Count Report. Youth with the East Point Youth Action Team in Fulton County, Georgia, examine disparities and inequalities that exist between schools in the Northern and Southern regions of their county (Fletcher, 2017).

Organizing educators and other adults into teams with youth as partners focused on learning outcomes for everyone positions project-based learning as a key avenue toward democracy building. Project-based learning centers classroom learning goals on creating, implementing, and assessing projects led by youth.

Project-based learning can position youth as partners with educators. These Student/Adult Partnerships, made of varying ages, abilities, genders, and interests, collaboratively decide how the teams function to achieve student learning.

Restorative justice is a student-led approach to resolving conflict in schools. It holds democracy at the center, with youth as planners, facilitators, and evaluators throughout the entirety of the process. Where many previous conflict resolution programs in schools were adult-led and student-driven, restorative justice programs elevate youth by increasing student agency through positioning learners as strategic owners of the entire process (Manchester et al., 2021, p. 12). Youth can call for restorative justice, plan its implementation, facilitate the process, and submit their feedback afterward. This is especially important to youth of color, of whom former US Secretary of Education Arne Duncan said, "…minority students across America face much harsher discipline than non-minorities—even within the same school…some of the worst discrepancies are in my hometown of Chicago." Many people believe historic ways of behavior management in schools are directly responsible for several realities for youth of color and low-income youth, including the achievement gap and zero tolerance policies, both of which encourage youth to drop out or face being pushed out of school. Restorative justice moves youth to engage with each other in powerful, responsive ways. The philosophy and practices of restorative justice bring youth who misbehave into structured, safe, and supportive conversations with youth who are affected by their misbehavior. This teaches accountability and interdependence while repairing the harm that was caused. It also prevents future behavior of a similar fashion, as youth become more responsible for their actions and responsive to the climate of the learning environment. Significant research supports all of this. Community organizations, individual schools, and districts across the United States are adopting this practice more frequently, including Voices of Youth in Chicago Education (VOYCE) and Oakland Public Schools.

When youth are seen as partners instead of recipients in service learning, this method can foster democracy when it is focused on transforming education. Service learning, which infuses classroom learning with meeting real community needs, can be ideal. Working with adults as partners, youth must identify challenges, research the issues, identify and create strategies, facilitate action, and infuse reflection throughout activities (Fletcher, 2004). Some approaches position youth in each strategy for democracy in schools, while others focus on enhanced Student/Adult Partnerships through service. Whichever way it goes, it is important for activities to focus on school improvement.

Youth are creating curriculum, teaching and facilitating, evaluating and promoting curriculum, textbooks, and other classroom learning. Expecting youth to be co-creators of the classes they learn in, student-created curriculum increases in student engagement, student agency, and critical thinking provide privileged learning and teaching experiences for youth and educators (Nelson & Fredrick, 1994). Youth on curriculum committees can have opportunities to create curricula or modify what currently exists. There is a long history of this though, with student involvement in curriculum writing extending back to the 1970s. This activity continues today, including elementary youth rewriting curriculum and other dynamic activities. Reading, analyzing, and learning required standards can give youth a basis for deepened learning and understanding, while partnerships with teachers ensure quality outcomes.

Given choices in how and what they learn, student-centered learning encourages youth to thrive from a direct connection between their own interests and classroom-based learning. Student-centered learning embodies democracy in schools by ensuring required content is mastered through Student/Adult Partnerships. Used to facilitate classroom activities, student-driven learning can be utilized throughout all grade levels and across all content areas. Rather than simply dumping learning responsibilities directly on youth right away though, teachers should gradually and increasingly invest in student capacity in order to ensure their knowledge and skills.

With increasing interest in student-driven classroom evaluation, more schools consider student evaluations of teachers viable. However, focus should also be on the potential effects of youth evaluating the entirety of the learning experience and education system. Engaging youth in evaluating classes and schools, teacher performance and efficacy, and self-performance and learning can be the keys to truly transforming learning, teaching, and leadership. When done in concert with educators' self-evaluation and peer evaluations among educators, there is a perfect space formed. This can include student-led parent-teacher conferences, student assessments of classrooms and curricula, as well as other approaches. There are examples from around the world. Youth at Lexington High School wanted to share their feedback with teachers. However, unable to find a school sanctioned way to do that, they created their own club and process. Approaching the process as allies to teachers, these youth devised their own evaluations and volunteered their evaluative services to teachers. Similarly, in 2010, the Boston School Committee passed the Boston Student Advisory Council's "Student to Teacher Constructive Feedback Policy" mandating that all high school teachers administer the "Friendly Feedback Form" in their classrooms. Every full-time high school teacher administers the constructive feedback survey at least once per year. The initial implementation was piloted using the paper survey that allows for anonymous completion. A professional development workshop was offered to provide school leaders with more information about the tool.

Right now, youth are facilitating professional development for teachers on a range of issues including service learning, LGBTTQQI culture, and using technology in the classroom. Youth teaching is evaluated by teachers and administrators in attendance and guided by supporting adults. At Vashon Island School District in Washington, high school youth from an alternative school taught teachers in the local, rural district about service learning. Returning from several state-wide professional developments they were encouraged to attend, these youth contributed greatly to the teachers' learning about the topic. In a small city school district in Massachusetts, youth led a complex process to help teachers become more effective. After conducting voluntary evaluations of their classes, youth provided coaching and training opportunities for teachers to become more effective in their classrooms.

Student empowerment is any attitudinal, structural, and cultural activity process or outcome where youth of any age gain the ability, authority, and agency to make decisions and implement changes in their own schools, learning and education, and in the education of other people, including fellow youth of any age and adults throughout education. There are countless ways this can happen as well as many potential outcomes, all of which feature learning, teaching, and leadership. Student empowerment happens in schools; child empowerment and youth empowerment happens outside of schools. Throughout society, adults act as the apex (top) power holders, using adultism to enforce their power. This is true within schools, too, where adults are ultimately responsible for all activities, outcomes, and processes. Student empowerment happens when adults share any amount of that power with youth. There are times when youth can attempt to grasp the power of adults without adults sharing it willingly, too. However, these are fleeting because of adults' ultimate grasp on power. Student empowerment generally happens through student authorization and student action. Student authorization happens when youth acquire the knowledge and positions they need in order to affect schools.

There are many barriers to school transformation reflecting student empowerment. They include the culture of schools, structures within education, adults throughout the system and youth themselves. There are also many ways to overcome these barriers. However, one of the barriers to student empowerment is the concept itself. By dispensing their power without discretion or well-informed intentions, well-meaning educators can actually do a moderate-to-severe disservice to youth themselves. Examining situations when youth are placed on a pedestal can reveal that these actions are often the reality that any power is better than no power, and that youth are devoid of power within schools right now. However, that is simply not the case, and learning about student empowerment before taking action can do a lot to improve youth's experiences with this approach. What many educators are actually striving for is not student empowerment at all, but ultimately, democracy. When student empowerment activities are most effective, they reflect democracy. Youth's ideas, knowledge, opinions, and experiences in schools and regarding education are actively sought and substantiated by educators, administrators, and other adults within the educational system. Adults' acknowledgment of youth's ability to improve schools is validated and authorized through deliberate teaching focused on learning about learning, learning about the education system and learning about democracy.

Across the United States and around the world, youth are organizing themselves into energized, focused, and powerful organizations to promote roles for youth in education reform in substantive and meaningful ways. Working with adults as allies, youth are stepping outside schools to organize youth and communities to improve schools. Leading sophisticated campaigns, they are compiling signature petitions, picketing school boards, holding teach-ins, and doing more to insist schools pay attention to social justice, promote equity among youth, deconstruct the school-to-prison pipeline, and more.

The Whole Child Approach is a distinct strategy within education today (Hendrick, 1992; ASCD, 2023). Built on professional collaboration among youth, between youth and adults, and among educators, administrators, and others, the whole child approach partners people from different perspectives in order to affect the entire student, rather than piece by piece. Schools that seek to meet the basic student needs of safety, belonging, autonomy, and competence are more likely to foster authentic student engagement. The Whole Child tenets argue for each student to ensure they enter school healthy and learn about and practices a healthy lifestyle; each student learns in an environment that is physically and emotionally safe for youth and adults; each student is actively engaged in learning and is connected to the school and broader community; each student has access to personalized learning and is supported by qualified, caring adults; and each student is challenged academically and prepared for success in college or further study and for employment and participation in a global environment (Dalton, Churchman & Tasco, 2008). The concept has been explored in simpler terms, too, which more closely reflects the systems thinking approach advocated throughout this book. For instance, in *Whole Child, Whole Life: 10 Ways to Help Kids Live, Learn and Thrive*, the authors explore how the contexts young people live in directly affect their day-by-day well-being by calling out "Time, big outside forces, systems and settings, and spaces where kids spend time" as the most important elements to recognize (Krauss & Herrera, 2023). However a person understands the approach, Whole Child provides a readily ascertainable way to wholistically understand the lives of children and youth. In turn, it can give us a reasonable way to frame the expansive steps needed to address the democracy deficit disorder. Infusing democracy into this approach can encourage adults in schools to align school goals and values through Student/Adult Partnerships that develop social skills and understanding for everyone involved. Youth and adults consequently contribute to the school and community and achieve goals together, including culturally, socially, and academically. Schools and communities must work together to ensure that student needs are met on all levels, including fundamental levels of health, safety, and belonging (Dalton, Churchman & Tasco, 2008).

These are just some methods for ensuring democracy throughout schools and beyond. Other things to remember are to teach youth about giving back what they have received, or reciprocity. This powerful transition moves young people from being those who are engaged to being those who engage others.

The positions young people occupy in society are generally unstable placemarks in time, with the forces of school, home, and social life pulling at their desires to be involved throughout their community. Consequently, many young people actually disengage from the involvement that can enrich and sustain them. It is essential for *them* to develop and maintain supportive relationships with young adults as they become adults. Adults need to encourage young adults to keep building democracy through concrete action and involvement throughout their communities. Adults should not simply let go of young adults, but instead spend time together so they learn what responsible adults do in a democracy, from living responsibly at home to participating in committees to leading protests. Help young adults learn that adulthood is also about democracy, responsibility, and privilege in equal measures.

Similarly, adults need education for democracy, too. Left to their own devices, adults including parents, teachers, youth workers, counselors, and others might be forced to make their own paths. If that is the case, it is good for this journey to begin by adults recognizing their personal responsibility for curing the democracy deficit disorder by setting out to be an ally to young people, even when they do not feel welcomed or accepted. There is more than one way to be an ally, including learning about youth activities in their own community, and trying to be a silent partner to a children or youth group by raising money among adult friends to donate to the group. In their professional or personal capacity, adults can write letters to the editor, speak to the city council, or talk with parents in favor of engaging young people in democracy building. When children or youth do accept adult allies, adults should embrace it fully.

Many young people today are imbued with the strength of conviction, the courage of passion, and the determination of justice required to defeat the threat posed by adultism, racism, classism, heterosexism, and other oppression working vehemently to unravel the power of the people embodied by democracy. Updating his 2015 scan of the history of youth activism, Barrett recently wrote,

> Though young people through the ages have routinely been dismissed because of their age, they've often been decades ahead of older generations in their thinking. It was adults, after all, who clung to slavery and segregation, who maintained violently unsafe workplaces, who launched every war in U.S. history, and who elected a TV game-show host to the country's highest office. Young people have not been without their own mistakes and missteps, but they have changed U.S. history for the better again and again, and they will continue to do so. (Barrett, 2019)

The positive, powerful effects of youth-led social change cannot be overstated. Today they are aimed toward making the world a better place, and everyone should be supporting and engaging with them. Then, as a world, we can cure the democracy deficit disorder.

How Civics Can Save and Strengthen Democracy

The *Reimagining Our Futures Together Report: A New Social Contract for Education* from the International Commission on the Futures of Education (UNESCO, 2021) attempts to view the role of international education writ large. In a companion report (Haste & Chopra, 2020) the focus was on the nature of change and the need for civic education to help learners manage the ambiguity and uncertainty that will accompany the many changes yet to come. They argue that developing the capacities to manage ambiguity and change are critical to enabling membership and participation within societies in the future and to be effective citizens. The main report states that youth-led and other activism movements have a role to play in education encouraging and assuring robust democratic citizenship, including those focused on anti-racism, decolonizing of curricula, and other aspects of diversity, equity, inclusion, and justice (Haste & Chopra, 2020).

If the warnings about the dire health of democracy have any legitimacy, then a search for solutions is necessary as these reports state. One data report from the latest National Assessment of Educational Progress scores demonstrate concern. The latest civics results from the Nation's Report Card are also lackluster. The overall score dropped one point, declining from 154 points in 2014 to 153 points in 2018. Though this change is not statistically significant, it reverses a streak of modest improvement since 2006. Also, the percentage of youth performing at or above the proficient level in civics remains low: Less than a quarter of youth demonstrated solid academic performance and competency in civics and government based on NAEP standards since 2006 (Brown Center Chalkboard: Hansen et al. 2020).

Evidence from various sources might conclude that what is needed are citizens who think critically, take responsibility for their actions, evaluate information, listen to oppositional arguments, and generally choose behavior that is in the best interests of society. Such skills and dispositions could be developed in civics classes and training. But what is civics and if taught in schools, for example, what would be taught?

In 1907 a California textbook had this as its preface:

> The social work of the school is often limited to training for citizenship and citizenship is then interpreted in a narrow sense as meaning capacity to vote intelligently, a disposition to obey laws. The child is to be not only a voter and a subject of law; he is also to be a member of a family...He is to be a worker engaged in some occupation which will be of use to society and will maintain his own independence and self-respect. He is to be a member of some particular neighborhood and community and must contribute to the decencies and graces of civilization wherever he is... To suppose...that a good citizen is anything more than a thoroughly efficient and serviceable member of society...is a cramped superstition which is it hoped may soon disappear from educational discussion. Training for citizenship is formal and nominal unless it develops the power of observations, analysis and inference with respect to what makes up a social situation and the agencies through which it is modified. (Dunn, 1907)

Without a clear understanding of the role each member of society can play, many seem to choose to stay as recipients of the commons rather than participants, even ignoring their responsibilities as they demand their rights. Huxley's warning is clear:

By means of ever more effective methods of mind-manipulation, the democracies will change their nature; the quaint old forms—elections, parliaments, Supreme Court—and all the rest—will remain. The underlying substance will be a new kind of non-violent totalitarianism. All the traditional names, all the hallowed slogans will remain exactly what they were in the good old days. Democracy and freedom will be the theme of every broadcast and editorial [...]. Meanwhile the ruling oligarchy and its highly trained elite of soldiers, policemen, thought-manufacturers and mind-manipulators will quietly run the show as they see fit. (Huxley, 1958, p. 25)

This warning is clear that participation and knowledge are key elements of a democracy and a civically engaged citizenry. Just as there are many perspectives about a definition of democracy, so too are there equally wide-ranging definitions and views about civics and civics education. It appears, however, that part of the national conversation centers around a concept that civics used to be taught, it needs to be taught again and with a renewed offering of civics education, young people will become civically engaged. Perhaps civics education can challenge Huxley's perspective?

With the resurgence of interest in civics, several individuals have become the voices for its renewal. Central among them is Joel Westheimer, professor, writer, and speaker. In his book, *What Kind of Citizen? Educating Our Children for the Common Good* (2019), he defines three kinds of citizens. They are Personally Responsible Citizens, Participatory Citizens, and Social Justice Oriented Citizens. Each category builds on the previous with the last being the most laudable. Westheimer believes that the dispositions for the last category can be taught. Those dispositions include the following; critically assessing social, political, and economic structures; exploring strategies for change; knowing about social movements and how to effect systemic change; seeking out and addressing areas of injustice; and solving social problems and improving society.

This last category is central to the kind of citizen behavior that many hope for. In December 2020 U.S. Senators Chris Coons (D-Del.) and John Cornyn (R-Texas) introduced landmark legislation to invest $1 billion annually in civics and history education from K-12 through higher education. The Educating for Democracy Act would create a variety of grants to states, non-profits, institutions of higher education, and civics education researchers to support and expand access to civics and history education in schools across the country. It would also strengthen policy makers' understanding of young Americans' achievement in civics education by increasing the frequency of and encouraging participation in the National Assessment of Education Progress exam. Companion legislation was introduced by U.S. Representatives Rosa DeLauro (D-Conn.) and Tom Cole (R-Okla.) in the House.

According to Senator Coons (2020), "Civic engagement is crucial for the health of our democracy. With expanded civics education in K-12 and higher education, this bill will equip new generations of Americans with a deeper understanding of their responsibilities as citizens and how to exercise their cherished rights" (Press release 12/2020). Senator Cornyn (2020) who co-sponsored that bill stated that "The United States continues to be a model for the world because we are taught from a young age the merits of democracy, our Constitution, the Bill of Rights, and the civic duties that are inherently part of being an American. This bill would help schools inspire the next generation of public servants and teach all young Texans the value of freedom, and I'm glad to work with Sen. Coons on this bipartisan legislation" (Press release 12/2020).

Westheimer and others have become clear spokespeople for civics education but this knowledge-based model is the polar opposite of the kind of learning environment that can promote a civically minded child. This adultist view of children in many ways indicates that traditional civic education mirrors a banking approach to education (Freire, 1968) where adults know how the larger public sphere operates and pass along knowledge without attending to the assets, capabilities, and concerns that young people bring to their communities.

It is impossible to encourage a view of an active citizen while young people are told what to do, when to do it, and how. As long as there is the assumption that young people need to be taught to be civically engaged, the point is missed. That point is that children are already engaged in civic behavior even when very young.

Much of what is considered "children and young people's participation today is part of a wider neoliberal project that emphasizes an ideal young citizen who is responsible and rational while simultaneously downplaying the role of systemic inequality and potentially reinforcing rather than overcoming children and young people's subjugation" (Hartung, n.d., p. xii).

But what defines "civic" behavior that is different from Westheimer and others? It is important to revisit Westheimer's notion of dispositions. If civics leads to reaching for the common good then children need to be seen as responsible, rationale individuals, not adults in waiting (Johansson, 2011, p. 1). The goal is to recognize that children are citizens and that they already behave civically. Processes need to be in place to respect young people for their behavior and that adults need to get out of the way. The civic behavior of young people is fully under-recognized and under-valued (Hart, 1992, p. 15).

The hidden world of the child is often invisible to adults, particularly to those who see children as simply people waiting to be adults (Jenks, 1996, p. 57). What is largely missing from the participation debate is an exploration of the multiple, messy, and mundane ways in which children actively engage in negotiating, contesting, and changing everyday spaces, relationships, and practices. By recognizing these skills and behaviors of children, it is possible to support their civic understanding rather than believing that they need to be taught.

Other views of children are wide ranging. Jans' perspective is,

> Due to changing social conditions active citizenship becomes a dynamic process rather than a standard, clear-cut set of rights and responsibilities. Furthermore, childhood presents itself more and more as an ambivalent social phenomenon. On the one hand, children are seen as autonomous individuals, on the other hand, as objects of protection. Nevertheless, today children can be seen as active citizens. Their ability to learn and play allows them to give active meaning to their environment. Accepting playful and ambivalent forms of citizenship, child participation presents itself no longer as an utopia, but as a fact. (Jans, 2004, p. 40)

Jans argues for a view that creates a concept of children sized citizenship to match the skills and practices that young people already engage in. So much of this field of thought is contested. Hartung (n.d.) argues that children and young people already possess power (p. 52) and that they are experts on their own lives. This is a contested perspective that is often argued when the United Nations Convention on the Rights for Children (UNCRC) is discussed.

During the development of the UNCRC the challenge then and now is the inability of adults to stop their adultism. Here is one conundrum: children can make their claim to be equal members of the citizen community through active participation in it, but in order to be able to participate they first need to be accepted as members of the citizen community. Fielding suggests that the emancipatory critique of the dominant neo-liberal position tend to argue that the current vogue for student voice is primarily an instrument of school effectiveness driven by adult purposes linked firmly to economic performance and the continued ascendency of those in position of power (2004, p. 205). With this perspective in mind it is clear that adults are not comfortable with children's participation which remains difficult for adults to accept. It is clear that no one would argue that children are the same as or identical to adults, but the recognition of the skills, rights, and achievements they possess is a long way from happening.

Article 12 of the UNCRC is significant for the discussion of the rights of a child (United Nations General Assembly Resolution 44/25, 1989):

1. States Parties shall assure to the child who is capable of forming his or her own views the right to express those views freely in all matters affecting the child, the views of the child being given due weight in accordance with the age and maturity of the child.
2. For this purpose, the child shall in particular be provided the opportunity to be heard in any judicial and administrative proceedings affecting the child, either directly, or through a representative or an appropriate body, in a manner consistent with the procedural rules of national law.

To Hartung (n.d.) the value of Article 12 is not only that it enunciates the specific right to meaningful participation, but it moves away from the dominant world view of children as silent, invisible, and passive "pre-citizens" to a world view of children as full human beings invested with agency, integrity, and decision-making capabilities (p. 53). Sadly, adulthood represents everything that children are not: Mature/immature and rationale/irrational and the right of the child to express their views freely assumes that children need to be supported, empowered, and educated by adults in order to learn how to act as political agents; that children need to be protected because they are incomplete, innocent, vulnerable, invisible, and apolitical. As Dewey once wrote, the understanding of children as immature may lead us to focus on what they lack rather than what they have (1916, p. 46). This deficit mindset diminishes their abilities as well as the responsibilities adults have for re-envisioning their roles throughout society.

Lester (2013, p. 28) argues that there is ample evidence that very young children are engaged in the most essential civic behaviors in their play. As they maneuver through their lives, their play processes require them to engage in sophisticated and nuanced ways. "By playing, children subject the taken-for-granted to scrutiny, injecting a critique of their subordinate position, while at the same time hiding away from, or playing with their assumed innocence in the company of adults, in 'infrapolitics' of the powerless" (Scott, 1990, p. 193). Mitra and Serriere (2015) reinforce and expand on this concept and suggest that young children are part of a continuum of engagement in democracy that can expand through a young person's educational experience from the youngest years onwards.

Lester's point of view is clearly supportive of a view that children are civically engaged, particularly as he views their actions in play. Play is their primary way of being actively engaged and can be viewed as "micro-political expressions in which children collectively participate to establish control over their immediate environment in order to make things different or better." In other words, play can be seen as a form of protest as they search for justice. Moss (2007, p. 12) argues that we need to bring democracy to the nursery (Millei & Kallio, 2018).

Others who study play argue that high quality play-based curricula create opportunities for young people to dialogue with one another and engage in problem solving (Payne, 2020, p 2). Such skills as conflict -resolution, negotiating and listening become developed. They develop the dispositions that are required for active citizenship although often in formal schooling there is little opportunity for independent engagement and decision making. Generally, the adults are in charge, giving young people little or no civically based opportunities. This is sadly a result of the socialization that teachers receive that prevent them from trusting children.

Some might argue that children are not ready to engage in the behaviors and practices that require facing difficult or messy ideas. Some argue that children are not developmentally ready to learn about the flaws and abuses of power in the world either writ large or at the community level. What is true, however, by pretending that institutions, policies, and practices in civic life are healthy, fair, or just is a disservice to children. They experience behaviors that are unfair, inappropriate, and inexplicable and so to validate their observations and felt reality can be a way to move them toward a stronger sense of themselves. Swalwell and Payne (2019, p. 127) ask educators to engage in Critical Civic education by helping children develop an understanding of injustice and to reflect on what matters to them and how they can make their ideas a reality.

Hart states that schools are more likely to be concerned with political indoctrination rather than with the kind of critical debate that would allow children to establish and practice their own beliefs (p. 36). One cannot be engaged if not exposed. However, as this book expressed earlier, there are practical ways schools can overcome Hart's concerns.

Why should adults engage with young people as they enact civics in their lives? What steps can be taken to learn from them? The value of participation is that it fosters the long-term development of citizenship and more specifically, a sense of local responsibility (Hart) and civic resilience.

The plea for participation by children and young people has its anti-moralizing side. The creation of opportunities for learning by experience, "learning by doing," gives young people the opportunity to work out their position about dominant value patterns in real and practical situations. In contrast to the abstract acquisition of knowledge, this presents opportunities to try out skills, develop attitudes, and test value judgments in real life situations. This is a way of learning in which social, cognitive, and moral education are closely linked (Winter, 1996, p. 157).

Democracy requires a knowledgeable citizenry and one that understands the civic responsibilities of a community. Young people can be encouraged to be active members of the community if their innate capacities such as independent thinking, fair play, questioning, and inquiry are encouraged. As adults in their lives continue to pressure children to do what they are told and given little or no autonomy, their innate ability to be civically engaged is defeated. Schools should encourage free play, student centered learning, and problem posing/solving opportunities. More important, however, is an understanding that young people are civically engaged (child sized civics) and need the space and encouragement to participate democratically. They are indeed future leaders—and today's leaders, too.

Conclusion

Democracy needs our immediate worldwide attention. The neoliberal juggernaut affecting the United States and quickly spreading around the world is poised to further undermine or even destroy democracies. We have described this concern as *democracy deficit disorder.*

Today there are countless examples of young people enacting their beliefs about their rights to support change and their need to be independent. These same youth often face massive roadblocks that prevent them from becoming democratically engaged throughout their communities. The belief that "Children are to be seen and not heard and to be told what to do" still remains to this day in homes and schools and community organizations. Adults seem to be afraid of youth and of losing control and power if they act.

For instance, when a young person takes on the work of serious challenges as Greta Thunberg has, she demonstrates the solution to democracy deficit disorder. A delightful conversation between Alexandria Ocasio-Cortez and Greta Thunberg in *The Guardian* illustrates what this looks like (Brockes, 2019).

> AOC: One of the things I'm interested in hearing from you is that often people say, "Don't politicize young people." It's almost a taboo. That to have someone as young as you coming out in favor of political positions is manipulative or wrong. I find

it very condescending, as though, especially in this day and age with the access to information we have, you can't form your own opinions and advocate for yourself. I'm interested in how you approach that—if anyone brings that up with you?

GT: That happens all the time. That's basically all I hear. The most common criticism I get is that I'm being manipulated and you shouldn't use children in political ways, because that is abuse, and I can't think for myself and so on. And I think that is so annoying! I'm also allowed to have a say—why shouldn't I be able to form my own opinion and try to change people's minds?

Becoming allies for youth has a history. After the horrors of World War I, Eglantyne Jebb and her sister Dorothy Buxton began the Save the Children Fund in London, which eventually became the International Save the Children Union (Kerbes-Ganse, 2015). Their work was also instrumental in the development of the Geneva Declaration of the Rights of the Child, enacted by the League of Nations in 1924.

In 1959, this document was succeeded by the Convention on the Rights of the Child, or UNCRC (United Nations, 1990). Supported by almost every nation in the world, the UNCRC codifies what governments of the world believe to be the rights of young people. Crafted over a ten-year period with many compromises related to cultural understandings of children, this 54-article document serves as a standard of expectation for all actions related to children.

However, while the UNCRC exists and many people agree with it in concept, there are many examples of childhood experiences that are not in alignment with the document. In fact, in societies worldwide children and youth are often still seen from the viewpoint of being looked down upon rather than from their viewpoint of looking up and forward. The social contract must be renegotiated to acknowledge the roles and possibilities inherent in every young person. Engaging young people in the democratic functions of the world will enhance civic engagement, empower communities, and enable deeper democratic action everywhere.

As Greta Thunberg and so many other youth activists have demanded over the years, children are more than inheritors of the planet: They are active, engaged people right now, not just in some ethereal future when adults deem them worthy of democratic rights. The democracy deficit disorder has allowed them to witness and experience non-democratic direction in every nation of the world. Thanks to social media and mass global cultural transmission, the evidence is clear to children and youth. The rise of right leaning actions, the return of the KKK and neo-Nazi groups, and the continued decimation of freedom in many countries gives significant pause among young people, because they can see what is ahead. We must challenge this adamantly and intentionally by providing opportunities for young people to do more than read about democracy or try it out in token classroom projects. Young people need to do democracy right now, and adults need to enable that action or get out of the way.

What happens when adults give young people some freedom without engaging in serious listening to their ideas and needs? These belittling and demeaning approaches are cynical to their core, providing only partial choice masked behind adult obfuscation. Even from the youngest ages and even without the education to express it effectively, young people know when sincerity is missing, when transparency is broken and when humility is gone. They know when adults are deceiving them. This is as true at home as it is in schools, and as obvious in schools as it is in the streets.

When young people are told what to do and how to do it and where to do it and with what to do it with, the most obedient will go along. They do not want to stand out and cause trouble because that is what we all have been taught and reinforced with for years and years. Whether they intend to or not, this conformity is what educators, youth workers, and others implicitly and explicitly transmit to students in schools and communities. But there are always young rebels who are the defiant ones who want to do things their way and have a different idea about what is to be done, whether it is learning, teaching, or leadership. The founders of this American democracy were unwilling to conform and may have been the best examples of rebels fighting for their freedom and responsibility. This is the antidote for democracy deficit disorder.

As described previously, in the 1930s, Korczak advocated that, "children are not the people of tomorrow, but people today. They are entitled to be taken seriously. They have a right to be treated by adults with tenderness and respect, as equals. They should be allowed to grow into whoever they were meant to be—The unknown person inside each of them is the hope for the future" (Korczak, 1929, p. 8).

This is evident in the well-intended, if poorly implemented, Article 12 of the UNCRC, which states:

> State Parties shall assure to the child who is capable of forming his or her own views the right to express those views freely in all matters affecting the child, the views of the child being given due weight in accordance with the age and maturity of the child. For this purpose, the child shall in particular be provided the opportunity to be heard in any judicial and administrative proceedings affecting the child, either directly, or through a representative or an appropriate body, in a manner consistent with the procedural rules of national law.

The wording alone shows why Article 12 is poorly implemented. Generally speaking, adults do not value the voices of young people, let alone our obligation to act on what they say. If we want young people to act civically then we cannot continue to prevent them from practicing the skills of action

Alexis de Tocqueville traveled throughout the United States in 1831 researching our prison system. Upon his return to France he penned what has become one of the most important histories of that period in our country. As impressed as he was with many aspects of our democracy, he leveled significant criticisms and warnings about the nature of a utopian vision that needed educated and engaged citizens to keep the republic working well. He wrote, "I know of no country in which there is so little independence of mind and real freedom of discussion as in America" (Tocqueville, 2006, p. 239).

This observation may help us understand why ignoring the advice and wisdom of our young people is part and parcel of our culture. This means attacking the longstanding and widely spread nature of the democracy deficit will be much more difficult than the simplistic, unsophisticated measures that have been taken before.

Benjamin Franklin (Kidd, 2017) would agree that we need to educate all residents, citizens, and immigrants to their responsibilities in preserving this experiment in democratic governance. As has been shown with adults for centuries now, it takes work, patience, attention, and shared vision to make shared governance successful. However, when we examine the latent and ignored power of children and youth, it is easy to show we have not done such as yet. The future however will not get better unless our young people come to understand the roles they must occupy throughout our society, working with adults as partners and allies to understand, critique, actualize, and transform what democracy looks like and why it should matter.

One of the major goals of this book was to help the reader find actions they can take right now to support every young person becoming engaged in democratic actions throughout our society. First, each of us must first examine our own view of children and youth and determine how we can become allies by listening to youth.

Are we comfortable creating ideas with young people as partners? Are we capable of standing with and for young people when they do not want to stand alone? Do we actually want to work with young people even if we do not agree with them? Can we practically respect the ideas of children and youth, help them actualize their personal and collective power, and create meaningful opportunities for young people to change the world?

Answering these questions can be the first steps we must take. They are critical if we are to become allies to our young people and to democracy as a whole. Democracy is fading right now, and it is no exaggeration to state that democracy deficit disorder needs our immediate attention and that of our entire community particularly our children and youth. The good news is that a deficit is fixable. We can infuse our democracy with the kinds of action, beliefs, and knowledge necessary to turn the disorder into a strength—but we need everyone to do so. This book offers one prescription for democracy deficit disorder: authentically engaging young people throughout our democracy.

Beyond problem-posing and critical examinations, we must take concrete action in order to cure the democracy deficit disorder. To do this, adults and young people can follow the five steps in Fletcher's "Cycle of Engagement" (Fletcher, 2023).

The first step is listening to young people. This is more than words. It means making space for youth voice, which is any expression of any young person about anything, anywhere, at any time. Youth voice is already being shared all the time, whether consciously or unconsciously, or through verbal, written, drawn, acted, danced, sung, graffitied, screamed, whispered, obviously or incidentally. Youth voice can also include attendance, participation, and behavior. By understanding that children and youth are already constantly sharing youth voice, adults assume the burden of learning to listen. Listening to young people can show what problems concern them, and how they think they can bring their strengths, identities, and gifts to that problem to help generate real solutions. Because of this, young people can also learn how to share youth voice in ways adults will hear them. Both are valid avenues toward curing the democracy deficit disorder—but they are not the only ones.

With this broad understanding of youth voice, adults need to understand that listening to youth voice happens during conversations, in-person and online forums, at art shows, via texting, on graffiti walls, in student newspapers, on the Internet, and in learning activities. It can also happen through acting out, in fights, while cheating on tests, while daydreaming, and in myriad other ways. It can occur in classrooms, at summer camp, during therapy, in out-of-school time programs, at friends' homes, through presentations, at home and during community events, as well as in foster care, juvenile diversion, in-school suspension, and during restorative justice circles. Look for spaces, programs, and activities both in-person and online where young people's voices are centered and they are asked to engage, build community, and impact outcomes.

The next step in the Cycle of Engagement is to validate young people. This happens when adults and others express genuine curiosity about what is being said and acknowledge the difference between their knowledge, opinions, wisdom, and ideas. Validating young people also means supporting them as they navigate the risks and opportunities of sharing their voices. When parents, teachers, youth workers, and other adults do this, they demonstrate their understanding that what young people care passionately about may or may not mirror adult interests or knowledge. Validating requires seeing young people as whole people and recognizing that what they are expressing matters to them. This allows them to be seen and heard. It can happen through simply saying yes, but that is not the only way. It can also mean saying no, and it can happen when we ask inquiring questions, examine basic assumptions, and identify biases with young people. Validating young people can mean connecting them to broader issues, activities, or movements, too.

Authorizing children and youth is the third step in this cycle. Young people are authorized when they are given the ability to tell their own stories. Adults routinely assume that ability, but the right of children and youth to tell their truths and share their realities is often metered, policed, and silenced by adults. Focused on fostering justice through equity, authorizing should acknowledge the ways in which race, class, trauma, ability, language, neurodiversity, and geography shape access for young people. It then can encourage young people to claim their emotions, knowledge, and actions. Practically speaking, authorizing young people can mean making ways for them to learn more obvious through classes, training, or encouraging self-driven learning. It can mean enabling them to follow up on the issues they care about on small and large scales and learn the meaning of their involvement. Authorizing young people can also mean giving them informal or formal positions and encouraging them to recognize the power and purpose of their involvement. Whether they are informally charged with researching issues that matter to them or formally voted to be a full-voting student member of a school board, as this book illustrated earlier, there are nearly countless positions for children and youth throughout our society. Shoring up, emboldening, and engaging the capacities of young people through knowledge-sharing and skill-building is very important during this step. Ultimately, authorizing young people should mean helping them see their strengths and identifying pragmatic ways that they can apply them to the issues they care about.

The Cycle of Engagement continues with taking action. This should be practical and obvious action that helps young people understand how to build bridges between personally meaningful concerns and collective action. The role of adult allies should become more blatant in taking action as they exert their influence to ensure young peoples' opportunities to engage with the systems, communities, and people who need to hear them. Taking action can happen in the most seemingly miniscule and insignificant ways or in the grandest, most reverberating ways, so long as it reflects the positive potential of democracy. In taking action, young people experience the positive power of Student/Adult Partnerships in concrete, practical ways. Taking action to defeat the democracy deficit disorder can look like the countless ways illuminated throughout this book, particularly through activist learning, which places practical, ascertainable lessons at the heart of social justice in action including young people and adults together conducting research, planning action, teaching lessons, evaluating everything, making decisions throughout systems, and advocating for change.

The final step in this cycle is reflection. Through reciprocal mentoring, young people can lead adults in asking serious questions about what has happened while adults can guide children and youth toward critical thinking on the outcomes of their efforts to defeat the democracy deficit disorder. Looking for young people reflecting on democracy, expanding horizons for nontraditional youth voice, and expanding the diversity of children and youth whose voices are engaged is essential. Reflection happens when young people and adults critically assess and analyze democracy. This empowers learning to become vibrant by challenging the intricacies of power in learning. Reflection can foster personal growth for children, youth, and adults, and can become a powerful lever for defeating the democracy deficit disorder transformation. It can happen at the beginning of activities, during a class or program, and at the end of activities or benchmarks, as well as throughout the entire course of events and further beyond the activities. Reflections can be public or private; used as explicit teaching opportunities or as passive reinforcement or exploration activities; be visual, audio, kinesthetic, musical, natural; and many other forms, too. Self-reflection provides an essential location for action as well.

When reflection is completed, what is learned should be applied to the beginning of the process, thus completing the cyclical nature of this process. Calling these "steps" is meant to embrace the practical nature of each one. However, they are not linear things that begin here and go there, and then are finished. Instead, they represent the cyclical nature of a spiral and each one can be done at any point, or on its own. Whether working to defeat the democracy deficit disorder at home, in school, throughout your neighborhood, place of worship, or in community and government programs, everyone has a place they can begin and places they can go. Pablo Picasso once wrote that, "Action is the foundational key to all success," which is why the Freechild Institute for Youth Engagement motto has been "Only through action do words take meaning" for almost 25 years. Whatever route is chosen, the most important part is to get to work to save democracy.

Appendix I: Glossary of Terms

These terms are defined for usage in this book.

Adolescence is the identification of people according to their relevance to adulthood; if they are becoming adults or experiencing situations like adults, they are in adolescence. This perspective diminishes the unique station of youth throughout society and diminishes the contributions, attitudes, knowledge, and actions due to age.

Adult is any person who is acknowledged as being in the age of majority either by law, culture, or other rite of passage.

Adult ally is any supportive person in the lives of young people who equitably, holistically, and appropriately empowers and engages children and youth of all ages. Designated by those young people as an ally, they can include friends, family members, youth workers, teachers, and others.

Adultism is the bias toward adults, including their ideas, actions, attitudes, beliefs, and outcomes. This can be internalized, subversive, and demonizing; it can also be appropriate sometimes.

Children are people between the ages of birth and 11 years old. The word also refers to the offspring of parents.

Child development is the linear growth or regression of skills, knowledge, and abilities all people experience in their youngest years. Visualized as a stairstep progression, child development pins down development according to conveniently identifiable markers in the life of a child.

Children's rights are specific opportunities endowed to people under the age of 12 simply because they are children.

Children's voices are the behaviors, actions, and words of the youngest people, from toddlers to middle school and beyond.

Civic education is any intentional or other learning seeking to influence ideas, beliefs, opinions, knowledge, or actions about living in communities.

Civic engagement happens when someone chooses to be connected with a community again and again, in any way, shape, or form.

Community youth development combines the developmental instincts of young people as they naturally desire to create change in their surrounding environments by partnering youth and adults to create new opportunities for youth to serve their communities while developing their personal abilities.

Democracy is a personal and group way to live that relies on individual autonomy—people controlling their own lives within reason—and equality, the idea that people should have the same opportunities to affect themselves, others, and society. It includes government on behalf of all the people, according to their "will" and individual control, authority, and leadership within their own lives.

Democracy education is an approach to learning, teaching, schooling, and education administration that actively, meaningfully, and sustainably integrates democracy throughout K-12 schools and education systems.

Democratic education is learning that uses democratic processes to foster student ownership of learning and student leadership in school governance.

Ephebiphobia is the fear of youth expressed inadvertently or explicitly, subversively, or obviously and by children, youth, adults, and older people.

Holistic youth development is a framework for considering the myriad ways children and youth grow, learn, and evolve while they are young.

Evolving capacities are the nonlinear processes fostering transitions that all people experience throughout their lives. Visualized as a spiral, the evolving capacities of children and youth identifies multiple skills, abilities, knowledge, and actions simultaneously instead of isolating progress or regression according to conveniently placed circumstances.

Experiential learning is the process of making meaning from direct experience, which may or may not be planned and does or does not have specific learning goals.

Holistic youth development is a framework for considering the myriad ways children and youth grow, learn, and evolve while they are young.

Meaningful Student Involvement is the process of engaging students as partners in every facet of school change for the purpose of strengthening their commitment to education, community, and democracy.

Participatory action research engages the people studied in creating, administering, and responding to action research projects.

Praxis is the mutual understanding of the problems, potentials, resources, activities, learning, and more that arises in any authentic attempt to challenge the democracy deficit disorder.

Project-based learning infuses deliberately planned hands-on activities focused on teaching and learning to foster youth success.

Service learning uses meaningful service throughout the community to help youth achieve clearly stated learning goals.

Student/Adult Partnerships are intentionally equitable learning relationships based on fostering and sustaining mutual respect.

Suffrage for young people is the elimination of the voting age, everywhere, at all times.

Youth are anyone between the ages of 12 and 18 in the United States; ages varying internationally. The word youth also refers to a frame of mind or is attributed to behavior, attitudes, styles, and more.

Youth-Industrial Complex is a phenomenon that summarizes the overlapping interests of non-profits, businesses, and government agencies which use public and private resources to create youth-serving activities to address economic, social, and political problems.

Youth empowerment is the attitudinal, structural, and cultural process whereby young people gain the ability, authority, and agency to make decisions and implement change in their own lives and the lives of other people, including youth and adults.

Youth action is any activity undertaken by youth intended to change their own lives, the lives of others, or the world.

Youth development is an intentional and coincidental process that defines the growth and evolution of young people, including their knowledge, skills, and other abilities. An extension of child development, youth development continues stairstep growth and regression according to easy-to-identify markers in the teen years.

Youth engagement is the sustained connection young people hold toward a particular thing, whether an idea, person, activity, place, or outcome. That sustained connection can be social, emotional, educational, spiritual, sentimental, or otherwise as long as its sustained.

Youth equity is the pro-active rebalancing of relationships between youth and adults to allow for appropriately empowered roles between youth and adults. It allows for a 40/60 split of authority, while everyone involved—young people and adults—are recognized for their impact in the activity, and each has ownership of the outcomes.

Youth infusion is the active, deep, and sustained integration of youth throughout an organization or community's structure and culture.

Youth involvement is any deliberate effort that centers on young peoples' ongoing attendance in personal, social, institutional, cultural, and other forms of structural action throughout society. Youth involvement is generally formal, often including specific roles, education, and outcomes.

Youth leadership is the practice of young people exercising authority over themselves or others, both in informal and formal ways. There is youth leadership beyond the scope of what adults recognize, appreciate, or foster; there is also youth leadership which is guided by adults.

Youth mainstreaming is a public policy strategy that acknowledges the roles youth can play and the issues affecting them across various sectors such as health, finance, economic development, housing, justice, foreign affairs, education, and agriculture.

Youth organizing is an approach that trains young people in community organizing and advocacy and assists them in employing these skills to alter power relations and create meaningful institutional change in their communities by employing activities such as political education and analysis, community research, campaign development, direct action, and membership recruitment.

Youth participation is the active attendance of young people in any mode throughout their lives or communities. Youth participation can happen through active decision-making, sports, schools, or faith communities. It can also happen in homes and among friends. Youth participation can be formal or informal; when it is formal, youth may not choose to attend something, but they choose whether to participate. When its informal, youth choose to join in on something.

Youth rights are the specific inalienable freedoms every person has between the ages of 12 and 18 years old, including opportunities and responsibilities.

Youth voice is any expression of any young person anywhere, at any time. This can include expressions that are verbal, written, visual, body language, or actions; expressions that are convenient and inconvenient for adults to listen to; and intentional as well as unintentional expressions. Youth voice does not require adult approval or acceptance.

References

Adams, Gordon. (1981). *The iron triangle: The politics of defense contracting.* Council on Economic Priorities.

Alinsky, S. (2010). *Rules for radicals: A pragmatic primer for realistic radicals.* Knopf Doubleday Publishing Group.

Ambar, S. M. (2016). *Malcolm X at Oxford union racial politics in a global era.* Oxford University Press.

American Psychological Association. (2004, June). *Consumerism: Driving teen egos and buying— through 'branding.'* Retrieved May 13, 2022, from https://www.apa.org/monitor/jun04/ driving

American University School of International Service. (2017, November 16). *In small places, close to home: The beginnings of universal human rights. International relations online.* Retrieved May 19, 2022, from https://ironline.american.edu/blog/our-basic-human-rights/

American Youth Congress. (1935). Declaration of the rights of American youth. *The City College Libraries.* Retrieved May 19, 2022, from https://www.jstor.org/stable/community.9286 533?mag=antiwar-posters-city-college-new-york&seq=1

AmeriCorps, Office of Research and Evaluation, & Hanson Schlachter, L. (2021). *Key findings from the 2019 current population survey: Civic engagement and volunteering supplement.* https://www.americorps.gov/sites/default/files/document/2019%20CPS%20CEV%20findi ngs%20report%20CLEAN_10Dec2021_508.pdf

Andersen, J. S. (2017, October 30). *Why democracy matters in movement and sport cultures.* Playthegame.org. Retrieved May 13, 2022, from https://www.playthegame.org/news/comments/2017/049_why-democracy-matters-in-movement-and-sport-cultures/

Annie E. Casey Foundation. (2017, July 27). *New study: The "adultification" of Black girls.* Annie E. Casey Foundation. Retrieved May 27, 2022, from https://www.aecf.org/blog/new-study-the-adultification-of-black-girls

Aquarone, F. (2021, May 7). Student experiences of democratic education and the implications for social justice. *Theory and Research in Educ*ation, *19*(1), 40–64. https://doi.org/10.1177/14778785211005695

Arnstein, S. R. (1969). A ladder of citizen participation. *Journal of the American Institute of planners, 35*(4), 216–224. Taylor & Francis Online. Retrieved June 29, 2022, from https://www.tandfonline.com/doi/abs/10.1080/01944366908977225

Aronowitz, S. (2015). *Against schooling: For an education that matters.* Taylor & Francis.

Associated Press. (2022, July 31). Sting warns during Warsaw concert of threats to democracy. *Billboard.* Retrieved December 12, 2022, from https://www.billboard.com/music/music-news/sting-warsaw-concert-warning-ukraine-war-1235120576/

ASCD. (2023). The ASCD whole child approach to education. *Association for Supervision and Curriculum Development.* Retrieved April 20, 2023, from https://www.ascd.org/whole-child

Association of Alaska School Boards. (2001). The power of an untapped resource: Exploring youth representation on your board or committee. *Alaska Department of Labor.* Retrieved June 28, 2022, from http://labor.alaska.gov/awib/Untapped_Resource.pdf

Augsberger, A. (2022). COVID-19 shines a light on health inequities in communities of color: A youth-driven photovoice inquiry. *Journal of Community Psychology.* https://doi.org/10.1002/jcop.22866

Avery, P. G., Levy, S. A., Simmons, A. M. M., & Scarlett, M. H. (2012). Adolescents' conceptions of democracy in central/eastern Europe and the United State*s. ERIC.* Retrieved May 26, 2022, from https://files.eric.ed.gov/fulltext/EJ1149755.pdf

Bachelet, M. (2022, April 19). COVID 19 recovery: Youth taking action for a sustainable future. *OHCHR.* Retrieved May 10, 2022, from https://www.ohchr.org/en/statements-and-speeches/2022/04/covid-19-recovery-youth-taking-action-sustainable-future

Bailey, R. (2014). *A. S. Neill.* Bloomsbury Publishing.

Baldwin, J. (1979, July 29). If Black English isn't a language, then tell me, what is? *The New York Times.*

Baldwin, J. (2017). *Notes of a native son.* Penguin.

Barnes, M. (2013). *Role reversal: Achieving uncommonly excellent results in the student-centered classroom.* ASCD.

Barrett, D. (2015). *Teenage rebels: Stories of successful high school activists, from the little rock 9 to the class of tomorrow.* Microcosm Publishing.

Barrett, D. (2019, February 13). How a year of youth activism has changed the country. *Teen Vogue.* Retrieved June 4, 2022, from https://www.teenvogue.com/story/youth-activism-changed-the-country-in-the-year-since-parkland

Bauman, Z. (2000). *Liquid modernity* (Polity Press, Ed.). Wiley.

Beaumont, M., Chalker, K., Clayton, L., Curtis, E., & Hales, H. (2021). Invisible youth during times of Covid. *BJPsych Bulletin, 45*(2), 123–124. https://doi.org/10.1192/bjb.2021.20

Benforado, A. (2023). *A minor revolution: How prioritizing kids benefits us all.* Crown Publishing.

Bernier, A. (Ed.). (2013). Introduction. In *Transforming young adult services* (pp. 1–29). American Library Association.

Biesta, J. J. G. (2015). Democracy in the kindergarten. Helping young children to be at home in the world. In J. Kaurel, T. Pålerud, & K. E. Jansen (Eds.), *Demokratiske praksiser i barnehagen* (pp. 21–45). Fagbokforlaget.

Black Youth Project. (2012, November 15). "Kids These Days" fighting against adultism and fostering cross-generational dialogue. *The Black Youth Project.* Retrieved May 25, 2022, from http://blackyouthproject.com/kids-these-days-fighting-against-adultism-and-fostering-cross-generational-dialogue/

Boateng, A. B., Klupe, J., Moore, J. C., Williams-Jackson, A., & Casey, I. B. (2021). *An education system built on the pillars of White supremacy and anti-Blackness: A collection of autoethnographic studies depicting how Black kids never had a chance.* The Institutional Repository Library (IRL) at the University of Missouri-St. Louis (UMSL) IRL@UMSL. Retrieved May 29, 2022, from https://irl.umsl.edu/cgi/viewcontent.cgi?article=2080&context=dissertation

Books, S. (Ed.). (2015). *Invisible children in the society and its schools.* Taylor & Francis.

Borden, L. M., Villarruel, F. A., Keith, J. G., & Perkins, D. F. (Eds.). (2003). *Community youth development: Programs, policies, and practices.* SAGE Publications.

Bort, R., & Aleah, K. (2020, December 14). Youth activists: Black lives matter inspires new protest movement. *Rolling Stone.* Retrieved May 23, 2022, from https://www.rollingstone.com/politics/politics-features/black-lives-matter-protests-new-generation-youth-activists-1099895/

Boyte, H. C. (2018). *Awakening democracy through public work: Pedagogies of empowerment.* Vanderbilt University Press.

Brake, M. (2013). *The sociology of youth culture and youth subcultures (Routledge revivals: Sex and drugs and Rock 'n' Roll?).* Taylor & Francis Group.

Breeze, M., Gorringe, H., & Rosie, M. (2017). Becoming independent: Political participation and youth transitions in the Scottish referendum. *The British Journal of Sociology, 68*, 754–774. https://doi.org/10.1111/1468-4446.12288

Brockes, E. (June 29, 2019). When Alexandria Ocasio-Cortez met Greta Thunberg: 'Hope is contagious,' *The Guardian.* Retrieved December 12, 2022, from https://www.theguardian.com/environment/2019/jun/29/alexandria-ocasio-cortez-met-greta-thunberg-hope-contagious-climate

Broumas, A. G. (2017, January 20). Social democratic and critical theories of the intellectual commons: A critical analysis. *Triple-C, 15*(1). https://ssrn.com/abstract=2910247

Burton, L. (2007). Childhood adultification in economically disadvantaged families: A conceptual model. *Family Relations, 56*(4), 329–345. http://www.jstor.org/stable/4541675

Butcher, J. (2009). *Dresden files: Turn Coat.* Penguin Publishing Group.

Cammarota, J., & Fine, M. (Eds.). (2010). *Revolutionizing education: Youth participatory action research in motion.* Taylor & Francis.

Cammarota, J., Ginwright, S., & Noguera, P. (Eds.). (2013). *Beyond resistance! Youth activism and community change: New democratic possibilities for practice and policy for America's youth.* Taylor & Francis.

Campus in Camps and Grupo Contrafilé. (2014). *The tree school.* http://www.campusincamps.ps/wp-content/uploads/2014/11/Tree-School_Digital-Book_FINAL.pdf

Carr, C., & Runciman, D. (2018, December 5). 129: Democracy for young people—talking politics. *Talking Politics.* Retrieved June 3, 2022, from https://www.talkingpoliticspodcast.com/blog/2018/129-democracy-for-young-people

Carroll, M. (2021). Childhood in history: Perceptions of children in the ancient and medieval worlds. *Childhood in the Past, 14*(1), 72–74. https://doi.org/10.1080/17585716.2021.1905885

CBC. (2019, September 28). Canadian Indigenous water activist Autumn Peltier addresses UN on clean water. *CBC.* Retrieved June 4, 2022, from https://cbc.ca/news/world/canadian-indigenous-water-activist-autumn-peltier-addresses-un-on-clean-water-1.5301559

Checkoway, B. (1996). *Adults as allies.* W.K. Kellogg Foundation.

Checkoway, B. (2010). What is youth participation? *Children and Youth Services Review, 33*(2), 340–345.

Checkoway, B., & Gutiérrez, L. M. (Eds.). (2012). *Youth participation and community change.* Taylor & Francis.

Chomsky, N. (2013). *On anarchism.* New Press.

Children's Voting Colloquium. (2023). *Who we are.* Retrieved April 20, 2023, from https://www.childrenvoting.org/

Christian, M. (1992). A global critical race and racism framework: Racial entanglements and deep and malleable whiteness. *Sociology of Race and Ethnicity, 5*(2), 169–185.

CIRCLE. (2017, March 26). *Civic deserts: 60% of rural millennials lack access to a political life.* CIRCLE—Tufts University. Retrieved July 14, 2022, from https://circle.tufts.edu/latest-research/civic-deserts-60-rural-millennials-lack-access-political-life

CIRCLE. (2021, April 29). *Half of youth voted in 2020, an 11-point increase from 2016.* CIRCLE—Tufts University. Retrieved May 12, 2022, from https://circle.tufts.edu/latest-research/half-youth-voted-2020-11-point-increase-2016

CIRCLE. (2022, May 9). *Major national issues like abortion may spur youth mobilization.* CIRCLE—Tufts University. Retrieved May 11, 2022, from https://circle.tufts.edu/latest-research/major-national-issues-abortion-may-spur-youth-mobilization

Closson, L. M. (2009). Aggressive and prosocial behaviors within early adolescent friendship cliques: What's status got to do with it? *Merrill-Palmer Quarterly, 55*(4), 406–435. Retrieved May 13, 2022, from http://www.jstor.org/stable/23096233

CNBC. (2019, August 12). Meet the millennial leaders of Hong Kong's protests. *CNBC.* Retrieved May 23, 2022, from https://www.cnbc.com/2019/08/12/meet-the-millennial-leaders-of-hong-kongs-protests.html

Cockburn, T. (2007, November). Partners in power: A radically pluralistic form of participative democracy for children and young people. *Children and Society, 21*(6), 446–457. https://doi.org/10.1111/j.1099-0860.2006.00078.x

Corbett-White, Mike. (2009). *'Capitalism is evil,' says new Michael Moore film*. Reuters. Retrieved April 19, 2023, from http://www.reuters.com/article/lifestyleMolt/idUSTRE5850F32 0090906

Collins, A. (2019). *Student rights in a new age of activism*. Greenhaven Publishing LLC.

Commonwealth Secretariat. (2017). *Youth mainstreaming in development planning: Transforming young lives*. The Commonwealth.

Cook, D. T. (2003, January 24). Monitor breakfast with James Carville and Stanley Greenberg. *Christian Science Monitor*. Retrieved June 3, 2022, from https://www.csmonitor.com/2003/ 0124/p25s04-usmb.html

Coons, C. (2020, December 1). Sens. Coons, Cornyn introduce landmark legislation to invest $1B annually in civics education. *U.S. Senate*. Retrieved May 6, 2022, from https://www. coons.senate.gov/news/press-releases/sens-coons-cornyn-introduce-landmark-legislation-to-invest-1b-annually-in-civics-education

Corney, T., Cooper, T., Shier, H., & Williamson, H. (2021, November 29). Youth participation: Adultism, human rights and professional youth work. *Children and Society*. Retrieved June 7, 2022, from https://onlinelibrary.wiley.com/doi/epdf/10.1111/chso.12526

Council of Europe. (1950). European convention on human rights. *European Court of Human Rights*. Retrieved May 19, 2022, from https://www.echr.coe.int/documents/convention_ eng.pdf

Counts, G. S. (1978). *Dare the school build a new social order?* Southern Illinois University Press.

Crawford, S. (2009, November 4). Medieval children. *Reviews in History*. Retrieved June 7, 2022, from https://reviews.history.ac.uk/review/254

Cummings, M. (2001). *Beyond political correctness social transformation in the United States*. Lynne Rienner Publishers.

Cushman, C., & Cervone, B. (2002). Moving youth participation into the classroom: Students as allies. *New Directions for Youth Development, 96*, 83–100.

Dahl, Robert A., & Shapiro, I. (2015). *On democracy*. Yale University Press.

Dalgaard, C. (2021, September 22). How I went from a teenage reposter to a real world activist. *PublicSource*. Retrieved May 10, 2022, from https://www.publicsource.org/social-media-rep ost-real-world-youth-activism-mental-health/

Dalton, L., Churchman, R., & Tasco, A. (2008). Getting students involved in creating a healthy school. *ASCD: Health School Communities Whole Child Initiative*. Retrieved December 12, 2022, from https://web.archive.org/web/20080607105756/http://www.healthyschoolcomm unities.org/HSRC/pages/navigationcontent/Resources.aspx?display=ResourcesLink10

Davies, Christie. (1989). Goffman's concept of the total institution: Criticisms and revisions. *Human Studies, 12*(1/2), 77–95.

de Kort, G. (2017, November 21). *Systematic participation of adolescents and youth in programming (MENA) nothing about us without us!* MENA Adolescent and Youth Hub. Retrieved May 11, 2022, from https://www.menayouthhub.org/sites/menayouthhub.org/files/webform/contr ibute_a_resource_to_nlg/448/eye2_systematic-participation-of-adolescents-and-youth-in-programming-%28mena.-nothing-about-us-without-us_esay2017.pdf

Delgado, M. (2019). *Urban youth trauma: Using community intervention to overcome gun violence*. Rowman & Littlefield Publishers.

Delgado, M., & Zhou, H. (2008). *Youth-led health promotion in urban communities: A community capacity-enhancement perspective.* Rowman & Littlefield Publishers.

Delgado, P. o. S. W. M., Delgado, M., & Staples, L. (2008). *Youth-led community organizing: Theory and action.* Oxford University Press.

Dellinger, D. (2017, December 22). Opinion: Dr. King's Interconnected World. *The New York Times.* Retrieved May 26, 2022, from https://www.nytimes.com/2017/12/22/opinion/martin-luther-king-christmas.html

Deleuze, G. (1986). *Foucault.* Translated by Sean Hand. Athlone.

Deresiewicz, W. (2012, April 15). The tyranny of freedom. *The American Scholar.* Retrieved May 12, 2022, from https://theamericanscholar.org/the-tyranny-of-freedom/

Dewey, J. (1916). *Democracy and education.* Macmillan.

Dewey, J. (1987). *John Dewey: The later works, 1925–1953* (Vol. 11, J. A. Boydston, Ed.). Southern Illinois University Press.

Dewey, J. (2008). *The middle works of John Dewey, volume 9, 1899–1924: Democracy and education, 1916 (collected works of John Dewey).* Southern Illinois University Press.

DiAngelo, D. R. (2018). *White fragility: Why it's so hard for White people to talk about racism.* Beacon Press.

Dimitrova, R., & Wiium, N. (Eds.). (2021). *Handbook of positive youth development: Advancing research, policy, and practice in global contexts.* Springer International Publishing.

Doherty, T. (1984, March 12). The exploitation film as history: Wild in the streets. *Literature/Film Quarterly, 12*(3), 186–194.

Dollar, B. (1975). *Youth participation: A concept paper. A report of the national commission on resources for youth to the Department of Health, Education and Welfare, Office of Youth Development.* National Commission on Resources for Youth.

DoSomething.org. (n.d.). *10 young racial justice activists you should know.* DoSomething.org. Retrieved June 4, 2022, from https://www.dosomething.org/us/articles/10-racial-justice-activists-you-should-know

Driskell, D. (2017). *Creating better cities with children and youth: A manual for participation.* Taylor & Francis.

Du Bois, W. E. B. (1947). No second class citizens. *Special Collections and University Archives, University of Massachusetts Amherst Libraries.* Retrieved May 27, 2022, from https://www.digitalcommonwealth.org/search/commonwealth-oai:h128ph45s

Dunn, Arthur W. (1907). *Civics: The community and the citizen.* W.W. Shannon, California Superintendent of State Printing.

Dweck, C., Bolton, J., & Domzalski, K. (2015, September 22). Carol Dweck revisits the 'Growth Mindset' (Opinion). *Education Week.* Retrieved May 1, 2022, from https://www.edweek.org/leadership/opinion-carol-dweck-revisits-the-growth-mindset/2015/09

Dweck, C. S. (2007). *Mindset: The new psychology of success.* Ballantine Books.

Earth Edition. (2022). *Meet HikingClub.CPT.* https://www.facebook.com/theearthissue/posts/7227482573991379

Eichsteller, G. (2009). Janusz Korczak—his legacy and its relevance for children's rights today. *The International Journal of Children's Rights, 17*(3), 377–391. https://doi.org/10.1163/15718 1808X334038

Emmerson, A. L. (2020, October 27). The fall of democracy: Opinion. *The Harvard Crimson.* Retrieved May 27, 2022, from https://www.thecrimson.com/column/fall-apart/article/2020/10/27/emmerson-fall-of-democracy/

Epstein, R. (2010). *Teen 2.0: Saving our children and families from the torment of adolescence.* Linden Publishing.

Eriksen, E. (2018). *Democratic participation in early childhood education and care—serving the best interests of the child.* Nordisk barnehageforskning. Retrieved May 11, 2022, from https://doi.org/10.7577/nbf.2319

Erlich, J., & Erlich, S. (Eds.). (1971). *Student power, participation and revolution.* Association Press.

Expósito, L. P. (2014, April 28). Rethinking political participation: A pedagogical approach for citizenship education. *Theory and Research in Education, 12*(2). https://doi.org/10.1177/1477878514530713.

Fabricant, N. (2022). *Fighting to breathe: Race, toxicity, and the rise of youth activism in Baltimore.* University of California Press.

Feldblum, S. (2019, May 15). Water democracy. *Dissent Magazine.* Retrieved May 10, 2022, from https://www.dissentmagazine.org/online_articles/water-democracy

Fielding, M. (2004). 'New Wave' student voice and the renewal of civic society. *London Review of Education.* https://doi.org/10.1080/1474846042000302834

Fisher, N., & Sudbury, K. (2017, November 26). Democratic education: Unschooling at school? *East Kent Sudbury.* Retrieved June 5, 2022, from https://eastkentsudbury.org.uk/opinion/democratic-education-unschooling-at-school/

Flanagan, C. A. (2013). *Teenage citizens: The political theories of the young.* Harvard University Press.

Fletcher, A. (2005). *Meaningful student involvement guide to students as partners* (1st ed.). Freechild Project and HumanLinks Foundation. https://soundoutorg.files.wordpress.com/2020/08/d45dc-msiguide.pdf

Fletcher, A. (2007). *Washington youth voice handbook.* CommonAction Publishing. https://adamfcfletcher.files.wordpress.com/2020/04/e79a2-abbreviatedwyvh.pdf

Fletcher, A. (2014a). *The practice of youth engagement.* CommonAction Publishing.

Fletcher, A. (2014b). *A short guide to holistic youth development.* Freechild Institute for Youth Engagement. Retrieved March 18, 2022, from https://adamfcfletcher.files.wordpress.com/2020/04/98b3c-asgthyd.pdf

Fletcher, A. (2014c). *The guide to student voice* (2nd ed.). CommonAction Publishing.

Fletcher, A. (2015). *Facing adultism.* CommonAction Publishing.

Fletcher, A., & Vavrus, J. (2006). *The Freechild project guide to social change led by and with young people.* CommonAction Publishing. https://freechildinstitute.files.wordpress.com/2020/12/0713b-socialchangeguide.pdf

Fletcher, A. F. C. (2015, March 30). Students as researchers—SoundOut. *SoundOut.* Retrieved May 10, 2022, from https://soundout.org/2015/03/30/students-as-researchers/

Fletcher, A. F. C. (2016, January 7). *Who are youth?—Freechild Institute.* Freechild Institute. Retrieved May 19, 2022, from https://freechild.org/2016/01/07/who-are-youth/

Fletcher, A. F. C. (2017). *Student voice revolution: The meaningful student involvement handbook.* CommonAction Publishing.

Fletcher, A. F. C. (2019). Chapter 6: Beyond revolution: Transforming whole schools to foster student power. In K. Harell, S. D. Wurdinger, J. C. McDermott, & H. Smith (Eds.), *Empowering our students for the future: Encouraging self-direction and life-long learning.* Rowman & Littlefield Publishers.

Fletcher, A. F. C. (2020). Chapter 10: Going beyond student voice through meta-level education transformation. In T. Lowe & Y. El Hakim (Eds.), *A handbook for student engagement in higher education: Theory into practice.* Routledge.

Fletcher, A. F. C., & Lesko, W. S. (2021, February 20). Youth infusion in systems. *Youth Infusion.* Retrieved May 30, 2022, from https://youthinfusion.org/2021/02/20/youth-infusion-in-systems/

Foa, R. S., Klassen, A., Wenger, D., Rand, A., & Slade, M. (2020). *Youth and satisfaction with democracy: Reversing the democratic disconnect?.* Centre for the Future of Democracy. Retrieved December 12, 2022, from www.cam.ac.uk/system/files/youth_and_satisfaction_with_democracy.pdf

Foucault, M. (1997). The birth of biopolitics. In P. Rabinow (Ed.), *Ethics: Subjectivity and truth. Essential works of Foucault, 1954–1984.* The New Press.

França, J. (2019, July 2). Henry Giroux: 'Those arguing that education should be neutral are really arguing for a version of education in which nobody is accountable.' *CCCB Lab.* Retrieved April 28, 2022, from https://lab.cccb.org/en/henry-giroux-those-arguing-that-education-should-be-neutral-are-really-arguing-for-a-version-of-education-in-which-nobody-is-acco untable/

Franklin, B. (1783). From Benjamin Franklin to Joseph Banks, 27 July 1783, U.S. National Archives. *Founders Online—National Archives.* Retrieved January 15, 2022, from https://founders.archives.gov/documents/Franklin/01-40-02-0236

Franklin, V. P. (2021). *The young crusaders: The untold story of the children and teenagers who galvanized the civil rights movement.* Beacon Press.

Freechild Institute for Youth Engagement. (n.d.A). *Action for youth engagement.* Freechild Institute for Youth Engagement. Retrieved March 18, 2022, from https://freechild.org/technical-ass istance/actions/

Freechild Institute for Youth Engagement. (n.d.B). *Freechild.org website.* Freechild Institute for Youth Engagement. Retrieved May 18, 2022, from https://freechild.org

Freechild Institute for Youth Engagement. (2016, January 5). *Youth equity—Freechild Institute.* Freechild Institute. Retrieved June 7, 2022, from https://freechild.org/2016/01/05/youth-equity/

Freechild Institute for Youth Engagement. (2016, January 7). *Glossary.* Freechild Institute. Retrieved May 27, 2022, from https://freechild.org/2016/01/07/glossary/

Freechild Institute for Youth Engagement. (2016, February 19). *What is youth mainstreaming?— Freechild Institute.* Freechild Institute. Retrieved June 6, 2022, from https://freechild.org/2016/02/19/chapter-i-what-is-youth-mainstreaming/

Freire, P. (1974). *Education for liberation and community.* Australian Council of Churches, Commission on Christian Education.

Freire, P. (1985, January). Reading the world and reading the word: An interview with Paulo Freire. *Language Arts, 62*(1), 15–21. https://www.jstor.org/stable/41405241

Freire, P. (1998). *Pedagogy of freedom: Ethics, democracy, and civic courage* (P. Clarke, Trans.). Rowman & Littlefield Publishers.

Freire, P. (2004). *Pedagogy of the oppressed*. Continuum.

Freire, P. (2015). *Pedagogy of indignation*. Taylor & Francis.

Frost, D., & Roberts, A. (2011, Spring/Summer). Student leadership, participation and democracy. *Leading and Managing, 17*(2), 66–84.

Funders Collaborative on Youth Organizing. (n.d.). Our mission. *FCYO.org*. Retrieved May 21, 2022, from https://fcyo.org/about/our-mission

Garcia, A., & Philip, T. M. (2018). Smoldering in the darkness: Contextualizing learning, technology, and politics under the weight of ongoing fear and nationalism. *Learning, Media and Technology, 43*(4), 339–344. https://doi.org/10.1080/17439884.2018.1534860

Gardner, H. (2008). A multiplicity of intelligences. In P. Mariën & J. Abutalebi (Eds.), *Neuropsychological research: A review* (pp. 17–23). Psychology Press.

Gatto, J. T. (1992). *Dumbing us down: The hidden curriculum of compulsory schooling*. New Society Publishers.

Gatto, J. T. (2017). *The underground history of American education, volume I: An intimate investigation into the prison of modern schooling*. Valor Academy.

Georgetown Law Center on Poverty and Inequality. (n.d.). *Adultification bias*. The Georgetown Law Center on Poverty and Inequality. Retrieved May 27, 2022, from https://genderjustic eandopportunity.georgetown.edu/adultification-bias/

Gillen, J. (2014). *Educating for insurgency: The roles of young people in schools of poverty*. AK Press.

Gillis, J. R. (2013). *Youth and history: Tradition and change in European age relations, 1770–present*. Elsevier Science.

Giroux, H. (2008). Disposable youth in a suspect society. *TruthOut*. https://truthout.org/articles/ disposable-youth-in-a-suspect-society/

Giroux, H. (2018). *Pedagogy and the politics of hope: Theory, culture, and schooling: A critical reader*. Taylor & Francis.

Giroux, H. A. (1981). *Ideology, culture and the process of schooling*. Temple University Press.

Giroux, H. A. (1999). *The mouse that roared: Disney and the end of innocence*. Rowman & Littlefield.

Giroux, H. A. (2009). *Youth in a suspect society: Democracy or disposability?* Palgrave Macmillan.

Giroux, H. A. (2011). Neoliberal politics as failed sociality: Youth and the crisis of higher education. *Logos Journal*. Retrieved May 11, 2022, from http://logosjournal.com/2011/neolibe ral-politics-as-failed-sociality-youth-and-the-crisis-of-higher-education/

Giroux, H. A. (2015a). *Dangerous thinking in the age of the new authoritarianism*. Taylor & Francis.

Giroux, H. A. (2015b). *Youth in revolt: Reclaiming a democratic future*. Taylor & Francis.

Gitlin, T. (2003). *Letters to a young activist* (T. Gitlin, Ed.). Basic Books.

Golarz, R. J., & Golarz, M. J. (1995). *The power of participation: Improving schools in a democratic society*. National Training Associates.

Gollop, M., Nairn, K., & Smith, A. B. (Eds.). (2000). *Advocating for children: International perspectives on children's rights*. University of Otago Press.

Gordon, H. R. D., & Schultz, D. (2020). *The history and growth of career and technical education in America: Fifth edition*. Waveland Press.

Gorn, E. J. (2015). *Mother Jones: The most dangerous woman in America*. Farrar, Straus and Giroux.

Grade, S. (2015). *Red pedagogy: Native American social and political thought*. Rowman & Littlefield Publishers.

Gross, B., & Gross, R. (Eds.). (1977). *The children's rights movement: Overcoming the oppression of young people*. Anchor Books.

Gruzd, A., & Hernández-García, Á. (2018, July). Privacy concerns and self-disclosure in private and public uses of social media. *Cyberpsychology, behavior, and social networking, 21*(7), 418–428. http://doi.org/10.1089/cyber.2017.0709.

Guggenheim, M. (2007). *What's wrong with children's rights*. Harvard University Press.

Guilbert, K. (2017, December 4). *Syrian boy wins children's peace prize for building refugee school in Lebanon*. Reuters. Retrieved June 4, 2022, from https://www.reuters.com/article/us-syria-lebanon-children-education/syrian-boy-wins-childrens-peace-prize-for-building-refugee-school-in-lebanon-idUSKBN1DY1RT

Guzman-Concha, C. (2012). The students' rebellion in Chile: Occupy protest or classic social movement? *Social Movement Studies, 11*(3–4), 408–415. https://doi.org/10.1080/14742837.2012.710748

Hansen, M., Quintero, D., & Vasquez-Martinez, A. (2020, April 27). Latest NAEP results show American students continue to underperform on civics. *Brookings*. Retrieved May 6, 2022, from https://www.brookings.edu/blog/brown-center-chalkboard/2020/04/27/latest-naep-results-show-american-students-continue-to-underperform-on-civics/

Hart, R. A. (1994). *Children's participation: From tokenism to citizenship. Innocenti essays No. 4*. UNICEF.

Hart, S. N., Newell, P., Power, F. C., & Durrant, J. E. (Eds.). (2005). *Eliminating corporal punishment: The way forward to constructive child discipline*. UNESCO.

Hartung, C. (n.d.). Conditional citizens. *Perspectives on Children and Young People*. https://doi.org/10.1007/978-981-10-3938-6

Haste, H., & Chopra, V. (2020). The futures of education for participation in 2050: Educating for managing uncertainty and ambiguity. *UNESCO Digital Library*. Retrieved 2022, from https://unesdoc.unesco.org/ark:/48223/pf0000374441/

Hayden, T. (2001). Co-opting the radical instinct: A warning. In N. Welton & L. Wolf (Eds.), *Global uprising: Confronting the tyrannies of the 21st century: Stories from a new generation of activists*. New Society Publishers.

Hefner, K. (1970). Declaration of wants, youth liberation movement of Ann Arbor, 1970. *Declaration Project*. Retrieved May 19, 2022, from https://declarationproject.org/?p=1642

Helmig, B., Ingerfurth, S., & Pinz, A. (2014). Success and failure of nonprofit organizations: Theoretical foundations, empirical evidence, and future research. *Voluntas, 25*, 1509–1538. https://doi.org/10.1007/s11266-013-9402-5

Hendrick, J. (1992). *The whole child: Developmental education for the early years*. Merrill.

Hendrick, J. (1992, March). EJ441890—where does it all begin? Teaching the principles of democracy in the early years, young children, 1992. *ERIC*. Retrieved May 13, 2022, from https://eric.ed.gov/?id=EJ441890

Hern, M. (Ed.). (1996). *Deschooling our lives*. New Society Publishers.

Heywood, C. (2018). *A history of childhood*. Wiley.

Hipolito-Delgado, C. P., Stickney, D., Zion, S., & Kirshner, B. (2022). Transformative student voice for sociopolitical development: Developing youth of color as political actors. *Journal of Research on Adolescence.* Retrieved May 23, 2022, from https://onlinelibrary.wiley.com/act ion/showCitFormats?doi=10.1111%2Fjora.12753

Hodge, S. A. (2010, August 4). *Which age groups bear the largest share of the tax burden?* Tax Foundation. Retrieved May 12, 2022, from http://taxfoundation.org/blog/which-age-gro ups-bear-largest-share-of-tax-burden

Holt, J. C. (1974). *Escape from childhood.* E. P. Dutton.

hooks, b. (2013). *Teaching community: A pedagogy of hope.* Taylor & Francis.

hooks, b. (2014a). *Teaching to transgress.* Taylor & Francis.

hooks, b. (2014b). *Yearning: Race, gender, and cultural politics.* Taylor & Francis.

hooks, b. (2018). *All about love: New visions.* HarperCollins.

Hoose, P. (2001). *We were there, too! Young people in U.S. history.* Farrar, Straus and Giroux (BYR).

Hoose, P. (2010). *Claudette Colvin: Twice toward justice.* Square Fish.

Hope, M. A., & Hall, J. J. (2018, July 10). *'Other spaces' for Lesbian, Gay, Bisexual, Transgendered and Questioning (LGBTQ) students: Positioning LGBTQ-affirming schools as sites of resistance within inclusive education.* Taylor & Francis Online. Retrieved May 14, 2022, from https:// www.tandfonline.com/doi/abs/10.1080/01425692.2018.1500273

Huxley, A. (1994). *Brave new world revisited.* Flamingo.

Institute of Development Studies. (2022, March 14). *Kids in charge? Age and power in Peru's movement of working children.* Institute of Development Studies. Retrieved May 25, 2022, from https://www.ids.ac.uk/events/kids-in-charge-age-and-power-in-perus-movement-of-work ing-children/

Inter-Tribal Council of Michigan, Inc. (2019). *WE R NATIVE.* Inter-Tribal Council of Michigan, Inc. Retrieved June 4, 2022, from http://www.itcmi.org/wp-content/uploads/2020/02/We-R-Native-2019-Edition-Print.pdf

Istvan, A. (2018, June). *Let's be real: Youth leadership as a promising practice for ending dating violence.* American Psychological Association. Retrieved May 10, 2022, from https://www.apa. org/pi/families/resources/newsletter/2018/06/youth-dating-violence

Izsák-Ndiaye, R. (2021). *If I disappear global report on protecting young people in civic space.* United Nations Office of the Secretary-General's Envoy on Youth. Retrieved December 12, 2022, from https://www.un.org/youthenvoy/wp-content/uploads/2021/06/Global-Report-on-Pro tecting.-Young-People-in-Civic-Space.pdf

Jacobo, J. (2019, August 2). Irish teen invents method to remove microplastics from ocean, wins $50K Google science fair prize. *ABC News.* Retrieved June 4, 2022, from https:// abcnews.go.com/Technology/irish-teen-invents-method-remove-microplastics-ocean-wins/ story?id=64731771

Jahanbegloo, R. (2018). *The revolution of values: The origins of Martin Luther King Jr.'s moral and political philosophy.* Lexington Books.

Jahns, M. (n.d.). Children as citizens: Towards a contemporary notion of child participation. *11*(1), 27–44. https://doi.org/10.1177/0907568204040182

Jenks, C. (1996). *Childhood.* Routledge.

Jens, A. (2015). *Adultism in architecture: Are children being discriminated against by our urban surroundings?* GRIN Verlag.

Jobs, R. I., & Pomfret, D. M. (Eds.). (2016). *Transnational histories of youth in the twentieth century.* Palgrave Macmillan.

Johannsen, C. (2011, April 22). Higher education under attack: An interview with Henry A. Giroux. *Truthout.* Retrieved May 11, 2022, from https://truthout.org/articles/higher-educat ion-under-attack-an-interview-with-henry-a-giroux/

Johansson, V. (n.d.). 'I'm in charge of the Truffula Seeds': On children's literature, rationality and children's voices in philosophy. *Journal of Philosophy of Education, 45*(2), 359–377. https:// doi.org/10.1111/j.1467-9752.2011.00802.x

Johnston, S. M. (2021). *The great resignation in teaching: Servant leadership impact on teacher retention, job satisfaction, and principal efficacy during the COVID-19 pandemic.* Jannetides College of Business and Entrepreneurial Leadership. Retrieved May 27, 2022, from https:// www.proquest.com/openview/813ae60b127f91affa9b140c8623df4d/1?pq-origsite=gscho lar&cbl=18750&diss=y

Kahne, J., & Westheimer, J. (2003). Teaching democracy: What schools need to do. *Phi Delta Kappan Magazine, 85,* 34–66.

Kennedy, R. F. (1966, June 6). Day of affirmation address (News Release Version), University of Capetown, Capetown, South Africa, June 6, 1966. *JFK Library.* Retrieved May 19, 2022, from https://www.jfklibrary.org/learn/about-jfk/the-kennedy-family/robert-f-kennedy/rob ert-f-kennedy-speeches/day-of-affirmation-address-news-release-version-university-of-capet own-capetown-south-africa-june-6

Kerber-Ganse, W. (2015). Eglantyne Jebb—A pioneer of the convention on the rights of the child. *The International Journal of Children's Rights, 23*(2), 272–282. https://doi.org/10.1163/15718 182-02302003

Kidd, Thomas S. (2017). *Benjamin Franklin: The religious life of a founding father.* Yale University Press.

Kim, J., Abdul-Matin, I., & Taha, K. (2002). *Future 500: Youth organizing and activism in the United States.* Subway Elevated.

King, M. L. (1968). *Where do we go from here: Chaos or community?* Beacon Press.

Klein, N. (2021). *How to change everything: The young human's guide to protecting the planet and each other.* Atheneum Books for Young Readers.

Klein, R. (2003). *We want our say: Children as active participants in their education.* Trentham.

Kohn, A. (1993, September). Choices for children: Why and how to let students decide. *Phi Delta Kappan, 75*(1), 8–16, 18–21. Retrieved May 11, 2022, from https://www.alfiekohn.org/arti cle/choices-children/

Koller, S. H., Petersen, A. C., Motti-Stefanidi, F., & Verma, S. (Eds.). (2016). *Positive youth development in global contexts of social and economic change.* Taylor & Francis.

Kraemer, D. (2021, November 5). Greta Thunberg: Who is the climate campaigner and what are her aims? *BBC.* Retrieved June 4, 2022, from https://www.bbc.com/news/world-europe-49918719

Krauss, S. M., & Herrera, M. S. (2023). *Whole child, whole life: 10 ways to help kids live, learn & thrive.* Corwin.

Krishnamurti, J. (1976). *Krishnamurti's notebook* (1st ed.). Harper & Row.

Kurth-Schai, R. (1988). The roles of youth in society: A reconceptualization. *The Educational Forum*, *52*(2), 113–133. https://doi.org/10.1080/00131728809335473

Kurth-Schai, R., & Green, C. R. (2016). *Re-envisioning Education and democracy*. Information Age Publishing, Incorporated.

Lansdown, G. (2005). *The evolving capacities of the child* (UNICEF. Innocenti Research Centre, Ed.). Save the Children.

Lehrer, A. (2022, May 9). SCOTUS 'Pissed Off the Wrong Generation': Gen Z activists protest threat to abortion rights. *The 74*. Retrieved June 5, 2022, from https://www.the74million.org/scotus-pissed-off-the-wrong-generation-gen-z-activists-protest-threat-to-abortion-rights/

Lerner, R. M., & Silbereisen, R. K. (Eds.). (2007). *Approaches to positive youth development*. SAGE Publications.

Lesko, W. (2001, December). Student activism for the next generation. *Educational Leadership*, *59*(4), 42–44. ERIC. https://eric.ed.gov/?id=EJ638998

Lesko, W., & Fletcher, A. F.C. (2022). Youth infusion blog. *Youth Infusion*. Retrieved May 11, 2022, from https://youthinfusion.org/blog/

Lesko, W. S. (2001). *Youth infusion intergenerational advocacy toolkit*. Activism 2000 Project.

Lesko, W. S., & Tsourounis, E. (1998). *Youth! The 26% solution*. Activism 2000 Project.

Lester, S. (n.d.). Rethinking children's participation in democratic processes: A right to play. *Youth Engagement: The Civic-Political Lives of Children and Youth*, 21–43. https://doi.org/10.1108/s1537-4661(2013)0000016006

Levine, E. S. (2000). *Freedom's children: Young civil rights activists tell their own stories*. Penguin Young Readers Group.

Levine, P., & Higgins-D'Alessandro, A. (2010). Youth civic engagement: Normative issues. In L. R. Sherrod, J. Torney-Purta, & C. A. Flanagan (Eds.), *Handbook of research on civic engagement in youth*. Wiley.

Lilleker, D. G., & Ozgul, B. A. (2021). *The psychology of democracy*. Routledge.

Lister, R. (2007). Why citizenship: Where, when and how children? *Theoretical Inquiries in Law*, *8*. https://doi.org/10.2202/1565-3404.1165

Longchamp, C. (2016, December 26). *The ten flops of democracy in 2016—SWI Swissinfo.ch*. SwissInfo. Retrieved May 27, 2022, from https://www.swissinfo.ch/eng/directdemocracy/trump-brexit_the-ten-flops-of-democracy-in-2016/42788274

Lourde, A. (1984). Age, race, class and sex: Women defining difference. *Sister Outsider*, *114*(23), 120.

Louv, R. (2008). *Last child in the woods*. Algonquin Books.

Love, B. L., Lane, J., & Pendharkar, E. (2020, June 12). An essay for teachers who understand racism is real (Opinion). *Education Week*. Retrieved June 7, 2022, from https://www.edweek.org/leadership/opinion-an-essay-for-teachers-who-understand-racism-is-real/2020/06

Males, M. A. (1996). *The scapegoat generation: America's war on adolescents*. Common Courage Press.

Males, M. A. (1999). *Framing youth: Ten myths about the next generation*. Common Courage Press.

Males, M. (2023). Los Angeles's astounding youth trends terrifying everyone. *LA Progressive*. Retrieved April 4, 2023, www.laprogressive.com/law-and-the-justice-system/astounding-youth-trends

Manchester, H. B., Aquino, E., & Wadhwa, A. (2021). *The little book of youth engagement in restorative justice: Intergenerational partnerships for just and equitable schools*. Good Books.

Markham, T. (2013, July 3). *The challenges and realities of inquiry-based learning*. MindShift.. Retrieved December 12, 2022, from https://www.kqed.org/mindshift/29714/the-challenges-and-realities-of-inquiry-based-learning

Marshall, T. H. (1992). Citizenship and social class (1950). In T. H. Marshall & T. Bottomore (Eds.), *Citizenship and social class* (pp. 8–17). Pluto Press.

Marten, J. A. (2018). *The history of childhood: A very short introduction*. Oxford University Press.

Martin-Kniep, G. (2008). *Communities that learn, lead and last: Building and sustaining educational expertise*. Jossey-Bass.

Martinez, S., & Steger, G. (2013). *Invent to learn: Making, tinkering, and engineering in the classroom*. Constructing Modern Knowledge Press.

McClellan, P. A. (2020). Portraits of Black girls: Reflections on schooling and leadership of a Black woman principal in an age of adultism. *Journal of Educational Administration and History*, *52*(3), 256–269. https://doi.org/10.1080/00220620.2020.1786357

McDermott, J. C., & Bird, L. B. (Eds.). (1999). *Beyond the silence: Listening for democracy*. Pearson Education.

McDermott, J. C., & Smith, H. (2010). Foxfire—no inert ideas allowed here. In T. Smith & C. Knapp (Eds.), *Sourcebook for experiential education: Key thinkers and their contributions*. Routledge.

McGuire, M. E. (2007). What happened to social studies?: The disappearing curriculum—Margit E. McGuire, 2007. *SAGE Journals*. Retrieved May 14, 2022, from https://journals.sagepub.com/doi/abs/10.1177/003172170708800815

Meckel, R. A. (1998). *Save the babies: American public health reform and the prevention of infant mortality, 1850–1929* (p. 118). University of Michigan Press.

Meyer, D. S. (2018, April 13). Perspective: The Parkland teens started something. How Can It become a Social Movement? *The Washington Post*. Retrieved May 11, 2022, from https://www.washingtonpost.com/outlook/2018/04/13/392feb24-3e55-11e8-974f-aacd97698cef_story.html

Millei, Z., & Kallio, K. P. (2016). Recognizing politics in the nursery: Early childhood education institutions as sites of mundane politics. *Contemporary Issues in Early Childhood*, *19*(1), 31–47. https://doi.org/10.1177/1463949116677498

Mitra, D. L. (2014). *Student voice in school reform: Building youth-adult partnerships that strengthen schools and empower youth*. State University of New York Press.

Mitra, D. L., & Serriere, S. C. (2015). *Civic education in the elementary grades: Promoting student engagement in an era of accountability*. Teachers College Press.

Moraitis, N. (2006). *Youth—activism—engagement—participation: Good practices and essential strategies for impact*. Amnesty International. Retrieved June 5, 2022, from https://www.amnesty.org/en/wp-content/uploads/2021/08/act760032006en.pdf

Moses, B. (2014). Foreword. In J. Gillen (Ed.), *Educating for insurgency: The roles of young people in schools of poverty*. AK Press.

Moss, D. A. (2019). *Democracy: A case study*. Harvard University Press.

Moss, P. (n.d.). *Democracy as first practice in early childhood education and care*. Centre of Excellence for Early Childhood Development.

Moyer, M. W. (2022, March 24). Kids as young as 8 are using social media more than ever, study finds. *The New York Times*. Retrieved June 8, 2022, from https://www.nytimes.com/2022/03/24/well/family/child-social-media-use.html

Murphy, J. (2017). *The boys' war: Confederate and union soldiers talk about the civil war*. Houghton Mifflin Harcourt.

Nagda, B. A., Gurin, P., & Lopez, G. E. (2003). Transformative pedagogy for democracy and social justice. *Race Ethnicity and Education*, 6(2), 165–191. https://doi.org/10.1080/1361332 0308199

National Youth Rights Association. (n.d.A). *Home—NYRA*. Retrieved May 19, 2022, from https://youthrights.org

National Youth Rights Association. (n.d.B). *About NYRA*. National Youth Rights Association. Retrieved May 19, 2022, from https://www.youthrights.org/about/

Ndlovu, S. M., & Peterson, B. (2016). *Students must rise: Youth struggle in South Africa before and beyond Soweto '76* (B. Peterson, A. Heffernan, S. M. Ndlovu, & N. Nieftagodien, Eds.). Wits University Press.

Neill, A. S. (1990). *Summerhill: A radical approach to child-rearing*. Penguin.

Neill, A. S. (2010). The idea of Summerhill. In A. S. Canestrari & B. A. Marlowe (Eds.), *Educational foundations: An anthology of critical readings* (pp. 133–141). Sage Publications.

Nelson, J. R., & Frederick, L. (1994). Can children design curriculum? *Educational Leadership*, February, 71–74.

New York Times. (2015, March 3). How to ensure and improve teacher quality. *New York Times*. https://www.nytimes.com/roomfordebate/2015/03/03/how-to-ensure-and-improve-teacher-quality

New Zealand Herald. (2020, March 2). My story: Cruz Erdmann, the 14-year-old young wildlife photographer of the year. *NZ Herald*. Retrieved June 4, 2022, from https://www.nzherald.co.nz/nz/my-story-cruz-erdmann-the-14-year-old-young-wildlife-photographer-of-the-year/FWGOBXT2CUWKH4WOWHEGSCUVO4/

Nishiyama, K. (2017, April 20). Deliberators, not future citizens: Children in democracy. *Journal of Deliberative Democracy*. Retrieved May 13, 2022, from https://delibdemjournal.org/article/id/539/

Nittle, N. K. (2020, July 28). *How the Greensboro four sit-in sparked a movement*. History.com. Retrieved June 4, 2022, from https://www.history.com/news/greensboro-four-sit-in-civil-rights

Ober, J. (2013). Democracy's wisdom: An Aristotelian middle way for collective judgment. *American Political Science Review*, 107(2), 104–122. https://doi.org/10.1017/S000305541 2000627

Osguthorpe, R., & Graham, C. (2003). Blended learning environments definitions and directions. *The Quarterly Review of Distance Education*, 43, 227–448.

Paglayan, A. S. (2021). The non-democratic roots of mass education: Evidence from 200 years. *American Political Science Review, 115* (1), 179–198. https://www.cambridge.org/core/journ als/american-political-science-review/article/nondemocratic-roots-of-mass-education-evide nce-from-200-years/8C8C594AA07996A00ED4BEFC66B133B7

Paine, A. (2006). *Mark Twain's notebook.* Read Books.

Park, J. G. (2020). *Aesthetic liberalism: Beauty and political action in the age of interest.* eCom-mons@Cornell. Retrieved May 10, 2022, from https://ecommons.cornell.edu/bitstream/ handle/1813/102931/Park_cornellgrad_0058F_12146.pdf?sequence=1

Paterson, J. (2021, March 9). *Student activism on the rise: NEA.* National Education Association. Retrieved May 23, 2022, from https://www.nea.org/advocating-for-change/new-from-nea/ student-activism-rise

Patten, A. (2022, March 11). America's teacher burnout problem looms. *WebShrink.* Retrieved May 27, 2022, from https://www.webshrink.com/general/general-news/americas-teacher-burnout-problem-looms

Payne, K. A. (n.d.). Starting with children's democratic imagination. A response to "That's My Voice! Participation and Citizenship in Early Childhood." *Democracy and Education, 28*(2), 6.

Pease, B. (n.d.). *Undoing privilege: Unearned advantage and systemic injustice in an unequal world.* Bloomsbury Publishing.

Perkins, D. F., Villarruel, F. A., Keith, J. G., & Borden, L. M. (Eds.). (2003). *Community youth development: Programs, policies, and practices.* SAGE Publications.

Peters, K. & Straus, T. (2009). *Visions and voices: American Indian activism and the civil rights movement.* Albatross Press.

Peto, T. (2020). *Too immature to vote?* Erasmus Law Review.

Pinchok, N., & Brandt, W. C. (2009). *Connecting formative assessment research to practice: An introductory guide for educators.* Learning Point Associates.

Posnick, S. (2020, December 11). *Innovator Jose Gonzalez.* California Teachers Association. Retrieved May 10, 2022, from https://www.cta.org/educator/posts/innov20-jose-gonzalez

Postman, N. (1994). *The disappearance of childhood.* Vintage Books.

Rathburn, M. K. (2015, January 11). *Building connections through contextualized learning in an undergraduate course on scientific and mathematical literacy.* ERIC. Retrieved May 12, 2022, from https://files.eric.ed.gov/fulltext/EJ1134658.pdf

Ray, R. (2020, February 14). Black Americans are not a monolithic group so stop treating us like one: Rashawn Ray. *The Guardian.* Retrieved May 27, 2022, from https://www.theguard ian.com/commentisfree/2020/feb/14/black-americans-are-not-a-monolithic-group-so-stop-treating-us-like-one

Reckmeyer, M. (October 30, 2019). *Focus on student engagement for better academic outcomes.* Gallup. Retrieved December 12, 2022, from https://www.gallup.com/education/267521/ focus-student-engagement-better-academic-outcomes

Redefy. (n.d.). About us. *Redefy.* Retrieved June 4, 2022, from https://www.redefy.org/about

Reulecke, J. (2001). History of youth movements. In *International encyclopedia of the social & behavioral sciences* (pp. 16671–16674). Pergamon. https://doi.org/10.1016/B0-08-043076-7/ 02730-3

Roberts, K. (2015). Youth movements. In J. D. Wright (Ed.), *International encyclopedia of the social & behavioral sciences* (pp. 837–841). Elsevier Science. https://doi.org/10.1016/B978-0-08-097086-8.32174-2

Roos, M. (2021, April 29). *Measuring white fragility—hill—2021—social science quarterly.* Wiley Online Library. Retrieved June 1, 2022, from https://onlinelibrary.wiley.com/doi/abs/10.1111/ssqu.12985.

Rosen, S. M., & Conner, J. (Eds.). (2016). *Contemporary youth activism: Advancing social justice in the United States.* ABC-CLIO.

Rousseau, J. J. (2013). *Emile* (p. 64). Dover Publications, Incorporated.

Ryder, J. (2013). *The things in heaven and earth: An essay in pragmatic naturalism: An essay in pragmatic naturalism.* Fordham University Press.

SABC News. (2021, June 18). Youth month: beauty pageants as a form of youth activism against substance abuse. *SABC News.* Retrieved June 4, 2022, from https://www.youtube.com/watch?v=6w1ZQpttSxw

Samimi, J. C. (2010). Funding America's nonprofits: The nonprofit industrial complex's hold on social justice. *Columbia Social Work Review, 1.*

Sanborn, H., & Thyne, C. (2014). Learning democracy: Education and the fall of authoritarian regimes. *British Journal of Political Science, 44*(4), 773–797. https://doi.org/10.1017/S0007123413000082

Sarkar, J., & Mendoza, B. (2005). Bolivia's children's parliament: Bringing participation to the national stage. *Children, Youth and Environments, 15*(2), 227–244. https://www.jstor.org/stable/10.7721/chilyoutenvi.15.2.0227

Schmidt, H. (1997, September 1). A universal declaration of human responsibilities. *InterAction Council.* Retrieved May 6, 2022, from https://www.interactioncouncil.org/sites/default/files/udhr.pdf

Scholastic. (n.d.). *Teaching kids how government works: Social studies, civics, and media literacy for students in grades 4–6.* "We the People." Retrieved May 14, 2022, from https://wethepeople.scholastic.com/grade-4-6.html

Schulman, S. (2006, November). *Terms of engagement: Aligning youth, adults, and organizations toward social change.* Diccionario Cambridge Inglés y Tesauro gratuitos. Retrieved May 12, 2022, from https://journals.lww.com/jphmp/fulltext/2006/11001/terms_of_engagement__aligning_youth,_adults,_and.7.aspx

Schwartz, S. (2011, April 28). *Youth and the "Arab Spring."* United States Institute of Peace. Retrieved June 5, 2022, from https://www.usip.org/publications/2011/04/youth-and-arab-spring

Scott, J. (1990). *Domination and the arts of resistance: Hidden transcripts.* Yale University Press. Retrieved December 12, 2022, from https://monoskop.org/images/0/0f/Scott_James_C_Domination_and_the_Arts_of_Resistance_Hidden_Transcripts_1990.pdf

Sharrow, V. (2000). *Encyclopedia of youth and war: Young people as participants and victims.* Oryx Press.

Stanford University. (2004, January 21). *What is democracy?: Larry diamond.* Larry Diamond. Retrieved May 26, 2022, from https://diamond-democracy.stanford.edu/speaking/lectures/what-democracy

Stephenson, P., Miles, G., & Gourley, S. (2004). *Child participation* (R. Blackman, Ed.). Tearfund.

Stewart, T. (2012). Adultism: Discrimination by another name. In A. P. Jackson, A. Nosakhere, & J. Jefferson (Eds.), *The 21st-century Black librarian in America: Issues and challenges*. Scarecrow Press, Incorporated.

Stoneman, D. (2002). The role of youth programming in the development of civic engagement. *Applied Developmental Science*, *6*(4), 221–226. https://doi.org/10.1207/S1532480XADS0604_9

Stoneman, D., & Bell, J. (1988). *Leadership development: A handbook from the youth action program of the East Harlem Block Schools*. East Harlem Block Nursery, Inc. http://files.eric.ed.gov/fulltext/ED313484.pdf

Stonewall Youth. (n.d.). *Overview*. Stonewall Youth. Retrieved June 5, 2022, from https://www.stonewallyouth.org/our-work

Straume, I. S. (2016). Democracy, education and the need for politics. *Stud Philos Educ*, *35*, 29–45. https://doi.org/10.1007/s11217-015-9465-4

Students for a Democratic Society. (1962). *Port Huron statement*. Hanover College History Department. Retrieved May 19, 2022, from https://history.hanover.edu/courses/excerpts/111huron.html

Sugarman, T. (2009). *We had sneakers, they had guns: The kids who fought for civil rights in Mississippi*. Syracuse University Press.

Swalwell, K., & Payne, K. (n.d.). Critical civic education for young children, multicultural perspectives. *Multicultural Perspectives*, *21*(2), 127–132. https://doi.org/10.1080/15210960.2019.1606641

Symonds, A. (2020, October 8). Why don't young people vote? *The New York Times*. Retrieved May 12, 2022, from https://www.nytimes.com/2020/10/08/upshot/youth-voting-2020-election.html

Taft, J. K. (2019). *The kids are in charge: Activism and power in Peru's movement of working children*. NYU Press.

TED Talks. (n.d.). Why art is essential to democracy [Playlist]. *TED*. Retrieved May 13, 2022, from https://www.ted.com/playlists/733/why_art_is_important_to_democracy

Terriquez, V., Kirshner, B., Valladares, S., Baca, K., Garcia, M., Valladares, M. R., Sanchez, J., & Kroehle, K. (2020). *The 2020 national youth organizing field scan*. Funders' Collaborative on Youth Organizing. Retrieved May 18, 2022, from https://fcyo.org/uploads/resources/20-years-of-youth-power-the-2020-national-youth-organizing-field-scan_resource_609d4a85ebe152ee0283274e.pdf

TIME. (2017, November 3). TIME's 30 most influential teens of 2017. *TIME*. Retrieved June 4, 2022, from https://time.com/5003930/most-influential-teens-2017/

Tocqueville, A. d. (2006). *Democracy in America* (J. P. Mayer, Ed.). HarperCollins.

Torres, C. A., & Assié, T. (1998, November). Democracy, education, and multiculturalism: dilemmas of citizenship in a global world: comparative education review. *The University of Chicago Press: Journals*, *42*(4). Retrieved May 14, 2022, from https://www.journals.uchicago.edu/doi/abs/10.1086/447522

Tufts University CIRCLE. (n.d.). *Youth activism and community change: CIRCLE.* Tufts' CIRCLE. Retrieved May 12, 2022, from https://circle.tufts.edu/our-research/youth-activism-and-community-change#2

UNICEF. (n.d.). *Young climate activists demand action and inspire hope.* UNICEF. Retrieved May 23, 2022, from https://www.unicef.org/stories/young-climate-activists-demand-action-insp ire-hope

United Nations. (n.d.). *Democracy.* United Nations. Retrieved May 26, 2022, from https://www. un.org/en/global-issues/democracy

United Nations. (1990). *Convention on the rights of the child.* UNICEF. Retrieved May 13, 2022, from https://www.unicef.org/child-rights-convention

United Nations. (1998, August 10). *Press Release.* Retrieved December 12, 2022, from https:// press.un.org/en/1998/19980810.sgsm6670.html

United Nations. (2010, August 12). *Secretary-general's message on international youth day: United Nations Secretary-General.* United Nations website. Retrieved May 19, 2022, from https:// www.un.org/sg/en/content/sg/statement/2010-08-12/secretary-generals-message-internatio nal-youth-day

United Nations For Youth. (n.d.). *Globalization WPAY.* The United Nations. Retrieved June 5, 2022, from https://www.un.org/development/desa/youth/globalization-wpay.html

United Nations General Assembly. (1948, December 10). *Universal declaration of human rights: United Nations.* United Nations website. Retrieved May 19, 2022, from https://www. un.org/en/about-us/universal-declaration-of-human-rights

United Nations General Assembly Resolution 44/25. (1990). *Convention on the rights of the child.* OHCHR. Retrieved May 6, 2022, from https://www.ohchr.org/sites/default/files/crc.pdf

United Nations International Children's Emergency Fund: History of Child Rights. (n.d.). UNICEF. Retrieved May 6, 2022, from https://www.unicef.org/child-rights-convention/history-child-rights

USA Today. (1988). Interview with Maya Angelou. *USA Today.*

U.S. Senate Impeachment Trial [TV series episode]. (2021, February 9). In M. Shriver (Executive Producer). C-SPAN 2. https://d.facebook.com/watch/?v=3690094327748734&_rdr

Vora, S. (October 6, 2022). Taking up the mantle of democracy. *The New York Times.* Retrieved December 12, 2022, from www.nytimes.com/2022/10/06/world/youth-democracy-movem ent.html

Wall, J. (2021). *Give children the vote: On democratizing democracy.* Bloomsbury Publishing.

Welton, N., & Wolf, L. (2001). *Global uprising: Confronting the tyrannies of the 21st century. Stories from a new generation of activists* (N. Welton & L. Wolf, Eds.). New Society Publishers.

Westheimer, J., & Kahne, J. (1998). *Teaching for social justice: A democracy and education reader* (J. A. Hunt, W. Ayers, & T. Quinn, Eds.). New Press.

Wikipedia. (2021a). *American youth congress.* Wikipedia. Retrieved May 10, 2022, from https:// en.wikipedia.org/wiki/American_Youth_Congress

Wikipedia. (2021b). *Sonia Yaco.* Wikipedia. Retrieved May 10, 2022, from https://en.wikipedia. org/wiki/Sonia_Yaco

Wikipedia. (2022a). *Students for a democratic society.* Wikipedia. Retrieved May 10, 2022, from https://en.wikipedia.org/wiki/Students_for_a_Democratic_Society

Wikipedia. (2022b). *Port Huron statement*. Wikipedia. Retrieved May 10, 2022, from https://en.wikipedia.org/wiki/Port_Huron_Statement

Wikipedia. (2022c). *Arab Spring*. Wikipedia. Retrieved May 10, 2022, from https://en.wikipedia.org/wiki/Arab_Spring

Wikipedia. (2022d). *Stoneman Douglas high school shooting*. Wikipedia. Retrieved May 10, 2022, from https://en.wikipedia.org/wiki/Stoneman_Douglas_High_School_shooting

Wikipedia. (2022e). *Liberal democracy*. Wikipedia. Retrieved May 11, 2022, from https://en.wikipedia.org/wiki/Liberal_democracy

Wikipedia. (2022f). *Age of candidacy laws in the United States*. Wikipedia. Retrieved May 11, 2022, from https://en.wikipedia.org/wiki/Age_of_candidacy_laws_in_the_United_States

Wikipedia. (2022g). *List of the youngest mayors in Canada*. Wikipedia. Retrieved May 11, 2022, from https://en.wikipedia.org/wiki/List_of_the_youngest_mayors_in_Canada

Wikipedia. (2022h). *National commission on resources for youth*. Wikipedia. Retrieved May 12, 2022, from https://en.wikipedia.org/wiki/National_Commission_on_Resources_for_Youth

Wikipedia. (2022i). *Holism*. Wikipedia. Retrieved May 12, 2022, from https://en.wikipedia.org/wiki/Holism

Wikipedia. (2022j). *Black lives matter*. Wikipedia. Retrieved May 13, 2022, from https://en.wikipedia.org/wiki/Black_Lives_Matter

Wikipedia. (2022k). *Children's rights*. Wikipedia. Retrieved May 19, 2022, from http://en.wikipedia.org/wiki/Children's_rights

Wikipedia. (2022l). *School corporal punishment*. Wikipedia. Retrieved May 25, 2022, from https://en.wikipedia.org/wiki/School_corporal_punishment

Wikipedia. (2022m). *2011–2013 Chilean student protests*. Wikipedia. Retrieved June 5, 2022, from https://en.wikipedia.org/wiki/2011-2013_Chilean_student_protests

Wikipedia. (2022n). *Wild in the streets*. Wikipedia. Retrieved June 7, 2022, from https://en.wikipedia.org/wiki/Wild_in_the_Streets

Will, M. (2022, February 25). Will there really be a mass exodus of teachers? *Education Week*, 12. https://www.edweek.org/teaching-learning/will-there-really-be-a-mass-exodus-of-teachers/2022/02

Willard, M., & Austin, J. A. (Eds.). (1998). *Generations of youth: Youth cultures and history in twentieth-century America*. NYU Press.

Winter, M. D. (n.d.). *Children as fellow citizens: Participation and commitment* (1st ed.). CRC Press. https://doi.org/10.1201/9781315381008

Wong, V. (2012). Social withdrawal as invisible youth disengagement: Government inaction and NGO responses in Hong Kong. *International Journal of Sociology and Social Policy*, *32*(7/8), 415–430. https://doi.org/10.1108/01443331211249057

Woods, P. (2013). Drivers to holistic democracy: Signs and signals of emergent, democratic self-organising systems. In S. Weber, M. Göhlich, A. Schröer, C. Fahrenwald, & H. Macha (Eds.), *Organisation und partizipation organisation und Pädagogik* (Vol. 13). https://doi.org/10.1007/978-3-658-00450-7_31

World Economic Forum. (2020, January 19). *Greta is not alone: Meet the teen campaigners at Davos 2020*. The World Economic Forum. Retrieved June 4, 2022, from https://www.weforum.org/agenda/2020/01/the-teenage-change-makers-at-davos-2020/

World Economic Forum. (2020, January 23). *End gun violence: The youngest participant told Davos: World Economic Forum.* The World Economic Forum. Retrieved June 4, 2022, from https://www.weforum.org/agenda/2020/01/we-deserve-better-than-this-what-the-youngest-delegate-told-davos-will-i-am/

Wray, M. (2021, December 20). *PEP fellow creates civic engagement guide for youth.* Sanford School of Public Policy. Retrieved May 10, 2022, from https://sanford.duke.edu/story/pep-fellow-creates-civic-engagement-guide-youth-0/

Young Wisdom Project. (2004). *Making space, making change: Profiles of youth-led and youth-driven organizations.* Movement Strategy Center. https://movementstrategy.org/b/wp-content/uploads/2015/08/MSC-Making_Space_Making_Change.pdf

Youth.gov. (n.d.). *Benefits for youth, families, and communities.* Youth.gov. Retrieved May 29, 2022, from https://youth.gov/youth-topics/afterschool-programs/benefits-youth-families-and-communities

YouthRights.net. (2012). *Youth Rights Wiki.* National Youth Rights Association and the Freechild Project. Retrieved April 17, 2021, from https://web.archive.org/web/20110430184100/http://youthrights.net/

YPulse. (2020, March 31). *Quarantined young consumers are fueling booms for these 6 industries.* YPulse. Retrieved June 8, 2022, from https://www.ypulse.com/article/2020/03/31/quarantined-young-consumers-are-fueling-booms-for-these-6-industries/

Zeldin, S., McDaniel, A., Topitzes, D., & Calvert, H. (2000). *Youth in decision making: A study of the impacts of youth on adults and organizations.* National 4-H Council.

Zheng, C. (2022, February 21). The paradox of youth. *Medium Magazine.* Retrieved May 12, 2022, from https://mediummagazine.nl/the-paradox-of-youth-an-uncertain-moment/

Ziblatt, D. (n.d.). *Challenges to democracy: Daniel Ziblatt.* Scholars at Harvard. Retrieved May 27, 2022, from https://scholar.harvard.edu/dziblatt/challenges-democracy

Zinn, H. (2018). *You can't be neutral on a moving train: A personal history.* Beacon Press.

Studies in Criticality

General Editor
Shirley R. Steinberg

Counterpoints publishes the most compelling and imaginative books being written in education today. Grounded on the theoretical advances in criticalism, feminism, and postmodernism in the last two decades of the twentieth century, Counterpoints engages the meaning of these innovations in various forms of educational expression. Committed to the proposition that theoretical literature should be accessible to a variety of audiences, the series insists that its authors avoid esoteric and jargonistic languages that transform educational scholarship into an elite discourse for the initiated. Scholarly work matters only to the degree it affects consciousness and practice at multiple sites. Counterpoints' editorial policy is based on these principles and the ability of scholars to break new ground, to open new conversations, to go where educators have never gone before.

For additional information about this series or for the submission of manuscripts, please contact:

Shirley R. Steinberg, General Editor
msgramsci@gmail.com

To order other books in this series, please contact our Customer Service Department:

peterlang@presswarehouse.com (within the U.S.)
orders@peterlang.com (outside the U.S.)

Or browse online by series:

www.peterlang.com

www.ingramcontent.com/pod-product-compliance
Lightning Source LLC
Chambersburg PA
CBHW050636280326
41932CB00015B/2668